18 0044828 X
WITHDRAWN FROM STOCK
PC UW
LLYFRGELL
LIBRARY
ABERYSTWYTH
AF741166
4D2/48. W9

STRATEGIC ASPECTS OF OLIGOPOLISTIC VERTICAL INTEGRATION

STUDIES IN MATHEMATICAL AND MANAGERIAL ECONOMICS

Editors

HERBERT GLEJSER

STEPHEN MARTIN

VOLUME 36

NORTH-HOLLAND
AMSTERDAM • LONDON • NEW YORK • TOKYO

STRATEGIC ASPECTS OF OLIGOPOLISTIC VERTICAL INTEGRATION

CHANGQI WU

THE HONG KONG UNIVERSITY OF SCIENCE AND TECHNOLOGY
KOWLOON, HONG KONG

1992
NORTH-HOLLAND
AMSTERDAM • LONDON • NEW YORK • TOKYO

ELSEVIER SCIENCE PUBLISHERS B.V.
Sara Burgerhartstraat 25
P.O. Box 211, 1000 AE Amsterdam
The Netherlands

Library of Congress Cataloging-in-Publication Data

Wu, Ch'ang-ch'i.
Strategic aspects of oligopolistic vertical integration / Changqi Wu.
p. cm. -- (Studies in mathematical and managerial economics ; v. 36)
Revision of thesis (Ph. D.)--University of Leuven.
Includes bibliographical references and index.
ISBN 0-444-89451-9 (alk. paper)
1. Vertical integration. 2. Oligopolies. 3. Strategic planning.
I. Title. II. Series.
HD2748.W8 1992
338.8'2--dc20 92-29630
CIP

Prifysgol Cymru
University of Wales
Aberystwyth
Acc. No. 1800448288
Class No. HD2748 W9

ISBN: 0 444 89451 9

© 1992 Elsevier Science Publishers B.V. All rights reserved.

No part of this publication may be reproduced, stored in a retrieval system or transmitted in any form or by any means, electronic, mechanical, photocopying, recording or otherwise, without the prior written permission of the publisher, Elsevier Science Publishers B.V., Copyright & Permissions Department, P.O. Box 521, 1000 AM Amsterdam, The Netherlands.

Special regulations for readers in the U.S.A. This publication has been registered with the Copyright Clearance Center Inc. (CCC), Salem, Massachusetts. Information can be obtained from the CCC about conditions under which photocopies of parts of this publication may be made in the U.S.A. All other copyright questions, including photocopying outside of the U.S.A., should be referred to the publisher.

No responsibility is assumed by the publisher for any injury and/or damage to persons or property as a matter of products liability, negligence or otherwise, or from any use or operation of any methods, products, instructions or ideas contained in the materials herein.

This book is printed on acid-free paper.

PRINTED IN THE NETHERLANDS

PREFACE

The purpose of this book is to present a unified treatment of some fundamental issues concerning the strategic impact of vertical integration in an oligopolistic setting. The book is divided into two parts: Part I consists of chapters 1 to 4, while Part II consists of chapter 5. Part I contains a systematic analysis of oligopolistic vertical integration when all firms have the objective of profit maximization. Part II discusses the issues of vertical relations in a mixed market, where firms pursue asymmetric objectives. In addition to these two parts, an Introduction chapter provides a brief review of the related literature and research methodology. A General Conclusions chapter at the end, summarizes the results and discusses their major implications and possible extensions.

In Part I, an analytical framework is introduced, which combines market transactions, supply contracts and vertical integration. By exploring a two-stage Cournot game, it is demonstrated, that vertical integration is the Nash equilibrium that applies in both the fixed input proportion model and the variable input proportion model. Although vertical integration reduces total profits of individual firms, the competing firms must integrate vertically. The reason is that the underlying game has the structure of *prisoners' dilemma*.

Part I also shows that vertical integration leads to a higher social welfare than other alternative vertical structures, such as market transactions, supply contracts and mixed integration. The total effect of vertical integration is separated into the anti-competitive effect of market elimination and the pro-competitive effect of pure vertical integration. The former can be represented by an exclusive contract as a type of vertical restraint. When the pre-integration vertical structure is characterized as a supply contract, the market elimination effect is absent. Hence, vertical integration process creates only the pure vertical integration effect. Distinguishing market transactions and supply contracts as two alternative pre-integration arrangements has important policy implications. When an anti-trust authority reviews a vertical integration case, attention should be paid not only to the vertical integration, but also to the pre-integration vertical arrangements in a specific industry.

The significance of public enterprises in some Western European economies, and the trend of economic transitions toward a market system in Eastern Europe,

PC ABERYSTWYTH LLYFRGELL

justify the efforts to analyze the vertical relations in a successive oligopoly when firms have asymmetric objectives. The existence of public firms with the objective of welfare maximization, in an industry otherwise characterised as a successive oligopoly, creates a mixed market. Subsequently, asymmetry in downstream firms' objectives, leads to a higher output of final products than when all firms have the objective of profit maximization. Moreover, competition between suppliers of intermediate goods intensifies.

Asymmetry in firms' objectives may also be one of the reasons for the existence in cost differences between public and private firms. It is shown that, although public firms typically pay more than private firms in equilibrium, the intermediate input prices become lower for both types of firms in the downstream industry. It is further shown that the active participation of a public firm, e.g. acting as a Stackelberg leader, proves to be a more effective way to control the successive oligopoly than by acting passively as a Cournot player or as a Stackelberg follower. An interesting result is that the profits of downstream private firms may increase when they act as a Stackelberg follower in such a game. A second-mover advantage of private firms helps to create a *win-win* situation for downstream firms as the result of erosion of market power of the upstream firms.

The implications of these contributions suggest that in an oligopolistic industry where firms have symmetric objectives, vertical integration may strengthen a firm's competitive position through strategic interactions. In industries characterised as mixed oligopolies, private firms may be better-off by taking a low profile and acting as followers. Public firms in mixed oligopolies may instead act as leaders by positively influencing the outcome of successive oligopolies in order to improve social welfare.

Acknowledgements

This book is a revised version of the dissertation which I submitted in 1990 to the Faculty of Economics and Applied Economics at the University of Leuven.

I am very grateful to my promoter, Raymond De Bondt for his insightful suggestions and ideas which significantly improved the results contained in this book. The same gratitude extends to Leo Sleuwaegen and Piet Vanden Abeele. Their constructive comments improved the intuitive appeal of the arguments put forward. I am also in debt to Herman Daems, Marcel Van Acoleyen, Patrick Van Cayseele and to Katrien Kesteloot and Reinhilde Veugelers for their useful comments and suggestions. Many people helped me in various ways, among them are Rita Sepelie, Geert Steurs, John Van de Kerckhove and Gordon Patzer.

I would like to express my profound gratitude to Stephen Martin, the Editor of this series. His extensive comments and suggestions on several versions of the manuscript improved the contents, exposition and the language of this book immensely.

I am grateful to the people at North-Holland, particularly to Economics & Business Editor Lilian van de Vaart for her help and encouragement. I am also grateful to Mary Carpenter, who handled the manuscript with expertise and experience.

Special thanks go to Hean Tat Ket for his superb research assistance. He prepared the index and proofread the entire manuscript.

I gratefully acknowledge the generous financial support from ABOS of Belgium and from the University of Leuven. In addition, the stimulating research environment and the first-rate research support at the School of Business and Management at the Hong Kong University of Science and Technology, particularly at the Department of Finance and Economics, have proven to be invaluable for writing this book.

The completion of this book provides me with a good opportunity to express my gratitude to my wife, Yanxia Song. First, she prepared all the diagrams and many of the computations. Second, her continuous support and encouragement made this book possible. Most of all, her love and devotion is reflected in each and every page of this book.

CHANGQI WU
Clear Water Bay, Hong Kong
June 1992

CONTENTS

List of Figures

List of Tables

Lists of Symbols

AC	Average cost
C_i	The total cost function of firm *i*, *i=1,2*
D_i	The *i*th downstream firm
G	Gross benefit
R_i	Reaction function of the *i*th firm.
U_i	The *i*th upstream firm.
V_i	The *i*th vertically integrated firm.
W	Social welfare.
a	Intercept of the linear demand function
c	Marginal cost of the upstream firms.
e	Elasticity of derived demand for input.
i	Index of firms, i=1,2.
m	Price cost margin.
mc_i	Marginal costs of the *i*th downstream firm.
p_i	Price of the final products produced by the *i*th firm.
q_i	Output quantity of the *i*th downstream firm.
q_α	Marginal product of the input factor α
q_β	Marginal product of the input factor β
s_i	Market share of the *i*th downstream firm.
v_i	The output of the *i*th vertically integrated firm.
w_i	Price of the intermediate inputs.
x_i	Quantity of intermediate goods produced by the *i*th upstream firm.
α	Intermediate input supplied by an oligopolistic industry.
β	Intermediate input factor supplied by a competitive industry.
γ	Distributive parameter.
ε	Demand elasticity of the final product.
θ	Product differentiation parameter.
λ	Welfare weight
π^d_i	Profit of the *i*th downstream firm.
π^u_i	Profit of the *i*th upstream firm.
π^v_i	Profit of the *i*th integrated firm.
σ	Substitution elasticity between intermediate inputs.
Σ	Sign of summation.
∂	Sign of partial differentiation.

INTRODUCTION

1. THE SUBJECT AND OBJECTIVES OF THE RESEARCH

The central focus of industrial organization theory is to analyze the economic organization under which economic activities are conducted. The organization or institutional arrangements between sequentially related production processes should be one of the central issues. But until recently industrial economists devoted only sporadic attention to the subject of vertical integration. Theoretical developments have been hampered by the divergence of opinions regarding the dominant incentives for vertical integration.

As Kaserman (1978) pointed out, the lack of coherence among economists may be attributed to two basic characteristics of the topic. First, the bringing together of potentially separable stages of production under a single administrative structure represents an anomaly under the standard assumptions employed in the theory of value, namely in markets where (a) transaction costs are absent, (b) all relevant costs and prices are known, and (c) firms are price-takers. Under these assumptions, there are no incentives for vertical integration. Second, the relaxation of any of these assumptions can result in the creation of such incentives, but the theoretical treatments and economic implications vary drastically when a particular assumption is dropped. The first two assumptions, or the lack of them, are major concerns of transaction costs economics, the economics of uncertainty and the economics of asymmetric information. Abandonment of the third assumption brings this issue directly to the domain of imperfect competition theory. The sensitivity of the theoretical implications of vertical integration to the type of specific assumption set adopted partly explains the difficulty and challenge of this topic.

After so many years of effort, economists have accumulated certain knowledge about the causes and consequences of vertical integration. As Williamson and others have argued, transaction costs indeed play a major role in the firm's vertical integration decisions. Because of the impossibility of comprehensive contracting, by reason of bounded rationality, and the need to adapt a supply relation through time in response to disturbances, firms tend to become vertically integrated when an efficient supply requires investment in special-purpose, long-life equipment or when the winner of the original contract acquires an advantage such as a unique location or learning, including the acquisition of undisclosed or proprietary technical and managerial procedures and task specific labor skills (Williamson, 1975, 1989). Uncertainty in the supply of the upstream good with the consequent need for information by downstream firms (Arrow, 1975) and the transfer of risks from one sector of the economy to another (Carlton, 1979) can also create incentives for vertical integration.

Analyses of vertical integration focusing on the relations between market structure and the firm's conduct have achieved some, but slow, progress. Most of the early works have been summarized by Blair and Kaserman (1983). In brief, the previous works tell us the following:

> *A monopolist has no incentive to integrate forward into a competitive industry if that industry employs a technology with fixed proportions of inputs.*
>
> *If substitutions between production factors are allowed in a competitive downstream industry, the upstream monopolist may have an incentive to integrate forward. By doing so, he eliminates the distortions created by the monopoly input price and obtains a higher profit.*
>
> *Under successive monopolies, vertical integration results in a higher profit for the monopolists, and a larger output and lower price for the consumers by eliminating cumulative mark-up.*
>
> *Under bilateral monopoly, the results become "indeterminate" because the final solution depends on the bargaining process between the monopolist and monopsonist.*

It is obvious that at that time the literature was not complete. Those simplified models may not provide clear and satisfactory policy implications for the market structures that we typically observe, which fall between the two extreme cases of perfect competition and monopoly. It is not surprising to find that the market structure and conduct of the firms in an oligopolistic industry influence the type of vertical relations between firms and their suppliers or buyers (retailers). It is also true that a carefully formulated vertical integration strategy of a corporation can provide a competitive advantage over its rivals. A number of cases illustrate that vertical integration strategy is one of the most important corporate strategies which determines the firm's long-run profitability in an imperfectly competitive environment. For instance, the computer giant, IBM, is a highly vertically integrated firm. The production activities of IBM cover a broad range, from semiconductors manufacturing to personal computers assembling. That may have contributed to its high profitability in the earlier stage of its development.

Nevertheless, rapid changes in technology development in the vertically related industrial sectors as well as consumer demand have forced IBM to reconsider its position on vertical integration[1].

Another interesting issue is that firms operating in imperfectly competitive markets typically demonstrate diversity in some other aspects in addition to their vertical structures. For instance, oligopolists competing in the same market may possess or choose deliberately different technologies and have different cost structures; they may market differentiated products, and so on. Firms can enjoy and/or create competitive advantages based on these differences. One issue that has not yet been looked at in the literature is that the firms may pursue different objectives when making their vertical integration decisions. An obvious example one can think of is public firms competing with private firms in various industrial sectors in Western European countries. For instance, in the Belgian insurance market, multinational enterprises, public firms and private insurance companies compete with one another (Veugelers, 1991). Another example is the Belgian and Italian television broadcasting industry where state-owned T.V. stations compete with several private television networks. These industries are characterized by objective asymmetry when public firms are created to maximize social welfare and private firms pursue their own profits[2].

This asymmetry in objectives is not limited to the Western economies. A recent development in several traditionally centrally planned economies is the move towards a market oriented system. During this transitional period, these economies can only be characterized by the heterogeneity of the ownership structures which are created by the gradual decentralization of the economy on the one hand and the incentive scheme adjustments on the other. These changes are bound to create asymmetries in the objectives of the firms. Objective asymmetry can also be amplified by increases in foreign direct investments from multinational enterprises following the gradual opening of the domestic economy in those countries. For instance, in the past ten years, foreign direct investments in China have reached a level of $30 billion. In some important industrial sectors such as the automobile, telecommunication equipments and electronics industries, the state-owned enterprises and subsidiaries of the multinational corporations are competing with each other and the pattern of dichotomy is highly visible (United Nations Centre on Transnational Corporations, 1988).

---

[1] See "The New IBM", *BusinessWeek*, December 16, 1991.

[2] The possibility of pursuing different objectives by public enterprises is discussed in Bös (1989).

The issue of the interface between multinational enterprises with the objective of profit maximization and public firms with the aim of maximizing social welfare appears to be most obvious in those industries characterized by globalization and oligopolistic competition, such as the telecommunication, computer and automobile industries. These industries are typically supported by equally important upstream industries which produce and supply intermediate goods, services or technologies (semiconductor industry, auto-parts industry etc.). Because of the strategic importance of these industries and the particularity of those "mixed economies", it is important for us to understand the economic and competitive consequences of objective asymmetry and their impact on the firms' conduct and performance when they select their vertical integration strategies. And it is equally important to assess correctly the impact of the asymmetry in objectives on social welfare.

The broad objective of this book is two-fold: First of all, to investigate the oligopolistic vertical integration when all firms are assumed to pursue the objective of profit maximization and to answer questions such as: Why would firms in an oligopolistic market seek vertical integration? Does vertical integration improve social welfare? Secondly, to understand the vertical integration issues in a mixed oligopoly in which public and private firms co-exist and compete against each other. The research questions are: What are the consequences of asymmetric objectives on firms' vertical integration decisions and their impact on the equilibrium outcome? How does the public enterprise influence the outcome of the market in a successive oligopoly?

2. REFINEMENT OF CONCEPTS

To facilitate our discussion, some concepts need to be clarified first. These frequently used concepts describe the types of vertical relations and the types of oligopoly. There are numerous types of vertical arrangements in business practices, such as fully owned subsidiaries, franchising agreements, exclusive selling agreements, joint ventures, spot and forward market transactions, etc. Through these arrangements, the transfers of goods and services between sequentially related production stages are accomplished. But the related concepts are often loosely described. Inconsistency in terminology appears in the literature occasionally. Confusion is created when the same phenomenon is described by different terminology and the same terminology is used to imply different issues by different authors.

Although there are several ways of classifying these vertical institutional arrangements, most economists put them into three general categories, each having distinctive economic properties. The two most often cited alternative vertical structures are administrative hierarchies and the market, often called *make-or-buy* decisions from the managerial point of view. In addition, there are different types of institutional arrangements, such as the exclusive selling agreements, tying, franchising, resale price maintenance, etc. (Katz, 1989; Perry and Porter, 1990). These kinds of vertical arrangements characterize more sophisticated contractual relations between buyers and sellers and fall in between the spot market and vertical integration. Sometimes, these kinds of hybrid systems are referred to as *vertical restraints* in the literature. The analytical distinction lies in the degree of ownership and control, which influences the level and methods of cooperation and coordination among the firms operating in the separable production processes. Each of these types of vertical relationships will be discussed further hereafter.

2.1. Vertical Integration

Vertical integration can be defined as the combination of technologically separable and sequentially related economic activities within the confines of a single firm. Vertical integration occurs when one firm merges either with a firm from which it purchases the inputs or with a firm to which it sells its output. When vertical integration occurs in the direction of production factors or supplies, it is referred to as *backward integration*. When integration involves acquiring facilities for distribution, fabrication, or finishing, it is referred to as *forward integration*. Forward integration involves the acquisition of a stage of the production process that is closer to the final consumer. The related units are often fully owned subsidiaries and the transactions of all or part of their requirements and products are carried out internally.

The term *vertical integration* sometimes can be misleading. On the one hand, the vertically integrated firm may not be able to exert complete control because some decision-makings must be delegated. On the other hand, there are other mechanisms which are able to achieve the same economic effect as vertical integration. For instance, without common ownership, two firms operating in successive production processes may cooperate to such an extent that the joint profit obtained is as high as in case of vertical integration (Blair and Kaserman, 1983).

We should be aware of the differences between vertical integration and the cooperation mechanism between vertically related firms, particularly their theoretical foundations. First of all, the foundation for a cooperative game between a buyer and a supplier without integration is the existence of a non-empty core which requires the satisfaction of group rationality and of each and every subgroup rationality. This means that the profitability of the group and of each and every cooperative partner has to be improved through cooperation if some kind of mechanism of side-payment does not exist. Because the integrating firms have lost their identities in the integrated firm, the decision of vertical integration becomes rational when the profit of the integrated firm is larger than the joint profits of non-integrating firms. The latter certainly is a much weaker condition. Secondly, the information and cost structures differ under these two types of practices. In the case of a cooperative agreement, the solution may not be found easily and it may require substantial bargaining costs when the joint profits have to be divided among the participants of the cooperation. In the case of vertical integration, these problems are suppressed by a unified ownership although the integrated firm may require more information for internal control. Thirdly, compared with a vertical cooperation arrangement, vertical integration requires more commitments in resources and is harder to reverse, therefore it is a more credible move. Finally, from the regulatory point of view, the two practices may face different legal restrictions.

In this study, the economic essence of *vertical integration* is defined as a process which puts the productive assets allocated among the different but sequentially related economic activities under a single ownership. The administration will obtain a unified control over all decision variables and achieve complete coordination and cooperation among the economic agents within one firm.

2.2. Market Transactions

The term *market transactions* is used to describe the situation when firms rely completely on the spot market for their supplies or sales. In the pure form of market transaction, all buyers are in contact with all possible suppliers and search for the best possible deals. They make their own decisions about which transactions to accept in order to maximize their payoffs. In addition to the spot market transactions, there are also the futures markets, which are beyond the scope of our analysis. In the U.S. semiconductor industry, for example, semiconductor manufacturers turned out some

US$ 25 billion of silicon chips in 1988[3]. Among them more than $ 18 billion worth of chips (72% of the market) were produced by *merchant* semiconductor companies, which sell chips on the open market, with the remaining $7 billion worth produced by captive manufacturers. In the downstream computer industry, a lot of other computer producers, which purchase chips from the merchant manufacturers, rely on the market to coordinate the same activities. The leading computer producer IBM is a vertically integrated firm and produces $3.1 billion worth of chips in-house instead.

2.3. Alternative Vertical Arrangements

This category includes a variety of vertical arrangements which fall between market transactions and vertical integration. The concepts and terms used in the literature have not yet been standardized. Although some economists refer to some of these arrangements as vertical restraints, this term is too general to include different incentives and mechanisms behind each of these complex vertical arrangements. Instead, we are going to discuss three concepts which fall in between the two extreme cases: quasi-integration, vertical disintegration and vertical separation.

Vertical quasi-integration. There are at least three different definitions of vertical quasi-integration in the literature. According to Blois, the earliest user of this concept, "vertical quasi-integration" describes a situation where some firms gain the advantages of vertical integration without assuming the risks or rigidity of ownership. For instance, a large customer takes a substantial portion of the output of a particular supplier when the market condition is characterized by oversupply. This supplier will be susceptible to considerable discipline from its customer. As a result, the large customer can gain the advantage of vertical integration by keeping its costs as low as possible within the bounds of ensuring a continuing supply of inputs (Blois, 1972).

Monteverde and Teece (1982) use "vertical quasi-integration" to describe a specific practice, particularly in the auto industry: "a common organizational form in industrial economies is what may be called quasi-vertical integration: the ownership by a downstream firm of the specialized tools, dies, jigs, and patterns used in the fabrication of components for larger systems". This practice can be justified on several grounds. First, it increases the flexibility of the downstream firm since the assembler

---

[3] See "The U.S. Chipmakers' Shaky Comeback", *Fortune*, June 20, 1988.

can move the tools from one establishment to another if one particular supplier's production is interrupted. Secondly, it increases entry barriers for the replacement market since each supplier must contemplate complete retooling if it wants to enter into an independent parts production. Thirdly, it reduces the amount of investment for specific assets from the suppliers and, therefore, increases the efficiency of the market. Quasi-integration differs from full vertical integration in that the downstream firm still contracts with a supplier for the actual manufacturing of the component, whereas with full vertical integration the production process itself is internalized.

According to Michael Porter (1980, p.301), "quasi-integration is to use debt or equity investments and other means to create alliances between vertically related firms without full ownership". Common forms of quasi-integration include: minority equity investment; loans and loan guarantees; pre-purchase credits; exclusive dealing agreements; specialized logistical facilities and cooperative R&D.

Vertical disintegration or *vertical separation* are two terms used to describe a situation where two adjacent stages of production (distribution) are deliberately kept under separate ownership and control in order to achieve certain strategic objectives, such as a more cooperative outcome for the upstream industry. For example, when choosing its distribution channel strategy, the manufacturers in an oligopolistic industry may find it more profitable not to engage in forward integration if that can avoid direct competition between rival manufacturers. The difference between vertical disintegration (vertical separation) and quasi-integration is that the former describes an institutional arrangement which separates two vertically related but separable production stages into two firms; each pursues its own objective, and at the same time an exclusive relation is kept between these two separated firms. The latter implies that a certain level of vertical cooperation takes place between firms in two related industries with or without common ownership.

The difference between various forms of hybrid vertical arrangements and market transactions is whether or not restraints exist between firms and their particular supplier(s) or buyer(s). These restraints may be deliberately created for certain strategic reasons or due to the existence of transaction costs. For instance, under a contract arrangement, a buyer (supplier) cannot switch from his existing supplier (customer) or he can only do so at substantial switching costs, whereas he could do so easily in a market transaction game.

In our analysis, the variety of vertical structures will be limited to three basic forms: market transactions, supply contracts and full integration. Supply contracts are used in a context similar to vertical disintegration. Once we understand the incentive implications behind these three forms of vertical relationships, other forms of vertical structures may be treated as the combination of these three basic forms.

2.4. Various Forms of Oligopoly

A so-called *successive oligopoly* describes a scenario in which two oligopolistic industries are vertically related. In addition to that, market power is assumed to be distributed asymmetrically among firms in these two industries. The upstream firms (suppliers) have the market power to decide price (quantity) of intermediate products. Taking the input price as given, the downstream firms have market power over consumers. If the market power of the upstream firm and downstream firm is reversed, a *successive oligopsony* is created.

A successive oligopoly differs from the scenario in which the upstream firms and downstream firms bargain over the price of the intermediate products, which is referred to as a *bilateral oligopoly*. As has been mentioned earlier, bilateral relations lead to an indeterminate outcome.

A *mixed oligopoly* refers to an imperfect market environment where the firms in the same industry pursue asymmetric objectives. Different objectives do exist between the vertically related firms, e.g. the retailer's and the manufacturer's objective functions are obviously different from each other. However, this is not called mixed oligopoly when both firms are profit maximizers. Therefore, mixed oligopoly is used only to indicate a scenario in which the welfare-maximizing public firms and profit maximizing private firms co-exist in the same industry.

3. THE STATE OF THE ART

In this section, we are going to provide an overview of recent developments in the economics of oligopolistic vertical integration and the latest research findings on mixed oligopoly. The economics of vertical integration focuses on the types of alternative vertical arrangements; in particular, their economic consequences and implications for corporate strategy and competition policy. As has been stated earlier, there are a variety of approaches we may take in order to tackle this issue; this survey instead is devoted exclusively to the studies on vertical integration in an oligopolistic setting. Some of the important studies of vertical integration may not be included when different approaches are adopted in those studies[4]. This approach will save space for original analysis, although it may have the drawback of de-emphasizing the relations between the different approaches to yjr analysis of vertical integration. As a remedy, the comparison between our results and other approaches, e.g. transaction cost economics, are provided whenever there is a need to help readers obtain a good understanding of our contribution. Table 0.1 summarizes some of the most important findings on the welfare effect of the vertical merger under different market structures and demand conditions.

One of the basic assumptions which distinguishes the different models concerns the degree of substitutability between intermediate inputs. This section covers the literature under the assumption of fixed proportions of inputs and the subsequent section covers the strand of the literature with variable proportions of inputs.

3.1. Oligopolistic Vertical Integration with Fixed Input Proportions

The fixed proportions input model is the most widely used model in the literature of vertical integration. This is mainly for two reasons. First of all, the models with the fixed coefficients technology, which correspond to a Leontief production technology, are much simpler analytically than the models which incorporate the substitutability between multiple inputs. Nevertheless, the technology with fixed proportions inputs can be seen as a special case of more general technology specifications. Some basic insights regarding vertical relations, revealed under fixed proportions of inputs, can still be useful to understand more general cases. In addition, there are a number of important industry sectors to which the fixed input proportions model can be applied. Such industries include the semiconductor, computer and petroleum industries, among others. More specifically, as in the petroleum industry, the quantity of crude oil remains approximately the same when the crude oil is shipped from oil fields to the refineries. This invariance also applies to the refined product if a pre-determined method for converting the crude oil into refined oil products is used. An important application of the fixed inputs proportions model, particularly in the more recent literature, is how to handle the relationship between manufacturers and distributors, the so-called distribution channel issues.

---

[4] A concise review on the literature of vertical integration can be found in Perry (1989).

Table 0.1. Alternative Models of Vertical Merger

Names	Production Function	Preference Structure	Market Structures	Merger Effect*
Warren-Boulton (1974)	Variable proportions C.E.S. production	Constant elasticity demand	Monopolist vs competitors	±
Greenhut-Ohta (1976)	Fixed proportions	Linear demand	Monopolist vs competitors;	0
		nonlinear demand	Monopolist vs monopolist;	+
			Monopolist vs oligopolists	+
Greenhut-Ohta (1979)	Fixed proportions	General demand	Oligopolists vs oligopolists	+
Mallela-Nahata (1980)	Variable proportions C.E.S. production	Constant elasticity demand	Monopolist vs competitors	±
Waterson (1982)	Variable proportions C.E.S. production	Constant elasticity demand	Monopolist vs oligopolists	±
Hamilton-Lee (1986a)	Fixed proportions	General demand	Dominant firm vs duopoly	±
Hamilton-Lee (1986b)			Monopolist vs monopolist	±
Quirmbach (1986a)	General production function	General demand	Monopolist vs contestable market	±
Quirmbach (1986b)			Monopolist vs competitors	±
Abiru (1988)	Variable proportions C.E.S. production	Constant elasticity demand	Oligopolists vs oligopolists	+
Salinger (1988)	Fixed proportions	General demand	Monopolist vs perfect competition	+
Bonanno-Vickers(1988)/ Lin (1988)	Fixed proportions	General demand	Duopolist vs duopolist	+
Ordover-Saloner Salop (1990)	Fixed proportions	General demand	Duopolist vs duopolist	±
Hart and Tirole (1990)	Fixed proportions	General demand	Duopoly vs duopoly	±

* The welfare effect of vertical merger may be positive "+", indeterminate "±", or zero "0".

Along these lines, the existing work can be divided into two groups. One is represented by the works of Greenhut and Ohta (1979), Hamilton and Lee (1986a; 1986b), and Salinger (1988) who look at a successive oligopoly and address the normative issues and welfare implications of vertical integration. Another research line deals with a specific issue of vertical integration, namely, the relationship between manufacturers and retailers (distributors).

Greenhut and Ohta (1979) depict a model with two successive industries, where both stages are Cournot oligopoly in selling and the downstream stage is characterized by perfect competition in buying. They show that in the case of fixed production coefficients, constant returns to scale and linear demand, industry output increases and the final product's price falls if a sub-group of firms merge vertically. The profits of the merging firms increase at the expense of the non-integrated firms, while industry profit falls. That reverses the results of successive monopoly, in which vertical integration is beneficial to both consumers and merging monopolists. They further demonstrate that if the merged firms act as a Stackelberg leader to the remaining non-integrated firms, the market equilibrium output increases further than in a Cournot world of oligopoly. Their results support the view that vertical integration is socially desirable.

Hamilton and Lee (1986a) develop a model of vertical merger by introducing the possibility of entry into the intermediate inputs market. In their model, the downstream final market is composed of two Cournot firms. Entry into this market is assumed to be impossible. The upstream input market has a dominant firm and a group of competitive fringe firms, with the entry rate into the fringe being a function of intermediate input price. They show that a merger of the dominant firm with one of the Cournot downstream firms places the non-integrated fringe firms at a position of competitive disadvantage. Vertical integration restricts their production and reduces their market shares. But this foreclosure effect is dominated by the welfare enhancing effect of decline in the input price perceived by the downstream firms. Since vertical integration reduces the input price, the merger does discourage entry. However, they show that the slower rate of entry is not able to counteract the welfare enhancing effect in the long run. The vertical merger still yields a permanent increase in economic welfare. In their second paper, Hamilton and Lee show that the welfare gain due to the elimination of the mark-up over the input may be limited if the degree of contestability in the intermediate input market is high. Hence, the vertical merger may reduce social welfare when the market foreclosure effect becomes dominant (Hamilton and Lee, 1986b).

Salinger (1988) considers a two-stage Cournot game with n firms, in which vertically integrated and non-integrated producers co-exist. Assuming a linear demand and fixed inputs proportions, he examines the price path for the final and intermediate products and shows that those prices depend on two contradictory effects of the vertical merger. One effect is the elimination of successive markup for a vertically integrated firm, which increases competition in the final products market and lowers the intermediate price as well as the price of the final goods. Another is the increase in concentration in the intermediate goods market for the non-integrated producers, which causes an increase of the intermediate goods price. In his model the effect of a vertical merger on the derived demand curve facing the non-integrated upstream producers outweighs the effect of the increase in concentration in the intermediate goods market, thus causing the intermediate goods price to fall.

A number of authors (McGuire and Staelin, 1983; Bonanno and Vickers 1988; Lin, 1988) focus on a specific type of vertical integration, the relation between manufacturers and retailers/distributors. The standard setting for this type of model is a two-stage Bertrand duopoly with differentiated goods. They choose price instead of quantity as the decision variable for two reasons. First of all, they argue that using output quantity as a decision variable in the fixed coefficients model may restrict the decision flexibility of the downstream players. Secondly, with differentiated products, equilibrium prices need not be identical and a specification of the industry demand function, like $p=f(\Sigma x_i)$, cannot be used. By defining the relationship between each retailer and manufacturer as a captive exclusive relation, they seek the equilibrium vertical structures with property of sub-game perfectness and their implications for corporate strategies. In these models, the retailers are assumed to be Bertrand oligopolists and competing non-cooperatively in the second stage by selecting retail prices, given wholesale prices. In the first stage, the manufacturers, knowing the possible reactions of their captive retailers, are able to choose the wholesale prices and to manipulate the relations with the retailers in order to maximize their profits.

McGuire and Staelin (1983) assume a linear demand and cost function with constant returns to scales and investigate the effect of product differentiation on the Nash equilibrium vertical structures between manufacturers and their retailers. They find that the manufacturers' profits depend on the degree of substitutability between the end products of two manufacturers. When demands are independent, each manufacturer is a monopolist. It is much more profitable for the monopolist to integrate vertically with his retailer. As the products become better substitutes, vertical integration is not the best strategy for manufacturers to follow. They conclude that the substitutability among competing goods does influence the equilibrium vertical structure.

If a retailer's action does not influence his competitor's demand, vertical integration will increase the total profit of the retailer and manufacturer by eliminating the harmful mark-up over intermediate inputs[5]. However, if the retail market is highly competitive, manufacturers in a duopoly are better off if they can reduce the level of competition by inserting independent retailers between themselves.

Bonanno and Vickers (1988), in a framework similar to that of McGuire and Staelin, assume that the manufacturers are able to extract profit from retailers by charging a fixed fee. The question then becomes, what kind of vertical structure can maximize the total profits of a manufacturer and its captive retailer. They show that because the retailer's prices are strategic complements in a Bertrand game, vertical separation would increase the possibility of cooperation between competitive manufacturers and lead to a higher final product price[6]. Hence, the manufacturers' profits increase after the manufacturers have separated from the retailers.

Vertical separation permits the manufacturers to charge wholesale prices higher than their marginal costs, which pushes the positively sloped reaction curves of the retailers to the right. Competition between the retailers is consequently weakened. Subsequently, cooperation among the manufacturers becomes easier. The final equilibrium retail prices as well as wholesale prices are higher, as are the profits of the manufacturers. Lin (1988) examines a similar scenario. In addition to independently obtaining the same results, he demonstrates that complete extraction of retailers' surplus is not a necessary condition to ensure that vertical separation is an optimal strategy.

A few remarks may help to clarify the differences between the research lines represented by Greenhut-Ohta and McGuire-Staelin. The work of Greenhut-Ohta, to a large extent, follows the traditional spirit by focusing on the welfare effect of vertical integration. The works of McGuire-Staelin and others try to explain the emergence of vertical integration under variety of circumstances. They search for the causes which lead to the existence of vertical structures which are sub-game perfect Nash equilibria.

---

[5] McGuire and Staelin mistakenly explain the profit increase of the manufacturer after integration by the profit transfer from retailers to manufacturers.

[6] See Bulow, Geanakoplos and Klemperer (1985) for discussion of strategic substitution and complementarity. The strategic variables in the product market subgame are strategic substitutes (strategic complements) if a disposition towards less aggressive behavior by one firm induces more aggressive (less aggressive) behavior in the rival.

With different objectives in mind, the game settings of the two differ as well. Greenhut-Ohta compare the equilibrium output quantities and final product prices under two exogenously determined vertical structures: market transactions and vertical integration. McGuire-Staelin employ a two-stage four-player game and assume that the relation between the manufacturer and its retailer is a principal-agent type of relationship. In addition to changing the wholesale price, manufacturers are able to influence the relationship with retailers in order to gain a competitive advantage conditional on the other player's actions. Therefore, an optimal vertical structure is endogenized in their model. The strategic variables used are also different. Greenhut and Ohta use output quantity as the strategic variable in a conventional Cournot-Nash scenario. McGuire and Staelin assume that the players select prices as strategic variables for final products as well as for intermediate inputs. And finally, the Greenhut-Ohta results can be seen as mixing the game changing effect and pure integration effect by ignoring the other possible vertical structures before vertical integration takes place. McGuire and Staelin highlight the pure effect of integration by comparing the profitability of the firms involved under an exclusive supply contract and under vertical integration.

Although the above models differ in several aspects, the basic conclusion is that the welfare enhancing effect of vertical integration dominates the anti-competitive effect. In contrast to the above results, several authors recently are able to show that the anti-competitive vertical integration is possible if such an integration can be used to achieve the purpose of foreclosure of downstream firms from an essential source of supply. These authors typically model the firms as sophisticated players who are able to use a wide range of strategies and counter strategies. Ordover, Saloner and Salop (1990) show that anti-competitive foreclosure can arise as an equilibrium strategy in a model with differentiated products and price-setting firms. In their model the sum of the profits of the foreclosed downstream firm and its supplier increases if the foreclosed firm's price rises. The rival's price adjusts optimally upwards because of the strategic complementarity of the prices. In the quantity-setting, homogeneous goods model, by contrast, the sum of those profits increases when the foreclosed firm's output increases. That lowers the final price. Hart and Tirole (1990) consider a successive duopoly model and show that vertical integration can be privately desirable yet socially undesirable in a more general strategy space than in Ordover, Saloner and Salop (1990).

3.2. Oligopolistic Vertical Integration with Variable Input Proportions

Studies of vertical integration with variable proportions concentrate on the impact of vertical integration on the direction of price changes and on its welfare implications. The substitutability between intermediate inputs is, in most cases, incorporated into the models with the constant elasticity of substitution (CES) production function in the downstream industry.

Waterson (1982) sets up a model with one input monopolist and *n* downstream oligopolists. He investigates the effect of vertical integration when substitution between the monopolized input and the competitively supplied input is possible. Based on computer simulation, he concludes that the overall effect of vertical integration is very likely to be beneficial as long as the elasticity of substitution remains fairly low, though the prices of the final goods often rise. When the substitution elasticity increases, welfare is less likely to be improved by unconstrained vertical integration. These results are consistent with the intuition that a high substitution elasticity between two inputs limits the market power of the input monopolist and, therefore, reduces the welfare loss which may be potentially regained by vertical integration.

Waterson's results have been criticized recently by Abiru (1988) for mixing the effects of vertical and horizontal merger. When an upstream monopolist starts to merge with more than one downstream firm, the number of independent oligopolists in the final product market declines. Abiru separates these two effects by employing a model where both the upstream and the downstream industries are oligopolistically structured. He investigates the effect of vertical integration on the price and quantity of the final product by looking at the price-cost margin in the downstream industry. He shows that vertical integration does not change the magnitude of the profit-cost margin of a downstream oligopolist. He also finds that vertical integration lowers the perceived marginal costs for this downstream oligopolist by eliminating the mark-up on one of the inputs. Combining the conditions of a constant price-cost margin and a lower perceived marginal cost, an oligopolist must lower his selling price to maximize his profit. Abiru concludes that the *pure* vertical integration effect causes an unambiguous decrease in the final product price and increases the final product output quantity and consumer welfare.

3.3. Asymmetric Objectives and Mixed Oligopoly

The literature on mixed oligopoly reflects the trend that the industrial organization theory has been penetrating into the field of economics of public enterprises. Although the earlier literature on public enterprises were strongly influenced by the second-best literature and regulatory issues, a game theoretical approach has been used in some more recent work.

The work of Merrill and Schneider (1966) is one of the earliest to look at the issue of mixed oligopoly in a price leadership model. They assume that there are three private firms of equal size producing homogeneous goods. The firms have identical constant marginal costs and capacity constraints. The linear demand curve is assumed to be located far enough to the right, so that if the price were as low as the marginal costs, the industry's capacity could not satisfy the total demand and the market could not reach an equilibrium. These firms are able to form a cartel and charge a monopoly price for their products. This leads to a less than full utilization of production capacity and substantial profits for the cartel.

Merrill and Schneider assume that the government wants to maximize the industrial output by nationalizing one private firm and directly controlling the price of the public firm. The remaining private firms, by acting as a cartel, are able to set their price once the public firm decides on its price. The private firms may set their own prices higher or lower than the price of the public firm depending on which will yield a higher profit for them.

They show that the entry of a public firm into such an industry can result in an improvement of the market performance by reducing price and increasing output. However, it may not be optimal for the public firm to set price equal to its marginal cost and produce at full capacity, if this leads to monopoly pricing by private firms over the remaining buyers. This is more likely to happen when a firm's capacity is small relative to the market size and when the public firm cannot sell exclusively to "higher price buyers". They argue that, in any case, the public firm cannot stimulate the industry to work at full capacity unless it owns all the capacities in the industry.

Harris and Wiens (1980) investigate the role of the public firm as a regulatory instrument by assuming the public firm to be a dominant firm. They argue that the first-best allocation can be achieved if the public firm can announce its output policy to the private firms which react to it. Under the assumptions of decreasing returns to scale with homogeneous goods and perfect information, the public firm computes the competitive output level of the industry, which means that the public firm's marginal cost equals its price, and announces the output policy of making up any difference between this target and the private firms' output level. The private firms, in fact, face a given price and will choose their output level such that their marginal cost equals the price. The problem of this solution is that it may not be credible since the public firm may face a huge loss for certain values of the private firms' output. They themselves also point out that when information is incomplete, the public firm may have difficulty deciding the output target. Moreover, the private firms may have incentives to produce less than they would otherwise. This leads the public firm to produce more than the first-best solution requires. And the rapid increasing marginal cost of the public firm may lead to a higher product price and lower industry output than in the case of perfect information.

Beato and Mas-Colell (1984) deviate from the traditional assumption that public firms always take the dominant position and investigate a mixed duopoly in which the public firm may be either a *leader* or a *follower*. When the public firm plays the role of a follower in a Stackelberg game, it takes the output of the private firm as given and is instructed by the government to use the marginal cost pricing rule for choosing its own level of output. The private firm, on the other hand, acts as a leader, maximizing its profit along the public firm's reaction curve. They assume that technology shows decreasing returns to scale. It is argued that when the public firm acts as a follower the social welfare level may not be always dominated by the welfare level when the public firm plays a reverse role. They prove that if the equilibrium output of the private firm increases or at least does not decrease after the role of the private firm is reversed from a follower to a leader, the social welfare will be higher or at least not lower than the social welfare level when the public firm plays the role of the leader. They show that by imposing certain regularities, the private firms can find an equilibrium along the reaction curve of the public firm that results in a higher output level of the private firm than the equilibrium output along the reaction curve of a profit maximizing firm. The reason is that the industrial output must be higher than otherwise if the private firm increases its output after taking the role of the Stackelberg leader. At the market clearing condition, the price will fall and social welfare will increase.

De Fraja and Delbono (1989) consider an industry formed by a single public firm and n private firms with linear demand and quadratic cost function. Unlike Beato and Mas-Colell who consider only the Stackelberg relation, De Fraja and Delbono allow the public firm to take on a whole range of strategies. They compare the social welfare levels under the following alternative scenarios: The public firm behaves as a Stackelberg leader, a Cournot-type welfare maximizer and a Cournot-type profit maximizer. They show that when the public firm acts as a Stackelberg leader the social welfare is higher than if it acts as a Cournot-type player when the public firm is a welfare maximizer. They further demonstrate that when the public firm is instructed to maximize the total surplus, social welfare may be either higher or lower than social welfare when the public firm is instructed to maximize profit in a Cournot game. In other words, a profit-maximizing public firm may lead to a higher social welfare than a welfare maximizing public firm can reach. The reason behind their results is that they assume a quadratic cost function in their model. The asymmetric objectives between the public firm and n private firms lead to asymmetric output levels between the two types of firms. The public firm will produce more output than each of the n private firms. This leads to a rapid increase in the marginal cost of the public firm. That is, the public firm produces at an output level which is inefficient from the welfare point of view. The increase in consumer surplus may not be high enough to compensate the efficiency lost on the supply side due to the asymmetry in the firms' output levels. This is more likely to happen when the number of private firms is relatively large. When the public firm acts as a profit maximizer, all $n+1$ firms become identical and produce an equal amount of output; the diseconomy of scale from the public firm is avoided.

Cremer, Marchand and Thisse (1989) look at a case of n private firms selling a homogeneous product and competing over quantity. They analyze the extent to which public enterprises can be used to improve resource allocation in such an imperfectly competitive market. In their model all firms have constant marginal costs plus a fixed cost F, but the public firm has to pay a premium c per unit of output. The public firm has a non-negative profit constraint. They argue that it is often socially optimal to nationalize one single firm in that n-firm industry, but the output expansion effect of nationalizing the private firm is limited by the non-negative profit constraint on a high cost producer. They further demonstrate that the increase in social welfare is not guaranteed by creating a new public firm in the industry. The entry of a public firm is desirable only when the fixed cost is not too high. When the fixed cost is high, the creation of a new public firm may lower net welfare. In a separate paper, the same authors analyze a mixed oligopoly with horizontal product differentiation and quadratic transport costs (Cremer, Marchand and Thisse, 1991). It is shown that it is only when $n=2$ or $n\geq 6$ that a mixed oligopoly with one public firm is socially preferable to the private oligopoly. Moreover, when $n\geq 4$, the best position for the public firm is to act as a Stackelberg follower.

This strand of the literature shows that the government may have a third choice when dealing with concentrated industries. Instead of using nationalization with complete state-ownership or regulating the complete private sector by government supervision and anti-trust laws, the government may regulate a concentrated industry by the participation of one or more public firms and the creation of a mixed oligopoly. In the models developed in the literature, the costs and demand functions which the firms face are imposed exogenously. Therefore, the analysis for the impact of the objective asymmetry is limited to one industry. Moreover, in these models the role of the private firm is not the focus of the analysis. The implications for corporate strategy for the private firms operating in such an environment are not properly addressed.

4. THE RESEARCH OUTLINE

The review of literature indicates that the study of vertical integration is far from complete and a substantial gap exists in our understanding of the incentives of vertical integration in the complete range of horizontal market structure particularly in the oligopolistic setting. There are a number of theoretical issues which need to be addressed more thoroughly, such as

What type of vertical relationship is the subgame perfect equilibrium structure in a successive oligopoly?
How does the equilibrium change when market structure changes?
How does the vertical structure influence the profits and strategic positions of the firm?
What are the welfare implications of vertical integration with or without the presence of substitutability between intermediate inputs?

The answers to these questions will allow us to move to the second group of questions which deals with vertical integration issues in a successive oligopoly with asymmetric objectives. Although these issues becomes increasingly important, particularly in the wake of the rapid developments in Eastern European and other traditionally centrally planned economies, few studies can be found in the existing literature. The questions, which can be raised, include:

What is the impact of asymmetry in objectives on the equilibrium intermediate input prices and on the final goods market?
What is the role of a welfare maximizing public firm in a mixed successive oligopoly?
What is the vertical strategy for the profit maximizing private firm in such a mixed successive oligopoly?
How does asymmetry in objectives influence the equilibrium outcome in a mixed market?

The answers to these questions will be relevant not only for Eastern European countries but also for countries characterized as mixed economies in general.

By setting the two-fold objectives so as to achieve a better understanding of oligopolistic vertical integration in general and to analyze the vertical integration with objective asymmetry in particular, the overall plan of the book is as follows.

In the next three chapters the various scenarios of vertical integration with fixed proportions of intermediate inputs are analyzed. By exploring a successive duopoly model, Chapter 1 looks at the equilibrium outcomes under the various types of vertical relations. The Nash equilibrium vertical structure is derived given spot market transactions, exclusive contracts and vertical integration. The possibility of using vertical integration as a sort of entry barrier is also considered. Chapter 2 then generalizes the results of the successive duopoly by considering an n-firm oligopoly, and thus allows us to look at the issues of interrelations between horizontal competition and the Nash equilibrium vertical structures. The strategic impact of product differentiation on the equilibrium outcomes is the major concern of Chapter 3.

Departing from the fixed input proportions model, Chapter 4 starts with a model of variable proportions of intermediate inputs and focuses on the strategic effects of substitutability on the firms' vertical structure in oligopolistic competition.

Based on the insights revealed in the first four chapters, vertical integration issues are investigated in Chapter 5 in a mixed successive oligopolistic setting when the asymmetric objectives are added as a new feature. In addition to Cournot competition which is one of the basic characteristics in the previous chapters, other solution concepts such as Stackelberg equilibria are also considered. The policy implications of the analysis and outcomes are demonstrated through an example of evaluating the welfare impact of foreign direct investment and technology licensing in a mixed economy. For illustrative purposes, Table 0.2 is constructed to highlight the contents and scope of this study.

Table 0.2. *Taxonomy of Oligopolistic Vertical Integration Analysis*

Chapter No.	Firm's objectives	Demand characteristics	Technology characteristics	Market structures	Vertical relations	Purpose of investigation
1				*Duopoly*	*Market transactions, supply contract, full integration*	*Equilibrium output quantities, prices, firms's profits, social welfare*
2	*Symmetric objectives*	*Linear demand with homogenous goods*	*Fixed proportions of inputs*	*Oligopoly*	*Market transactions, supply contracts, mixed integration, full integration*	*Impact of horizontal market structure on equilibrium, mixed integration game, endogeneity of vertical structure*
3		*Linear demand with differentiated goods*		*Duopoly*	*Supply contracts, mixed integration, full integration*	*The impact of type and degree of product differentiation on equilibrium outcomes*
4		*Constant elasticity demand with homogenous goods*	*Variable proportions of inputs*	*Duopoly*	*Market transactions, supply contracts, full integration*	*Equilibrium outcomes with substitutability between intermediate inputs*
5	*Asymmetri c objective*	*Linear demand with differentiated goods*	*Fixed proportions of inputs*	*Duopoly*	*Supply contract, mixed integration, full integration*	*Impact of objective asymmetry on firms' profits and social welfare*

5. METHODOLOGY

One of the features of this work is the use of noncooperative game theory, which has revolutionized theoretically research in industrial economics. Although controversy continues on the usefulness of game theory in economic analysis, most economists would agree that the introduction of game theoretic concepts into the study of oligopolistic competition has made it possible to analyze in greater depth a whole range of questions that was not previously amenable to economic analysis[7]. The game theoretical paradigm standardizes and simplifies the formulation of problems and provides a way of modelling and analyzing scenarios in which each player's optimal decision depends on his conjecture of his rival's actions. Instead of simply following the fashion, a special reason for adopting the game theoretical framework in vertical integration analysis is the requirement for the explicit specification of the payoff functions of the game players. This is one of the most important elements in the whole analysis. That makes it easy to analyze the conduct of and interactions between the economic agencies with symmetric and/or asymmetric objectives and the resulting economic performance.

When discussing the vertical integration issues in our non-cooperative game theoretical model, Nash equilibrium concept is used. The firms modeled as players in a non-cooperative game may have complex strategies and payoffs. A *Nash equilibrium* is a set of strategies if, holding the strategies of all other firms constant, no firm can obtain a higher payoff by choosing a different strategy (Johansen, 1982; Friedman, 1989).

The two-stage game theoretical model is used somewhat differently from other studies that assume the same players are able to decide over one or more strategic variables in an intertemporal fashion. For instance, the rival firms may choose in the first period the level of the firms' research and development expenditure and in the second stage the same firms make the output decision over quantity or price (De Bondt and Veugelers, 1991). In our vertical integration analysis, the *two-stage game* refers to the interactions between the firms in two successively related industries. Although the game is played intertemporally, the players in the different stages may or may not be the same.

---

[7] The debate between Fisher (1990) and Shapiro (1990) symbolizes the different opinions among economists; also see Rubinstein (1991).

As has been documented in the literature of game theory, the information structure of the game has critical impact on the outcome of the game. In our study, *almost perfect information* is used to characterize the basic information environment.

To understand this information structure, it is important to clarify some basic concepts of information structure which are relevant in our analysis and which a game player may possess in any given game. First of all, *complete information* versus *incomplete information* refers to whether or not each player knows (a) who the set of players are, (b) all actions available to all players , and (c) all potential outcomes for all players. Essentially, complete information is obtained when each player knows (a), (b), and (c). *Perfect information* is a very strong information requirement. Games with perfect information represent situations in which individuals move one at a time and, whenever a player moves, he knows the past moves of all other players as well as his own past moves. All moves are sequential. A game with *imperfect information* implies simultaneous moves of players (Myerson, 1991). In a two-stage game, *almost perfect information* describes a combination of perfect information between stages and complete but imperfect information within each of the separate stages (Tirole, 1988).

In our vertical integration game, the firms in both the upstream industry and the downstream industry are assumed to know who their rivals are, what the possible actions they as well as their rivals may take and all the possible outcomes of their actions. In other words, the three conditions for complete information are satisfied in each separate industry. But in each of these two industries, the firms are assumed to make simultaneous moves when choosing their output quantities (prices). Therefore, a player has complete but imperfect information.

The information environment between the industries is quite different. First, the upstream firms are assumed to decide the output quantity (price) of the intermediate input by taking into account the optimal reaction of the downstream firms. Then, the downstream firms make their own decisions based on the known price of the intermediate inputs. The moves of the firms in different industries are sequential. Therefore, perfect information is obtained.

Because of the complexity of the game structure, the analysis starts with the simplest scenario possible, and the complications are gradually added in the following chapters. Chapter 1 analyzes a successive duopoly model with homogeneous goods and symmetric objectives. The settings become more complicated in the following three chapters when changes in market structure, product differentiation and substitutability are added sequentially. Asymmetric objectives are absent from the analysis until chapter 5, which analyzes a mixed successive duopoly. That not only helps us to see how the additional factor can influence the results, but also provides a clear picture for the presentation of the results.

It is not difficult to find the difference between our approach and other similar studies in the spirit of transaction costs economics. The basic conclusion of transaction cost economics states that the governance structure of an institution should economize the transaction costs arising from the task of carrying out an exchange. The comparison can be made between transaction costs if exchanges happen between two independent parties (market transactions, independent distribution channels) and when they happen between two parties working for the same firm (vertical integration).

Transaction cost analysis begins with the assertion that in a wide range of circumstances the free, competitive give-and-take process works better than administrative direction, i.e. *a priori*, the market is more efficient than vertical integration. The bias towards market transaction is overturned (vertical integration becomes more efficient) when (a) the both parties in a transaction must invest in transaction-specific assets which may encourage opportunistic behavior; (b) the evaluation of performance is difficult; and (c) there is substantial uncertainty involved.

It is clear that while transaction cost economics focuses mainly on the issue of economic efficiency reflected in the bilateral relations, our study emphasizes not only the bilateral relations between vertically related firms but also their strategic impact on competitive positions in the related industries. Moreover, one of the fundamental assumptions of transaction costs economics is that of asymmetric information between buyers and sellers, which encourages opportunistic behavior. But in our model the information structure between industries is assumed to be perfect. Finally, transaction cost economics often assumes that the firms engaged in transactions tend to choose the type of institutional arrangement that economizes transaction costs. The economics of oligopolistic vertical integration shows that the private incentives of the firm may not be consistent with the goal of social welfare under certain conditions. Therefore, public policy implications are important aspects of oligopolistic vertical integration that appear to be less significant in the studies of transaction cost economics.

PART I

OLIGOPOLISTIC VERTICAL INTEGRATION WITH SYMMETRIC OBJECTIVES

Chapter 1

VERTICAL INTEGRATION IN A SUCCESSIVE DUOPOLY WITH FIXED PROPORTIONS OF INPUTS

1. INTRODUCTION

In this chapter we are going to examine some controversial issues involing vertical integration by exploring a simple successive duopoly model. These issues, such as the impact of vertical integration on the prices of final goods and on the firms' profits, are cornerstones for further discussions of implications for corporate strategy as well as for public policy. From this model, we can derive the Nash equilibrium vertical structure of an oligopolistic industry. A successive duopoly model is considered mainly because it is analytically simple but at the same time it allows us to represent the underlying game in its strategic form. Hence, it facilitates the discussion and the presentation of the results.

One of the features in this and the following two chapters is that the production functions are characterized by fixed coefficients. One merit of this assumption is the simplification of the analysis. A more important reason for us to look at the case of fixed proportions of inputs is that the technology with fixed proportions of inputs is an approximate description for some important industries, such as the petroleum, transport, computer and semiconductor industries and for the relationship between manufacturers and retailers (distributors) in general.

In this Chapter, we will first specify our basic successive duopoly model. Then, discussions of four different types of game settings follow. These games differ in the vertical relations between firms in adjacent industries. The equilibria under a variety of game scenarios are used to develop some propositions that shield light on the vertical relations through which the firms in both industries interact strategically.

2. A BASIC SUCCESSIVE DUOPOLY MODEL

Imagine there are two adjacent industries. One industry produces goods closer to final consumers. An example of such an industry is the computer hardware industry.

Another industry produces intermediate goods, for instance, the semiconductor industry. When the structure of both industries is characterized as a duopoly, we call it a *successive duopoly*. The two firms in the downstream industry, denoted by D_1 and D_2, produce homogeneous final products with output quantities q_1 and q_2. The two upstream firms, denoted by U_1 and U_2, produce intermediate goods with quantities x_1 and x_2 respectively. The producers of the final goods face a downward-sloping linear demand curve

$$p=a-b(q_1+q_2) \tag{1.1}$$

where $a>0$, $b>0$ and p is the uniform price that consumers pay. The linear demand function allows the model to be solved in its closed form. The solution of this special case may provide some results that are otherwise less transparent under a more general demand scheme. The downstream firms' marginal costs, which are equal to their average costs, are denoted by mc. The marginal costs are the costs for purchasing intermediate inputs and there is no cost specific to the downstream production. There may be more than one kind of input used to produce the final products. Under the assumption of the fixed proportions of inputs, derived demands for all intermediate inputs are linear functions of the final output. Thus, different types of inputs can be normalized as one representative input with no changes in the basic results of our analysis. Hence, in the following discussion we only consider one input factor for production of the final goods. The price of the intermediate good is denoted by w. The upstream firms U_1 and U_2 employ a type of production technology with constant returns to scale and their marginal costs are determined exogenously and are represented by a constant c.

This actually posits a framework of a 4-player game. Now we can specify the types of games played at each of these two adjacent industries and the types of vertical relations between them. The distribution of market power between these two industries is represented by a Stackelberg relation where the firms in the upstream industry play the role of *leader*. As such they have the power to set the price or quantity of the intermediate goods by taking into account the reactions of the downstream firms. The downstream firms, having the market power with respect to the final consumers, are competitive buyers of the intermediate goods. Each firm is assumed to maximize its own profit.

Our model differs somewhat from some of the models in the literature (Bonanno and Vickers, 1988; Lin, 1988; Ordover, Saloner and Salop, 1990) in the sense that these models represent a two-stage duopoly with differentiated goods under Bertrand competition, while we consider a two-stage duopoly with homogeneous goods and Cournot competition (a scenario with differentiated goods will be considered later). Our approach can be justified based on a number of grounds. First of all, it has been shown by Kreps and Scheinkman (1983) that if firms must, for technological reasons, decide production capacity before they make their pricing decisions, such price competition with production capacity constraints produces the equilibrium outcomes of Cournot competition. Although their result has been criticised as depending critically on the assumption on rationing rules of the residual demand (Davidson and Deneckere, 1986; Van Cayseele, 1991), quantity competition can still be interpreted as a surrogate for long-run competition through the choice of technological scale (Maskin and Tirole, 1982). Secondly, it is well known that price competition and the quantity competition produce different equilibrium outcomes in the case of an oligopoly, *ceteris paribus*. This result has been generalized by Bulow, Geanakoplos and Klemperer (1985) in their model of strategic substitutes and strategic complements. Our quantity competition model can improve the understanding of oligopolistic vertical integration by providing a systematic study which is complementary to the existing literature. Finally, in some industries, such as the petroleum industry, the competition in several adjacent production processes is typically characterized as quantity competition.

3. THE ANALYTICAL FRAMEWORK

One challenge of analyzing vertical integration is that we have to consider a number of vertical structures even under a very simple model such as a successive duopoly. In the framework of a successive duopoly we characterized earlier, at least four types of vertical structures can be discussed. First of all, two intermediate input producers may sell their goods through an intermediate goods market. In that market, the equilibrium is reached through a bidding process. There are no transaction costs, nor are there vertical restraints. This is described as a *market transactions game*. Secondly, each of the two intermediate input producers may serve only one specific buyer and then there is a long-term contractual relationship between the suppliers and buyers, but no vertical cooperation exists between them. This is described as *supply contracts game*.

Thirdly, one pair of supplier and buyer may integrate vertically, while other firms continue to rely on external suppliers or buyers. This is a *mixed integration game*. In the case of the mixed integration game, the vertically integrated upstream firm may or may not be able to supply the other downstream firm, depending on whether or not the supply contract is exclusive. When all buyers and suppliers integrate vertically, the game is described as a *full vertical integration game*. Detailed game rules are discussed below, after which the equilibrium will be worked out subsequently.

3.1. Market Transactions Game

In this scenario, the transactions of the intermediate goods between these two adjacent industries are accomplished in an arms-length spot market. The structure of the market transaction game is illustrated in Figure 1.1.

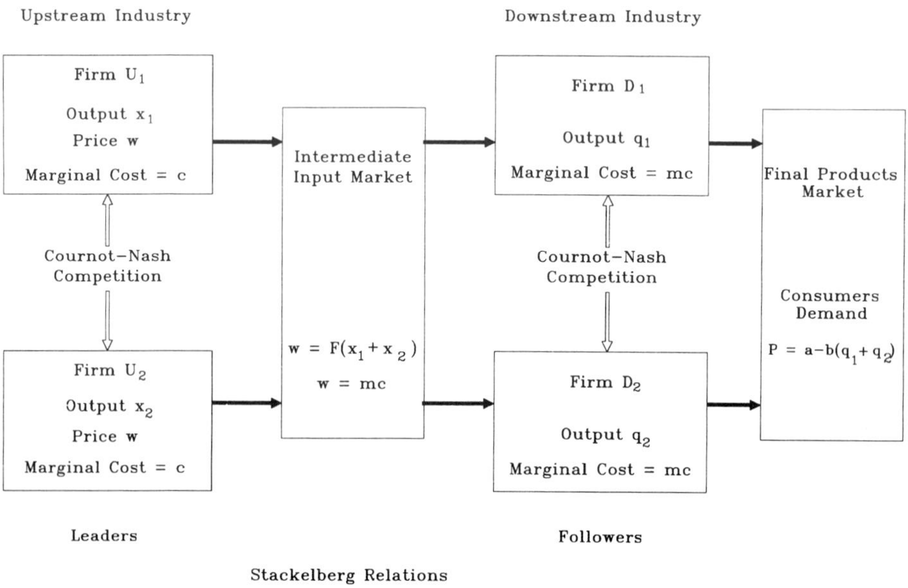

Figure 1.1. Market Transaction Game under a Successive Duopoly

The game starts from the first stage when the upstream firms U_1 and U_2 act noncooperatively to decide the Nash equilibrium output quantity of the input by overlooking the possible responses from the downstream industry. This leads to the market clearing price of the intermediate input, w. In the second stage, the downstream firms decide what quantity of final goods to produce after knowing the intermediate input price w. Finally, the Cournot game between the downstream firms ends with the subgame perfect Nash equilibrium.

To find the subgame perfect Nash equilibrium output quantity, we follow the backward sequential solution procedure and start from the second stage. For the two downstream firms D_1 and D_2, profit functions are

$$\pi_i^d = (p - mc_i)q_i \qquad i=1,2$$

where mc_i stands for the marginal costs of the ith downstream firm. The first order conditions of profit maximization for these two firms are

$$\frac{\partial \pi_i^d}{\partial q_i} = p + q_i\frac{\partial p}{\partial q_i} - mc_i = 0 \qquad i=1,2$$

Substituting p by the final demand function in equation (1.1), the first order conditions can be rewritten as

$$a - 2bq_1 - bq_2 - mc_1 = 0$$

$$a - bq_1 - 2bq_2 - mc_2 = 0$$

These first order conditions can be seen as the implicit form of the reaction functions of firms D_1 and D_2 in the quantity space. We can write these reaction functions explicitly and have the final output of one downstream firm as the function of its rival's output

$$q_1 = \frac{a - bq_2 - mc_1}{2b}$$

$$q_2 = \frac{a - bq_1 - mc_2}{2b}$$

The intersection of these reaction functions in the quantity space provides the Cournot-Nash equilibrium output quantities q_1 and q_2 in the second stage of the game. Once the intermediate input prices are known we can easily determine the actual quantities of these equilibrium outputs as follows:

$$q_1 = \frac{a - 2mc_1 + mc_2}{3b}$$

$$q_2 = \frac{a + mc_1 - 2mc_2}{3b}$$

Because of the uniform input price and the symmetry of the model, we can add up q_1 and q_2 and write the Nash equilibrium output of the downstream industry in a standard Cournot game as

$$q_1 + q_2 = \frac{2(a - mc)}{3b} \tag{1.2}$$

This equation reflects the aggregate optimal response of the downstream firms towards the changes in their marginal costs. The fixed coefficient production technology requires a linear relationship between the output quantity of the final goods and the quantity of intermediate inputs used to produce the final goods. In mathematical terms, $q_1+q_2=\alpha(x_1+x_2)$ where α stands for a constant coefficient of production. Simply by rescaling and letting $\alpha=1$, the output quantities of the final products q_1+q_2 will be equal to the quantity of the intermediate goods, x_1+x_2. In this case, the marginal cost of final products *mc* must be equal to the price of intermediate input *w*. This allows us to rewrite equation (1.2) as

$$x_1 + x_2 = \frac{2(a - w)}{3b} \tag{1.3}$$

Equation (1.3) is the derived demand function perceived by the upstream duopolists since it illustrates the relations between the input price and the quantity demanded for that input. We can rewrite equation (1.3) in the form of the inverse demand function,

$$w = a - \frac{3b}{2}(x_1 + x_2) \tag{1.4}$$

In the upstream industry (the first stage of the game), the intermediate input price *w* is determined by the outcome of the Cournot-Nash game between firms U_1 and U_2. Similar to the sub-game between the downstream firms, firms U_1 and U_2 act to maximize their profits $\pi^u_1=(w-c)x_1$ and $\pi^u_2=(w-c)x_2$ by adjusting their output quantities x_1 and x_2 until their marginal profits equal zero, or

$$\frac{\partial \pi_1^u}{\partial x_1} = 2a - 6bx_1 - 3bx_2 - 2c = 0$$

$$\frac{\partial \pi_2^u}{\partial x_2} = 2a - 3bx_1 - 6bx_2 - 2c = 0$$

The Nash equilibrium output quantities of the inputs will then be determined by solving the above equations simultaneously, which gives

$$x_1 = x_2 = \frac{2(a - c)}{9b}$$

When the equilibrium output of the intermediate input is known, the price of that input is no more than the market clearing price at the input market. Recalling equation (1.4), we know immediately that the equilibrium price of the intermediate input becomes

$$w = c + \frac{a - c}{3}$$

When $c = 0$, the intermediate input price becomes $a/3$.

The sequential solution procedure guarantees that the Nash equilibrium is subgame perfect. Once we know the subgame perfect intermediate input price, the equilibrium results concerning the quantity and price of the final product and the profit of each firm can be easily found by substituting this price back into the corresponding equations. These results are summarized below,

$$q_1 = q_2 = \frac{2(a - c)}{9b}$$

$$p = c + \frac{5(a + c)}{9} = w + \frac{2(a - c)}{9}$$

$$\pi_1^d = \pi_2^d = \frac{4(a - c)^2}{81b}$$

$$\pi_1^u = \pi_2^u = \frac{2(a - c)^2}{27b}$$

3.2. Supply Contracts Game

In the supply contract game, the downstream firm D_1 establishes an exclusive contractual relationship with upstream firm U_1, as does the firm D_2 with firm U_2. The structure of the game is illustrated in Figure 1.2.

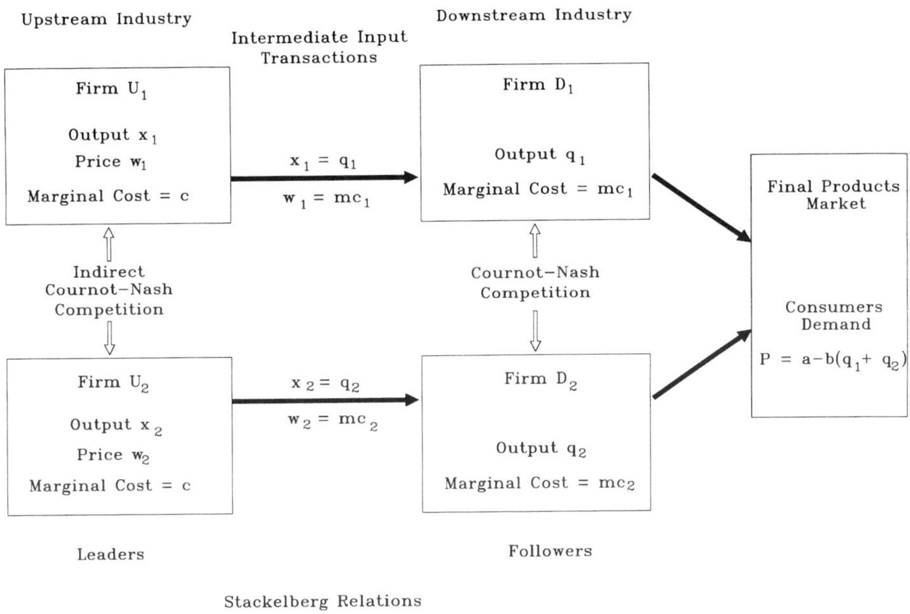

Figure 1.2. Supply Contracts Game under a Successive Duopoly

The contractual relationship specified here prevents the downstream firm D_1 from switching its source of intermediate inputs from U_1 to another supplier. Similarly, the upstream supplier U_1, after signing a supply contract with its customer D_1, is not allowed to sell the intermediate goods to the rival of its customer. This type of exclusive relationship may arise for a number of reasons. Transaction costs in general and sunk costs in particular are the main factors which hamper the functioning of the intermediate goods market, particularly in the high-tech industries. Different technical specification is another possible reason[8]. This type of market imperfection occurs even when the number of firms is sufficiently large (Williamson, 1975; 1985). This configuration of vertical relation provides an additional advantage because any impact of market foreclosure on equilibrium outcome is excluded (Tirole, 1988, p.193).

In this scenario, two upstream firms U_1 and U_2 cannot observe the actions of their competitors directly because of the lack of an intermediate input market. However, since the two downstream firms' decision rules are known, each upstream firm can infer its rival's move from the observed output in the final goods market. As a result, the direct competition between the intermediate goods producers U_1 and U_2 is replaced by the indirect competition via their customers D_1 and D_2. The intermediate input prices are w_1 and w_2, the transfer prices of the intermediate goods between upstream firms U_1 and U_2 and their exclusive buyers.

To derive the equilibrium outcomes, we have to look at this problem more closely. The subgame in the final product market is an ordinary Cournot game and the equilibrium outcomes are similar to those in the market transaction game. The difference is that the marginal costs of the downstream firms may not be the same as in the market transaction game because now each of the downstream firms faces its exclusive supplier. Therefore, the first-order conditions of profit maximization for the downstream duopolists are

$$a - 2bq_1 - bq_2 - mc_1 = 0$$

$$a - bq_1 - 2bq_2 - mc_2 = 0$$

We know that the first order conditions can be seen as the implicit reaction functions between downstream firms D_1 and D_2. After solving the above equations simultaneously, we obtain the Nash equilibrium in the output of the final products as

[8] An example of these technical differentiations and consequently the exclusive supply relations, is the IBM PC compatibles which use the Intel designed CPU chips while Apple computers use only the Motorola designed CPU chips.

$$q_1 = \frac{a - 2mc_1 + mc_2}{3b} \tag{1.5}$$

$$q_2 = \frac{a + mc_1 - 2mc_2}{3b} \tag{1.6}$$

Under the assumption of fixed proportions inputs, we can replace the marginal costs of the downstream firms mc_1 and mc_2 by the input prices w_1 and w_2. After making these changes, equations (1.5) and (1.6) represent the derived demand functions of the upstream firms. The determination of these two intermediate input prices depends on the equilibrium outcome of the subgame in the upstream industry, given these derived inverse demand functions.

The upstream firms may or may not choose the same strategic variable as the downstream firms. The equilibrium prices for the intermediate inputs differ if the upstream firms use quantity or price as their strategic variable. To see these differences, we are going to derive the equilibrium results under alternative choices of strategic variables.

(a) Upstream firms act as Cournot players. When the upstream firms choose quantity as their strategic variable, the first stage game becomes a Cournot game. In the first stage Cournot game, the players are able to foresee the outcome of rivalry in the second stage. These equilibrium results are reflected in the derived demand for the intermediate input. The derived demand system can be found as follows. Under the assumption of fixed input proportions, output quantity of the final goods is equal to the quantity of the intermediate inputs at equilibrium. Substituting q_1 and q_2 by x_1 and x_2 in equations (1.5) and (1.6) and noticing $mc_1=w_1$, $mc_2=w_2$, we can transform equations (1.5) and (1.6) into

$$x_1 = \frac{a - 2w_1 + w_2}{3b} \tag{1.7}$$

$$x_2 = \frac{a + w_1 - 2w_2}{3b} \tag{1.8}$$

The relations between the prices of the intermediate inputs and the quantities produced, therefore, can be written explicitly in the form of inverse derived demand functions as

$$w_1 = a - 2bx_1 - bx_2 \tag{1.9}$$

$$w_2 = a - bx_1 - 2bx_2 \tag{1.10}$$

After knowing the derived demand, the Cournot upstream duopolists choose outputs to maximize their own profits. The first order conditions for profit maximization are

$$\frac{\partial \pi_1^u}{\partial x_1} = w_1 + x_1 \frac{\partial w_1}{\partial x_1} - c = 0$$

$$\frac{\partial \pi_2^u}{\partial x_2} = w_2 + x_2 \frac{\partial w_2}{\partial x_2} - c = 0$$

Using equations (1.9) and (1.10), these first order conditions for profit maximization become

$$a - 4bx_1 - bx_2 - c = 0$$

$$a - bx_1 - 4bx_2 - c = 0$$

The quantities of the intermediate inputs x_1 and x_2 which satisfy the first order conditions of profit maximization are then found to be

$$x_1 = x_2 = \frac{a - c}{5b}$$

When the two stage game starts, the upstream firms U_1 and U_2 announce the pre-determined output quantities x_1 and x_2 as in the above equation, and the Nash equilibrium prices of the intermediate inputs w_1 and w_2, under which the intermediate goods are transferred between the exclusive buyers and suppliers, are then found to be

$$w_1 = w_2 = c + \frac{2(a - c)}{5}$$

After knowing the input prices, the downstream firms D_1 and D_2 compete in the final products market. At equilibrium, the prices and profits for all firms are determined. The equilibrium results in this two stage game in terms of quantity, price and profit are found as follows:

$$q_1 = q_2 = \frac{a - c}{5b}$$

$$p = c + \frac{3(a-c)}{5} = w + \frac{a-c}{5}$$

$$\pi_1^d = \pi_2^d = \frac{(a - c)^2}{25b}$$

$$\pi_1^u = \pi_2^u = \frac{2(a - c)^2}{25b}$$

(b) Upstream firms act as Bertrand players. If the intermediate goods producers behave like Bertrand duopolists, the two stage game becomes asymmetric. In the first stage, the firms U_1 and U_2 choose the intermediate input prices w_1 and w_2 as their

strategic variables to maximize their own profits. In the second stage of the game, the downstream firms still play an ordinary Cournot game[9].

When determining their selling prices of the intermediate goods w_1 and w_2 in the first stage Bertrand game, the upstream firms choose their price at such level that the derivative of own profit with respect to own price equals zero. The Nash conjectural variation implies that upstream firm U_1 tries to find w_1 which maximizes $\pi^u{}_1(w_1,w_2)$ with respect to w_1 by assuming that the supplier will not respond to its price changes or $\partial w_2/\partial w_1=0$. This requires

$$\frac{\partial \pi_1^u}{\partial w_1} = x_1 + (w_1 - c)\frac{\partial x_1}{\partial w_1} = 0$$

Replacing x_1 by equation (1.7) and taking the first derivative, we have the first order condition for profit maximization as,

$$\frac{\partial \pi_1^u}{\partial w_1} = \frac{a - 4w_1 + w_2 + 2c}{3b} = 0$$

After some rearrangement, the reaction function of firm U_1 can be written as

$$w_1 = c + \frac{a - c + (w_2 - c)}{4}$$

This reaction function shows that firm U_1 will respond to changes in the input price of U_2, despite the fact that the exclusive contractual relations prevent direct competition between the intermediate inputs suppliers. Symmetrically, firm U_2's reaction function is

[9] A two-stage Bertrand game for homogeneous goods does not interest us because under the assumption of constant returns to scale the competitive outcome is expected.

$$w_2 = c + \frac{a - c + (w_1 - c)}{4}$$

By finding the intersection of the reaction functions of firms U_1 and U_2, we have the equilibrium prices,

$$w_1 = w_2 = c + \frac{(a - c)}{3}$$

When the game starts, the upstream firms announce the pre-determined prices w_1, w_2 and supply whatever amount their customers need. Then, the downstream firms D_1 and D_2 compete in the final products market before the equilibrium outcome is determined.In fact, once the subgame perfect equilibrium prices of the intermediate inputs are known, the remaining equilibrium values such as the output quantities of the final products and the profitability of individual firms can be found easily. They are

$$q_1 = q_2 = \frac{2(a - c)}{9b}$$

$$p = c + \frac{5(a - c)}{9}$$

$$\pi_1^d = \pi_2^d = \frac{4(a - c)^2}{81b}$$

$$\pi_1^u = \pi_2^u = \frac{2(a - c)^2}{27b}$$

As we can see, the changes in strategic variables indeed produce different equilibrium outcomes. The strategic implications for these results will be discussed later.

3.3. Mixed Integration Game

In the mixed integration game, the upstream firm U_2 integrates forward with the downstream firm D_2 to form a new firm V_2, but the upstream firm U_1 still operates independently and sells all its products to its exclusive buyer, the downstream firm D_1. The vertical structures of the upstream and downstream firms become asymmetric, as is illustrated in Figure 1.3.

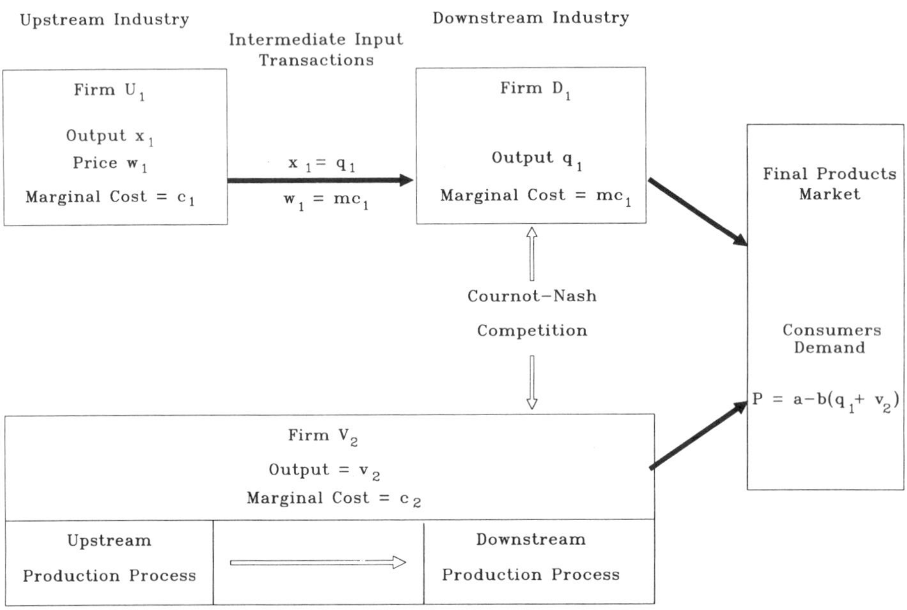

Figure 1.3. Mixed Integration Game under a Successive Duopoly

The reason for us to look at the mixed integration setting is that such a type of vertical structure can often be observed in reality. For instance, IBM and DEC are vertically integrated firms in the computer industry while other major computer producers are largely not vertically integrated[10]. If mixed integration can be shown

[10] See "Who's Ahead in the Computer Wars" *Fortune*, February 12, 1990.

as an equilibrium vertical structure in such a successive duopoly, the insights obtained may help to improve our understanding of this phenomenon. Otherwise, mixed integration may be explained by other reasons such as transaction costs differences, product differentiation, industrial evolution, etc.

To derive the equilibrium results, we first look at the Cournot game between these two asymmetrically structured firms: the non-integrated downstream firm D_1 and the vertically integrated firm V_2. These two firms will act to maximize their profits by choosing own output conditional on the output of their rival.

For the non-integrated downstream firm D_1, the payoff function is

$$\pi_1^d = (p - mc_1)q_1$$

After noticing the linear demand function as $p=a-b(q_1+v_2)$, we can write the first-order condition for profit maximization for firm D_1 as

$$\frac{\partial \pi_1^d}{\partial q_1} = a - 2bq_1 - bv_2 - mc_1 = 0 \tag{1.11}$$

For the integrated firm V_2, the first-order condition for profit maximization as

$$\frac{\partial \pi_2^v}{\partial v_2} = a - bq_1 - 2bv_2 - c = 0 \tag{1.12}$$

From (1.12), we can see that because vertical integration eliminates the markup in the intermediate inputs, the marginal cost of the vertically integrated firm becomes a constant c.

After rearranging equations (1.11) and (1.12) we obtain the reaction functions of firm D_1 and V_2,

$$q_1 = \frac{a - bv_2 - mc_1}{2b} \tag{1.13}$$

$$v_2 = \frac{a - bq_1 - c}{2b} \tag{1.14}$$

The intersection of these two reaction functions in the quantity space is the Nash equilibrium in the downstream industry. It is obvious from (1.13) and (1.14) that the Nash equilibrium output quantity of the final products depends on the marginal costs of firm D_1. Therefor, the subgame perfect equilibrium cannot be determined unless the non-integrated upstream firm U_1 decides its output quantity of intermediate inputs.

When deciding its output quantity, the upstream firm U_1 has to overlook the competition and equilibrium conditions in the final products market. These conditions are reflected in firm D_1's derived demand for the intermediate input. Because the marginal cost of firm D_1 is equal to the price of the intermediate input, any action of U_1 can also influence the outcome of the equilibrium in the final products market.

As a result, the upstream firm U_1, with its payoff function $\pi^u_1=(w_1-c)x_1$, will decide its output such that the first-order condition of profit maximization is satisfied, which means

$$\frac{\partial \pi_1^u}{\partial x_1} = w_1 + x_1 \frac{\partial w_1}{\partial x_1} - c = 0$$

After recalling that $mc_1 = w$ and using equation (1.11), we can write the intermediate input price $w = a-2bq_1-bv_2$. The first order condition of firm U_1 becomes

$$a - 4bx_1 - bv_2 - c = 0$$

This can be rewritten in the form of the reaction function of the upstream firm U_1. In this reaction function, firm U_1 will adjust its output optimally conditional on the vertically integrated firm's output v_2,

$$x_1 = \frac{a - bv_2 - c}{4b} \tag{1.15}$$

Because of the fixed proportions of the inputs, the quantity of the intermediate input purchased by firm x_1 is equal to its output q_1. This allows us to solve equation (1.14) and (1.15) as simultaneous equations. We then find the sub-game perfect output quantities as:

$$x_1 = \frac{a - c}{7b}$$

$$v_2 = \frac{3(a - c)}{7b}$$

When the game starts, firm U_1 announces its decision about the output quantity of the intermediate input. Then, the non-integrated downstream firm D_1 competes with the integrated firm V_2 in the final products market. The equilibrium outcomes concerning the prices of intermediate inputs and final products, as well as the firm's profits, can be determined consequently as follows,

$$w_1 = c + \frac{2(a-c)}{7}$$

$$p = c + \frac{3(a-c)}{7} = w + \frac{a-c}{7}$$

$$\pi_1^d = \frac{(a-c)^2}{49b}$$

$$\pi_1^u = \frac{2(a-c)^2}{49b}$$

$$\pi_2^v = \frac{9(a-c)^2}{49b}$$

3.4. Full Vertical Integration Game

The vertical integration game describes the scenario where the downstream firm D_1 and the upstream firm U_1 integrate vertically as V_1, and the downstream firm D_2 and the upstream firm U_2 integrate as V_2. In this case, the two-stage game degenerates into an ordinary one stage Cournot duopoly. The transactions of intermediate inputs between firms in two vertically related industries now become the transactions between two production processes within the confines of a single firm. In the case of full vertical integration, the perceived marginal costs of all firms become c. The structure of this full integration game is illustrated in Figure 1.4.

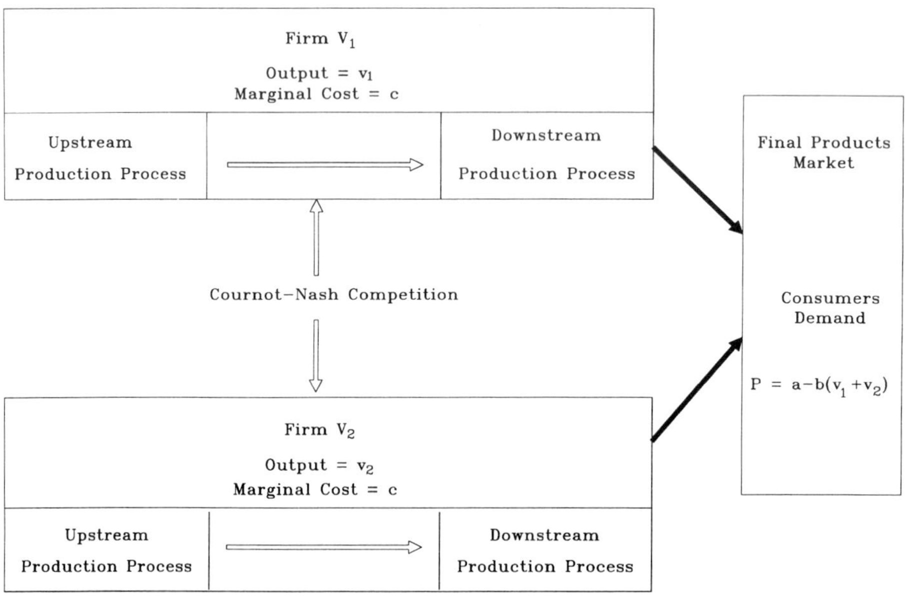

Figure 1.4. Full Integration Game under a Successive Duopoly

The Nash equilibrium outcomes in this one-stage game can be easily worked out. In fact, we can use the equilibrium results in the market transaction game and rewrite them as follows

$$v_1 = v_2 = \frac{a-c}{3b}$$

$$p = c + \frac{a-c}{3}$$

$$\pi_2^v = \pi_2^v = \frac{(a-c)^2}{9b}$$

4. SOME PRELIMINARY RESULTS

The equilibrium results such as prices and output quantities of the final products and the intermediate goods, the individual firm's profit and the industrial profit under the alternative game settings are summarized in Table 1.1. These results reveal the relationships between the firms' vertical structures and the equilibrium output quantities, prices and the firms' profits. The implications of different vertical structures on social welfare and corporate strategy can also be discussed based on these results.

4.1. Impact of Supply Contracts

Contractual relations between the suppliers and buyers are one of the most common transaction modes. Long term contracts and the spot market are often used as alternative ways to complete business transactions. Obviously, transaction costs differ when different methods of transactions are used. That is why transaction cost economists believe that firms can use the magnitude of the transaction costs as the criterion to decide whether they should use spot market or rely on contractual relations.

What we intend to show here is that, in addition to transaction costs, there are strategic reasons behind the distinctive characteristics of market transaction and vertical integration. The equilibrium results in Table 1.1 regarding the impact of supply contracts can be summarized as the following proposition.

Proposition 1.1. *In a successive Cournot duopoly with (1) linear demand for homogeneous final products, (2) fixed inputs proportions, and (3) constant returns to scale, the equilibrium output of the final goods is larger with market transactions of intermediate goods than with supply contracts.*

Proof. It is clear that the intermediate input price with the property of subgame perfect Nash equilibrium is $c + (a-c)/3$ when the vertical structure between two industries is characterized as a market transaction. It becomes $c + 2(a-c)/5$ when the vertical relations are characterized as supply contracts. Technically, it is trivial to verify that the former is always smaller than the latter. That is to say the equilibrium input price of the downstream firms in the market transaction game is always lower than that in the supply contract game. The reason is the absence of direct competition between the upstream firms in the intermediate input market.

When the market transaction game is transformed into the supply contract game, competition between two upstream firms becomes weaker. The exclusive contractual relations between buyers and sellers prevents direct competition from taking place. Instead, direct competition is replaced by indirect interactions via their downstream buyers.

When its rival firm's output of intermediate input remains unchanged, the profit maximizing output of an upstream firm is smaller when it sells its goods to its exclusive buyer than when it sells them in the intermediate goods market. The reason is that the exclusive contract, as a type of vertical restraint, prohibits the buyer from purchasing the intermediate inputs from other than its exclusive supplier. The indirect competition between the input producers continues through their downstream buyers, but it creates a more collusive situation. Consequently, the decrease of the output of the intermediate goods and the increase of their prices will unambiguously increase the marginal costs perceived by their customers in the downstream industry. It reduces further the equilibrium output of the final goods in the second stage of the game.

Table 1.1. Game Specifications and Equilibrium Prices, Quantities and Profits

Games and Vertical structure	Intermediate goods price	Final product price	Quantity	Firm U_1's profit	Firm D_1's profit	Firm U_2's profit	Firm D_2's profit	Total profit
Market transactions	$\frac{a+2c}{3}$	$\frac{5a+4c}{9}$	$\frac{4}{9}S$	$\frac{2}{27}T$	$\frac{4}{81}T$	$\frac{2}{27}T$	$\frac{4}{81}T$	$\frac{20}{81}T$
Symmetric supply contracts[1]	$\frac{2a+3c}{5}$	$\frac{3a+2c}{5}$	$\frac{2}{5}S$	$\frac{2}{25}T$	$\frac{1}{25}T$	$\frac{2}{25}T$	$\frac{1}{25}T$	$\frac{6}{25}T$
Asymmetric supply contracts[2]	$\frac{a+2c}{3}$	$\frac{5a+4c}{9}$	$\frac{4}{9}S$	$\frac{2}{27}T$	$\frac{4}{81}T$	$\frac{2}{27}T$	$\frac{4}{81}T$	$\frac{20}{81}T$
Mixed integration	$\frac{2a+5c}{7}$	$\frac{3a+4c}{7}$	$\frac{4}{7}S$	$\frac{2}{49}T$	$\frac{1}{49}T$	$\frac{9}{49}T$		$\frac{12}{49}T$
Full vertical integration	c	$\frac{a+2c}{3}$	$\frac{2}{3}S$	$\frac{1}{9}T$		$\frac{1}{9}T$		$\frac{2}{9}T$

[1] Both downstream and upstream firms are Cournot type players.
[2] Downstream firms are Cournot type players and upstream firms are Bertrand type players.
* $S = (a-c)/b$, $T = (a-c)^2/b$

In short, when all firms' outputs are positive, a higher intermediate input price pushes up the marginal costs of the downstream duopolists. As a consequence, the downstream firms have to reduce their output quantities. Therefore, the market price of the final products increases. Q.E.D.

This proposition can be related to the traditional view on vertical integration. Traditionally, vertical integration and the market mechanism are treated as two alternative institutional arrangements to realize the transactions of the intermediate goods between vertically related firms. The phrase *make-or-buy* decision has been widely used as a synonym for vertical integration or disintegration choices. But it may not correctly characterize that different ways of *buying*. The methods of purchase may have important implications for the equilibrium outcomes.

Some authors argue that if *buying* is chosen, transactions are governed at the aggregate level by the market supply of and demand for the intermediate products and at the disaggregate level by the bilateral negotiation and contracting process that occurs between individual buyers and sellers (Blair and Kaserman, 1983, p.11). In the case of a successive monopoly, the vertical relation is relatively simple and there is actually no intermediate input market. But when the number of firms increases in both industries, market transactions and supply contracts are two mechanisms which are different from vertical integration. As Proposition 1.1 shows, the prices and output quantities of the final goods are not the same when they are determined by supply and demand in the input market and when they are determined by the negotiation and contracting process between individual buyers and sellers.

4.2. Pure Effect of Vertical Integration

The difficulty of assessing the economic effect of vertical integration arises when several factors interact in determining the consequences of the integration. Among them, the horizontal merger effect has been identified as one source that frequently causes the incorrect estimation of the economic vertical integration (Abiru, 1988). Another source of mistakes in an oligopolistic setting is the market elimination effect created by exclusive relations between the buyers and sellers. To assess the pure effect of vertical integration, we need to exclude the possibility of an interaction of the vertical integration effect and the market elimination effect. This requires a direct comparison of the equilibrium results under the full integration game and the supply contract game. The result is summarized in the following proposition.

Proposition 1.2. *In a successive Cournot duopoly with (1) linear demand for homogeneous final products, (2) fixed inputs proportions, (3) constant returns to scale, the subgame perfect Nash equilibrium output of the final products increases when firms integrate vertically instead of relying on supply contracts for their intermediate goods.*

Proof. We first look at one pair of firms, U_2 and D_2. In the supply contract game, these two firms try to maximize their own profits. From equation (1.6), we know that the profit of firm D_2 is maximized when it sets its output quantity at $q_2=(a+w_1-w_2)/3b$. When firm D_2's marginal cost changes, its profit maximizing output level must change as well. Recall that the marginal cost of firm D_2 is equal to the intermediate input price w_2. When these two firms are not vertically integrated, the non-integrated upstream firm U_2 must act to maximize its own profit. This leads to the input price being higher than the marginal costs to produce such input, or $w_2>c$.

After firms U_2 and D_2 integrate vertically to form a new firm V_2, the marginal cost of the new firm becomes c because of the elimination of markup over the intermediate input. The replacement of w_2 by c lowers the price of intermediate inputs from the perspective of the downstream firms. This increases the output of the final goods unambiguously from q_2 to v_2.

For the downstream firm D_1 with equilibrium output $q_1=(a-2w_1+w_2)/3b$ (1.56), the decrease in the marginal cost of its rival w_2 will lead to a reduction in its output quantity q_1. But the stability conditions of the Nash equilibrium guarantee that the direct effect of strategic variable changes on the firm's output itself is stronger than the strategic effect or interaction effect on competing firms[11]. Thus, partial integration has a positive effect on the total output of the industry. By the same token, when the downstream firm D_1 and the upstream firm U_1 merge vertically and the partial integration become a full vertical integration, the Nash equilibrium industrial output increases further. Therefore, the output of final goods increases and the price decreases when the characteristic of the vertical structure changes from being a supply contract game to a full integration game.

---

[11] The stability condition of the Nash equilibrium requires that for any small changes in the value of strategic variables the strategic effect is smaller than the direct effect. This is always satisfied under linear demand and constant marginal cost.

Although similar conclusions, drawn from proposition 1.2, appear in a number of studies on oligopolistic vertical integration (e.g. Greenhut and Ohta, 1979), our results offer a different explanation. In those studies, the market mechanism and vertical integration are used as alternative vertical structures. Unavoidably, the anti-competition effect of market elimination and the pro-competition effect of vertical integration interact. By excluding the effect of market elimination on the vertical contractual relations, we are able to show in Proposition 1.2 that the positive effect of pure vertical integration is much larger than what was originally thought.

4.3. Relation between Strategic Variables and Vertical Structures

It is well known that the type of competition in the final products market may lead to a different vertical structure in a successive oligopoly. Vertical integration is typically the equilibrium vertical structure in quantity competition. Vertical separation may also be a Nash equilibrium vertical structure if the firms engage in price competition in the final products market (Bonanno and Vickers, 1988; Lin, 1988). In fact, not only can the producers of the final products choose whether or not they are going to compete over price or quantity, but the upstream firms may also be able to decide the types of competition they may engage in, namely whether they use quantity or price of the intermediate inputs as their strategic variable. The change of strategic variables in the upstream firm may take place at the same time as the vertical structure changes. One possible outcome is stated in Proposition 1.3.

Proposition 1.3. *In a Cournot successive duopoly with (1) linear demand for homogeneous final products, (2) fixed inputs proportions, (3) constant returns to scale, the equilibrium outcome under the market transactions game duplicates that under the supply contracts game if, at the same time, the upstream firms change their strategic variable from quantity to price.*

Proof. Comparison between these equilibrium results is easily made by looking at the first and third rows in Table 1.1. It is surprising to note that all equilibrium results under the supply contract game with Bertrand behaved upstream firms duplicate those of the market transaction game.

What Proposition 1.3. tells us is that the impact of supply contracts on the level of competition and resource allocation depends critically on the type of strategic variables selected by the upstream firms. When quantity is selected as the strategic variable, the substitution of competition in the input market by exclusive contractual relations restricts the effectiveness of the market. This leads to the decrease in final good output.

If the upstream firms change their vertical relationship with the downstream firms from market transactions to exclusive contracts and, at the same time, change their strategic variable from quantity to price, the final equilibrium may not change. This is because the competition-reducing effect of exclusive contractual relations is exactly compensated by the competition-enhancing effect of strategic variable change from quantity to price.

This result may have important implications for controversial issues related to exclusive contracts. Proposition 1.3 tells us that, although exclusive contractual relations *per se* may have certain anti-competitive effects, the expected gain in economic welfare may not be realized by forbidding exclusive contractual relations if upstream firms change their strategic variable from price to quantity.

4.4. Equilibrium Vertical Structure of the Industry

The private incentives for firms to choose their vertical structures depend on whether or not a particular type of vertical structure increases their profits. A Nash equilibrium vertical structure is the vertical structure from which no individual firm would have private incentive to deviate.

Proposition 1.4. *In a successive Cournot duopoly with (1) linear demand for homogeneous final products, (2) fixed inputs proportions, (3) constant marginal cost, vertical integration is a Nash equilibrium.*

Proof. To prove Proposition 1.4., we need to compare the payoffs of the players under alternative vertical structures. Figure 1.5 depicts the underlying game in its strategic form[12].

[12] See e.g. Myerson (1991) for discussion of different ways of representing a game.

		Firm U_2		
		Market	*Contract*	*Integration*
Firm U_1	*Market*	*12.3*, *12.3*	*12*, *12*	*6.1*, *16.3*
	Contract	*12*, *12*	*12*, *12*	*6.1*, *18.1*
	Integration	*18.3*, *6.1*	*18.3*, *6.1*	*11.1*, *11.1*

Figure 1.5. Strategy and Payoffs Matrix in a Successive Duopoly

This matrix shows that the strategy set of each player consists of three pure strategies: market transaction, supply contract and vertical integration. The payoffs in this matrix are the profits of the vertically integrated firms when firms take on the strategy of vertical integration. Otherwise, they are the joint profits of one upstream firm and one downstream firm under all other strategy combinations. The payoffs under different strategy combinations correspond to the equilibrium profits in Table 1 after all items are divided by a common denominator T/100. The payoff matrix can also be interpreted as the payoffs of the upstream firms when they are able to extract all economic profits from the downstream firms.

It is clear that vertical integration is a Nash equilibrium vertical structure. The reason is that vertical integration is a *dominant strategy* for each player to follow. The dominant strategy means that no matter what kind of strategy the rival takes, the payoff for a player by following this particular strategy is always higher than by following any other possible strategies. It is well known that the dominant strategy is always a Nash equilibrium from which no player is willing to deviate unilaterally.

This result is consistent with the observation that in an oligopolistic market firms often show a tendency towards vertical integration, especially when competitor(s) have already done so. The conventional argument goes as follows. The originally non-integrated firm is willing to integrate vertically because it is under the threat of foreclosure from intermediate goods supply or under profit *squeezing* which may be imposed by the competitors who have operations in both stages of production. The strategic form of the game illustrates that a rational manufacturer tends to integrate vertically even when he is not under the direct threat of "foreclosure". The reason for him to choose vertical integration is that individual rationality tells each firm that vertical integration is a dominant strategy. In other words, it is the best possible move any firm can take regardless of the rival's action.

A closer look at Figure 1.5. shows that the profits are higher when the industry vertical structure is not a full vertical integration than when all the firms are vertically integrated. In other words, vertical integration leads to a reduction in the firms' profits. This is because the vertical integration game has the characteristic of the *Prisoners' Dilemma* game. In the Prisoners' Dilemma game the payoffs of the players at Nash equilibrium are at a suboptimal level, but no one is willing to deviate from this Nash equilibrium. In our vertical integration game, the total profits of all firms are highest when they all choose the vertical strategy of market transactions. But this strategic combination is not a Nash equilibrium. Each individual firm has incentive to deviate from this strategy combination and pursue the objective of individual profit maximization by integrating vertically. If both firms are vertically integrated, the profits of all firms become lower. This result differs substantially from the outcome under successive monopoly, in which vertical integration increases the joint profit of the merging firms and improves consumer welfare (Blair and Kaserman, 1983).

We should point out that our model is a two-stage model. It can easily be demonstrated that the cooperative solution can be reached and the "prisoners' dilemma" be avoided when the game with such a structure is played repeatedly, when the discount factor is sufficiently close to one and when the time horizon is infinitely long. If such conditions are satisfied, vertical disintegration, such as supply contracts, may become the Nash equilibrium vertical structure.

5. CONCLUSIONS

By exploring a simple successive duopoly model, we are able to show in this chapter that the economic consequences of vertical integration depend on how the intermediate inputs transactions are organized before vertical integration takes place. If the vertical structure is governed by market transactions, the total impact of vertical integration can be separated into a market elimination effect and a pure vertical integration effect, with the former represented by an exclusive contractual relationship. The pure vertical integration effect always increases the output of final goods and economic welfare; the market elimination effect does just the opposite. Moreover, the welfare effect of supply contracts depends on the type of game played between the upstream firms. If the upstream firms change their strategic variable from quantity to price, supply contracts may do no harm to final consumers. Economic welfare can be improved if this type of contract is replaced by some other mechanisms such as vertical integration.

It is demonstrated that vertical integration is the only Nash equilibrium vertical structure in a successive Cournot duopoly. Since the underlying game has a structure of the *prisoners' dilemma*, the profits of all firms become lower if they integrate vertically. More importantly, vertical integration generates a higher economic welfare than other alternative vertical structures. Hence, vertical integration should not be prevented if this model resembles the real world situation.

The discussion of vertical integration through a successive duopoly model reveals some additional insights concerning the functioning of the market mechanism and the interactions of competitive forces within and between two adjacent industries. The largely simplified nature of the model, on the one hand, facilitates the analysis, but, on the other hand, it omits some important aspects of vertical integration in an oligopoly setting. The following chapters continue the investigation. The analysis will be extended in three dimensions. First, the successive duopoly model, so far extensively discussed, is generalized into an n-firm oligopoly in the next chapter. Secondly, product differentiation is introduced in Chapter 3. Thirdly, substitution between the intermediate inputs is allowed.

Chapter 2

VERTICAL INTEGRATION IN A COURNOT SUCCESSIVE OLIGOPOLY

1. INTRODUCTION

In this Chapter, we examine a successive oligopoly model by allowing the horizontal market structure to change from a simple duopoly to an n-firm oligopoly. Changes in market structure enrich the original duopoly model. The relations between the horizontal market structure and the vertical structure of a successive oligopoly will be the focus of this chapter.

As in the previous chapter, we posit a two-stage game theoretic model to characterize the relations between two adjacent industries. While demand conditions, production technology and the solution concept remain unchanged, the horizontal market structure differs. In the upstream industry, there are now n firms producing intermediate goods which are used by the same number of firms in the downstream industry to produce homogeneous final products. Although the number of firms in any upstream and downstream industries is rarely identical, existing studies on vertical integration have shown that inequality in the number of firms at different levels mixes the horizontal merger effect and the vertical integration effect in an oligopolistic setting. The controversy over the price path of the final goods in the process of vertical integration is largely caused by this effect (Abiru, 1988). Because of that and the focus of this study, the number of firms in both industries is deliberately kept identical to avoid any mixing of vertical and horizontal merger effects in analysis. We assume that there are three basic types of vertical structures from which each individual firm may choose, namely, market transaction, supply contract and vertical integration. The characteristics of these vertical structures have been described in the previous chapter.

In addition, we assume that one industry may be composed of firms with different types of vertical structures. This creates three types of mixed integration scenarios. First of all, some firms may integrate vertically while other firms are bound by supply contracts. Secondly, some firms integrate vertically while others continue to rely completely on the intermediate goods market. Thirdly, some upstream and downstream firms are bound by exclusive supply contracts and the remaining firms rely only on the market for intermediate goods.

We are seeking answers to the following research questions: (1) What is the impact of horizontal market structure, or the change of it, on the equilibrium results when the industry consists of firms with an identical vertical structure; (2) What is the impact of the degree of vertical integration when the total number of firms is constant and the vertical structure is characterized as a mixed integration; (3) What is the endogenously determined equilibrium vertical structure of the industry? In other words, without imposing external restrictions, what would a self-selected vertical industrial structure look like?

2. HORIZONTAL MARKET STRUCTURE AND GENERIC VERTICAL INDUSTRIAL STRUCTURES

In this section we investigate the equilibrium characteristics in three generic vertical structures: market transactions, supply contracts and full integration. The equilibria of these generic vertical structures are derived and the impact of the horizontal market structures on the equilibria is analyzed.

2.1. Equilibria under Three Generic Vertical Structures

(i) Market Transaction Game

The market transaction game is the scenario in which the intermediate goods transactions between these two industries are carried out in a well functioning market. In this market, there are n independent downstream firms which act as buyers and the same number of firms which act as suppliers. The intermediate input producers decide the output quantities of their products but compete directly against one another as Cournot players. The downstream firms have no market power over the intermediate input suppliers, but decide their own output quantities of the final product. They purchase the intermediate inputs on the intermediate goods market in which the Cournot behaved upstream firms compete against one another.

The structure of such a game is depicted by Figure 2.1.

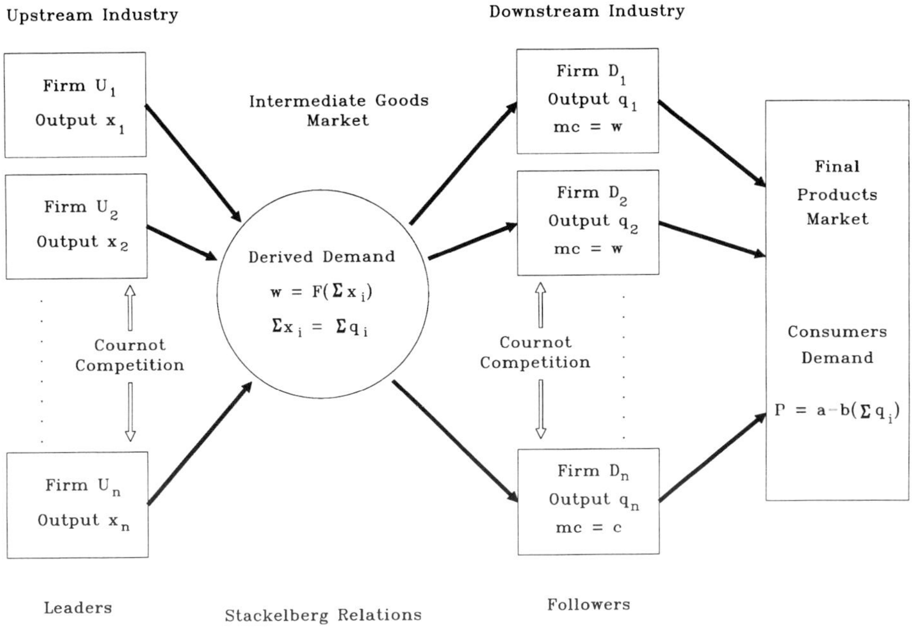

Figure 2.1. Market Transactions Game

To derive the subgame perfect Nash equilibrium under such a vertical structure, we have to start from the downstream industry, or the second-stage Cournot game.

The market demand for the final product is described by a linear inverse demand function

$$p = a - b(\sum_{i=1}^{n} q_i) \tag{2.1}$$

For the ith downstream firm, profit is

$$\pi_i^d = (p - w) q_i \qquad i=1,2,...n$$

where w is the market price of intermediate goods. The first-order condition of profit maximization for the ith Cournot-type firm requires that

$$\frac{\partial \pi_i}{\partial q_i} = a - b\sum_{j=1}^{n} q_j - bq_i - w = 0$$

After knowing the first order conditions for all n firms, we can derive the equilibrium output of the final products. The total output of the final products is

$$\sum_{i=1}^{n} q_i = \frac{n(a-w)}{(n+1)b} \tag{2.2}$$

Equation (2.2) reveals the linear relationship between the market clearing price w in the intermediate inputs market and the output of the final products. Given the fact that a fixed coefficient technology is used in the downstream industry, the output of final products is restricted by the supply of intermediate inputs. In fact, the market clearing condition requires that the total demand for intermediate goods must be equal to the total supply. Hence, equation (2.2) can be rearranged as the derived inverse demand function of the upstream firms after q_i is replaced by x_i,

$$w = a - b\frac{(n+1)}{n}\sum_{i=1}^{n} x_i$$

In the first stage of the game, the perceived profit of the ith Cournot-type behaved upstream oligopolist $\pi^u_i = (w - c)\, x_i$ can be written as

$$\pi^u_i = [a - b\frac{(n+1)}{n}(\sum_{j=1}^{n} x_j) - c]x_i \qquad i = 1,2,...n$$

where c is the marginal cost of the intermediate input. Each of these n upstream Cournot-type oligopolists acts to maximize its own profit after taking into account the possible reactions from its rivals. This requires the firm's perceived marginal profit to be zero. As a result, we can write the first-order conditions of profit maximization for all upstream firms as

$$\frac{\partial \pi_i^u}{\partial x_i} = [a - b\frac{(n+1)}{n}(\sum_{j=1}^{n} x_j) - c] - b\frac{(n+1)}{n}x_i = 0 \qquad i = 1,2,...n$$

Summing up these i equations and dividing by the number of upstream firms n, we find that the subgame perfect Nash equilibrium output of the upstream industry becomes

$$\sum_{i=1}^{n} x_i = \frac{n^2(a-c)}{(n+1)^2 b} = \frac{1}{(1+\frac{1}{n})^2}\frac{(a-c)}{b}$$

It can be verified that when $n=1$, the equilibrium output quantity of the industry becomes $(a-c)/4b$. That is the outcome under a successive monopoly. It is well known that for a linear demand and constant marginal cost, the output of a successive monopoly is only half that of the one stage monopoly (Martin, 1988; Scherer and Ross, 1990). When the number of firms n goes to ∞, we find the equilibrium outcome goes to $(a-c)/b$, which is the competitive solution. The equilibrium output of a successive oligopoly falls between these boundaries.

(ii) The Supply Contract Game

Now let us look at the second type of the generic vertical integration game, the supply contract game. The vertical structure of this game is illustrated in Figure 2.2.

In this scenario, each of the upstream firms supplies the intermediate goods to a specific downstream firm. The vertical relationship between buyers and sellers is characterized by exclusive contractual relations. We can imagine that there exists a market for contracts and there are n contracts available in this market. Each upstream firm is associated *ex ante* with one downstream firm. Any firm without a contract cannot participate in the sequential stages of the game. The equilibrium of this supply contract market will lead to a situation in which each upstream firm signs a supply contract with each downstream firm. When the market for contracts clears, the supply contract game follows.

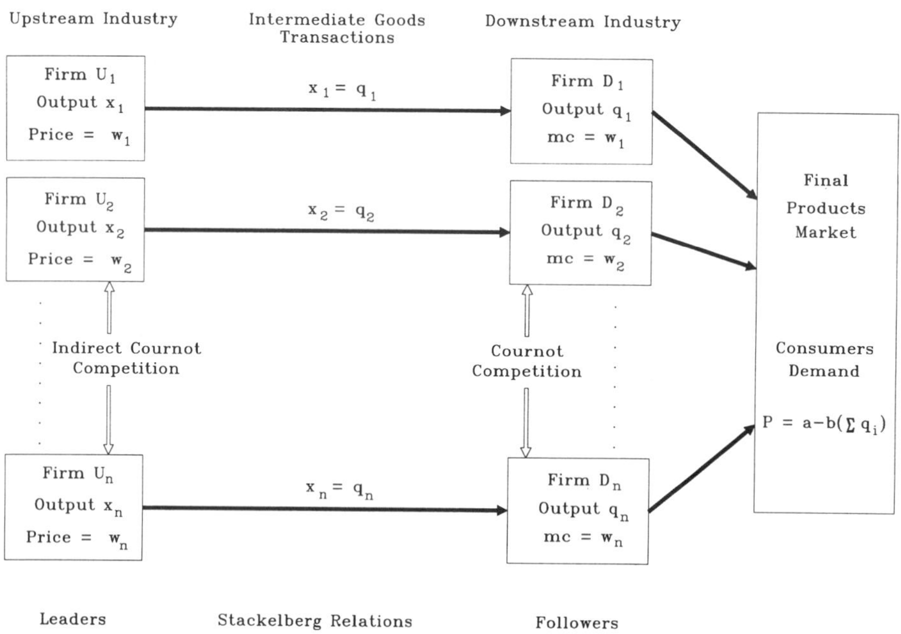

Figure 2.2. Supply Contracts Game

The difference between this scenario and the market transaction game is that the intermediate goods market is replaced by exclusive contractual relations between the upstream and the downstream firms. Consequently, the marginal costs of the downstream firms may differ among the firms since the transfer prices of intermediate goods are set between individual buyers and suppliers. Since the payoff function of the ith downstream firm is $\pi^d_i = (p-w_i)q_i$, the first order conditions for profit maximization take the form

$$\frac{\partial \pi_i^d}{\partial q_i} = a - 2bq_i - b\sum_{j=1}^{n} q_j - w_i = 0 \qquad i=1,2,...n,\ i{\neq}j$$

where w_i is the transfer price of the intermediate goods prevailing between the *i*th downstream firm and its exclusive supplier. From these first order conditions, the upstream firms can obtain information regarding the decision rule of their customers and the type of competition in the downstream industry. This information will help them make their production decisions for intermediate goods. To obtain their derived demand functions, we replace q_i with x_i because of the fixed coefficient production technology. The inverse demand for the intermediate input becomes

$$w_i = a - 2bx_i - b\sum_{j=1}^{n} x_j \qquad i=1,2,...n;\ i{\neq}j$$

Facing this derived demand function and with the objective function $\pi^u_i=(w_i - c)\,x_i$, the upstream firms try to maximize their own profits. The first order condition for profit maximization for the upstream firm is

$$\frac{\partial \pi_i^u}{\partial x_i} = a - 4bx_i - b\sum_{j=1}^{n} x_j - c = 0 \qquad i = 1,2,...n;\ i{\neq}j$$

The reaction function of the *i*th upstream firm can be derived from the above first order condition:

$$x_i = \frac{a - c - b\sum_{j=1}^{n} x_j}{4b} \qquad i = 1,2,...n;\ i{\neq}j \tag{2.3}$$

After some rearrangement, the equilibrium output of the upstream industry is

$$\sum_{i=1}^{n} x_i = \frac{n}{(n+3)} \frac{(a-c)}{b}$$

It is clear when *n=1*, the industrial output quantity is that of a successive monopoly. When *n* goes to infinity, the competitive outcome prevails.

(iii) The Full Integration Game

The full vertical integration game describes a scenario when each downstream firm integrates with an upstream firm. In the full integration game, the two-stage Cournot game degenerates into a one-stage game. The structure of the game is illustrated in Figure 2.3.

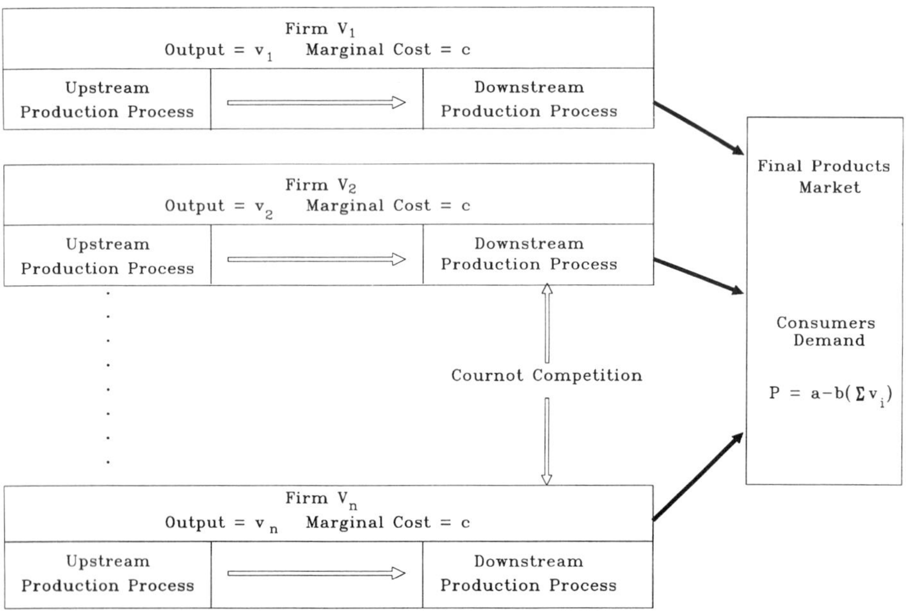

Figure 2.3. Full Integration Game

The equilibrium output quantity of an n-firm Cournot-Nash oligopoly can easily be found as

$$\sum_{i=1}^{n} q_i = \frac{n}{(n + 1)} \frac{(a - c)}{b}$$

We should note that the output quantity of the final product is used in this expression because the production of intermediate goods has become one production process under a single administrative structure after vertical integration takes place.

2.2. Comparison of the Equilibrium Outcomes under Three Generic Vertical Industrial Structures

Two comparisons are carried out in this section, through which we can see how the equilibria differ under alternative vertical structures and how these differences vary when the horizontal market structure changes. First of all, the equilibrium output quantities of the industry under three generic vertical structures are compared when the market structure is given. Secondly, the changes in the equilibrium output and the magnitude of changes under these alternative vertical structures are investigated when the horizontal market structure changes.

In a successive Cournot oligopoly, the equilibrium output quantities under the three generic vertical structures are summarized in Table 2.1.

Table 2.1. Equilibrium Output Quantities under Three Vertical Structures

Type of Game	Market	Contract	Integration
Output Quantity	$[n/(n+1)]^2 S$	$n/(n+3) S$	$n/(n+1) S$

Ignoring the common factor $S=(a-c)/b$ in Table 2.1, the comparison of the output quantities under the three alternative generic vertical structures produces the following results:

$$\frac{n}{(n+1)} > \frac{n^2}{(n+1)^2} > \frac{n}{(n+3)} \qquad \textit{for } \infty > n > 1$$

These inequalities show that output quantities under the vertical structures of market transactions (*M*), supply contracts (*C*) and full integration (*I*) in the present framework satisfies the following relation for any given number of firms

$$Q_I > Q_M > Q_C \qquad \textit{for } \infty > n > 1$$

where *Q* denotes the total output of final products. This inequality is reversed when the prices of the final products are compared.

The result in Table 2.1 illustrates the relations between the types of industrial vertical structures and the Nash equilibrium output quantity of the industry under Cournot competition, which can be summarized in Proposition 2.1.

Proposition 2.1. *In a successive Cournot oligopoly with linear demand and fixed inputs proportions, the output level with vertical integration is higher than that with market transactions, while the latter leads to a higher output level than with supply contracts.*

To understand the intuition behind Proposition 2.1, we may recall the existing findings concerning vertical integration in a successive oligopoly. Traditional treatments of vertical integration typically look at the possibilities of full vertical integration and market transactions as the only alternative institutional arrangements. These studies conclude that vertical integration, as would be expected, increases output and improves economic welfare (Greenhut and Ohta, 1979).

What Proposition 2.1 tells us is that the traditional treatment of the vertical integration effect can and should be decomposed into the pro-competitive effect of vertical integration (cooperation) and the anti-competitive effect of market elimination. Effective separation of these two effects is achieved by looking at the three generic vertical structures of two successive industries. The traditional view looks only at the combined effect. Although the combined effect leads to a higher industrial output and improves social welfare, the two forces move in opposite directions. Hence, the positive effect on social welfare of "pure" vertical integration is larger than was previously thought.

This result also shows that although vertical integration may improve social welfare in the framework posited, the extent of this improvement depends critically on pre-integration conditions. From our setting, it is clear that if vertical integration is used to replace exclusive supply contracts as the vertical structure in a successive oligopoly, the welfare gain is much larger than if it replaces market transactions.

Now, we can look at the effect of the horizontal market structure on the Nash equilibrium output quantity. To investigate the response of equilibrium output to changes in the number of firms, we make a study of comparative statics by analyzing the first derivative of equilibrium output under the different vertical structures. Table 2.3 summarizes the results.

Table 2.2. Comparative Statics of Equilibrium Output Quantities

Type of Game	Market	Contract	Integration
dQ/dn	$2n/(n+1)^3\ S$	$3/(n+3)\ S$	$1/(n+1)\ S$

The positive signs of the first derivatives indicate that the total output of the final products always increases when the number of firms increases. A comparison of the results of comparative statics from Table 2.2 leads to the following inequality,

$$\frac{dQ_C}{dn} > \frac{dQ_M}{dn} > \frac{dQ_I}{dn} > 0 \qquad \textit{for } \infty > n > 1$$

The relations between final price and the number of firms can be found in a similar way. The outcome of comparative statics is summarized in Proposition 2.2.

Proposition 2.2. *Under the assumptions of linear demand and fixed coefficients technology, when the number of firms increases, the output quantity of the final products increases under all three vertical structures; the magnitude of increase is larger under supply contracts than under market transactions and smallest under full vertical integration.*

It has been established that the Cournot oligopoly model possesses a kind of quasi-competitive behavior in which economic performance (measured by industry output or price) is positively related to the number of firms. When there are no scale economies, the model also generates the perfectly competitive solution as the number of firms goes to infinity (Ruffin, 1971). But the investigation of the relation between economic performance and market structure is limited to a one-stage Cournot oligopoly.

Based on the result in Proposition 2.2, we can argue that the speed of convergence toward the competitive outcome under a multi-stage oligopoly differs from that under a single stage oligopoly. Moreover, this convergence depends not only on horizontal market structure, but also on the type of vertical structure of the underlying industry.

The results in this section may have important implications for public policy. It is well known in the regulatory literature that when the conditions for marginal cost pricing cannot be satisfied, the regulators may apply the second best principles to improve the economic performance of the firms and social welfare (Baron, 1989; Joskow and Rose, 1989). When facing direct regulatory costs, the antitrust authority may have to decide which industry sectors to regulate or intervene in order to correct the distortions created by market imperfections. This requires us to measure correctly the welfare losses which can be regained by using regulatory mechanisms. Following this, we can design or select the most efficient instruments. These instruments, which reduce the barriers to entry, may change the horizontal market structure and encourage competition. What Proposition 2.2 tells us is that the sharpest improvement in economic welfare is expected to be achieved in the industry sectors characterized by exclusive contractual relations in an oligopolistic industry. Therefore, vertical relations as well as horizontal market structure should be considered when antitrust policies are deliberated and formulated.

3. DEGREE OF VERTICAL INTEGRATION AND EQUILIBRIA IN MIXED INTEGRATION GAMES

The purpose of this section is to look at three different mixed integration scenarios and to derive the equilibrium outcomes under these mixed integration games. Mixed vertical integration implies that firms are asymmetric as far as their vertical structures are concerned. Some firms may find that their rival firms adopt different types of vertical structures. Three different types of mixed integration will be discussed. The first is when some firms integrate vertically while other firms are bound by contracts. The second type of mixed integration is when some firms integrate vertically while others rely on the intermediate goods market. And the third type of mixed integration is when some upstream and downstream firms are bound by supply contracts and the remaining firms rely on the intermediate goods market for their supplies.

The merit of a successive oligopoly model, compared with the duopoly model which we discussed in the previous chapter, is that it allows us to investigate the impact of the degree of vertical integration on equilibrium outcomes. The degree of vertical integration is high when a large proportion of vertically related firms has established close relationships; otherwise, the degree of vertical integration is low.

3.1. Mixed Integration with Supply Contracts and Market Transactions

We posit a type of mixed integration game such that there are $n \geq 3$ firms in each industry. Firms are separated into two groups. Exclusive contractual relations are established among the first group of firms. The second group of firms relies on the intermediate goods market for their supplies and/or sales of the intermediate goods. This scenario does not appear in the successive duopoly model because after one upstream firm establishes an exclusive contractual relation with a downstream firm, the remaining firm has no other choice but to sell to (buy from) its only customer (supplier). The structure of this game is depicted in Figure 2.4.

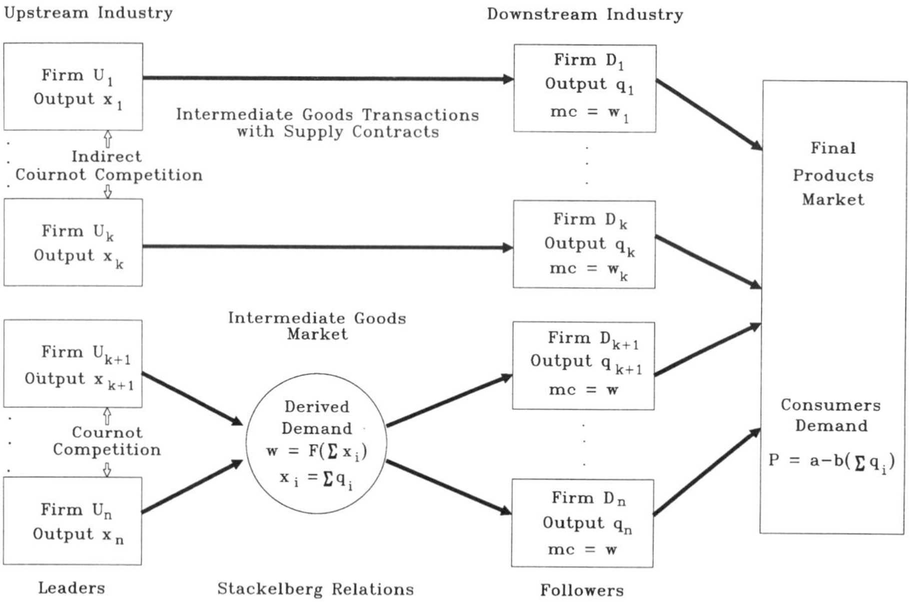

Figure 2.4. Mixed Integration Game (1): Supply Contracts vs Market Transactions

Suppose that k firms ($1 \le k \le n$) in both the upstream and the downstream industries are tied to each other by supply contracts. Given the fact that the payoff functions of the k downstream firms are $\pi^d_i=(p-w_i)\ q_i,\ i=1,...k$, the first order condition of profit maximization for the k downstream firms require

$$\frac{\partial \pi_i^d}{\partial q_i} = p + q_i \frac{\partial p}{\partial q_i} - w_i = 0 \qquad i=1,2,...k$$

where w_i can be interpreted as the transfer price of the intermediate goods between the ith downstream firm and its supplier.

The payoff functions of the remaining *n-k* firms can be written as $\pi^d_i = (p-w)q_i$, $i=k+1,...n$. Because they buy their intermediate inputs from the spot market, their marginal costs are identical. The first order conditions of profit maximization for these *n-k* firms become

$$\frac{\partial \pi_i^d}{\partial q_i} = p + q_i \frac{\partial p}{\partial q_i} - w = 0 \qquad i=k+1,...n$$

where *w* is the market price of the intermediate goods. Because the transfer prices between the buyers and suppliers involved in the contractual relations are set between individual firms, the prices of intermediate inputs, therefore, may differ among these types of firms. After some rearrangements, the first-order conditions of profit maximization for downstream firms become

$$\begin{aligned}
a - b[\sum_{i=1}^{k} q_i + \sum_{i=k+1}^{n} q_i\,] - bq_1 &= w_1 \\
a - b[\sum_{i=1}^{k} q_i + \sum_{i=k+1}^{n} q_i\,] - bq_2 &= w_2 \\
&\cdots\cdots \\
a - b[\sum_{i=1}^{k} q_i + \sum_{i=k+1}^{n} q_i\,] - bq_k &= w_k \\
a - b\sum_{i=1}^{k} q_i - b\frac{(n-k+1)}{(n-k)}\sum_{i=k+1}^{n} q_i &= w
\end{aligned} \tag{2.4}$$

These *k+1* equations determine equilibrium in the second-stage of the Cournot game. It is clear that the equilibrium output quantity in the second stage depends critically on the input prices. Any price changes of the intermediate inputs will cause a change in the second stage equilibrium. From the viewpoint of the upstream firms, this system consists of derived demand functions, which reflect the relationship between the prices of the intermediate goods and the quantity demanded of the intermediate inputs. The strategic interactions among the downstream firms are already reflected in these equations.

Like the downstream firms, these n upstream firms can be divided into two groups. The first k firms set the transfer price for their buyers after taking into account the strategic interactions among their downstream buyers and other firms which compete in the intermediate inputs market. With objective functions like $\pi^u_i=(w_i-c)x_i$, we find the first order conditions of profit maximization of these two types of firms to be

$$\frac{\partial \pi_i^u}{\partial x_i} = w_i - \frac{\partial w_i}{\partial x_i} x_i - c = 0 \qquad i=1,2,...k$$

$$\frac{\partial \pi_i^u}{\partial x_i} = w - \frac{\partial w}{\partial x_i} x_i - c = 0 \qquad i=k+1,...,n$$

To find the subgame perfect equilibrium, we replace w_i and w by the first order conditions in (2.4), and then we have

$$a - b\frac{(k+3)}{k}\sum_{i=1}^{k} x_i - b\sum_{i=k+1}^{n} x_i = c$$

$$a - b\sum_{i=1}^{k} x_i - b\frac{(n-k+1)^2}{(n-k)^2}\sum_{i=k+1}^{n} x_i = c$$

The aggregate reaction functions between the two types of upstream firms become

$$\sum_{i=1}^{k} x_i = \frac{(a - c)}{b} - \frac{(n - k + 1)^2}{(n - k)^2} \sum_{i=k+1}^{n} x_i$$

$$\sum_{i=k+1}^{n} x_i = \frac{(a - c)}{b} - \frac{(k + 3)}{k} \sum_{i=1}^{k} x_i$$

After solving these reaction functions simultaneously, we derive the subgame perfect Nash equilibrium group outputs

$$\sum_{i=1}^{k} x_i = \frac{(2n - 2k + 1)kS}{(n - k + 1)^2(k + 3) - (n - k)^2 k} \tag{2.5}$$

$$\sum_{i=k+1}^{n} x_i = \frac{3(n - k)^2 S}{(n - k + 1)^2(k + 3) - (n - k)^2 k} \tag{2.6}$$

Because of the fixed proportions of inputs, the final output quantity is known to be equal to the output of the intermediate goods. The total output of the final products is

$$Q = \frac{[(n - k + 1)^2 k - (n - k)^2(k + 3)]S}{[(n - k + 1)^2(k + 3) - (n - k)^2 k]}$$

It can be easily verified that when $k=0$, $Q = Q_M$ and when $k=n$, $Q = Q_C$ as shown in Table 2.1. Once the equilibrium output quantity of the final product for given k is known, we can do some comparative statics excercises by taking the first derivative of total output with respect to the number of firms with contractual relations, k. By doing this we can find the impact of the degree of vertical integration on the equilibrium output. The first derivative of the Nash equilibrium output is

$$\frac{\partial Q}{\partial k} = \frac{-3[2(n-k)^2 + 2(n-k) - 1]S}{[(n-k+1)^2(k+3) - (n-k)^2 k]^2} < 0$$

The negative sign of this comparative statics tells us that, in the two-stage Cournot oligopoly, the prevalence of contractual relations in the intermediate goods market reduces the final output. The relationship between the output quantity and changes in the vertical structure is summarized in Proposition 2.3.

Proposition 2.3. *In a successive Cournot oligopoly with linear demand and fixed coefficients technology, if the vertical structure is characterized by a mixed integration with contracts and market transactions, the total output quantity of the final goods decreases as more and more firms commit themselves into contractual relations.*

Intuitively, the decrease of the industry output is due to two factors. Firstly, since the supply contracts tie the downstream firm to a specific supplier, the upstream firm, therefore, may view the downstream firm as a captive customer and try to set a higher transfer price. Secondly, concentration in the market becomes higher as more firms are tied by contracts, which tends to increase the market price of intermediate goods. Both these factors tend to increase the marginal costs of the downstream firms, thereby reducing the industrial output of final products.

3.2. Mixed Integration with Vertical Integration and Supply Contracts

In this type of mixed integration scenario downstream firms are divided into two groups. One group consists of k integrated firms operating in both industries and each firm produces final goods with quantity v_i, $i=1,2,...k$. The second group consists of n-k firms which operate only in the downstream industry; each firm produces the final product with quantity q_i, and purchases its intermediate inputs from a specific upstream firm that produces the intermediate goods x_i, $i=k+1,...n$. These fully integrated firms are assumed to be horizontally independent to avoid any mixing-up between vertical and horizontal merger effects. The structure of this type of game can be found in Figure 2.5.

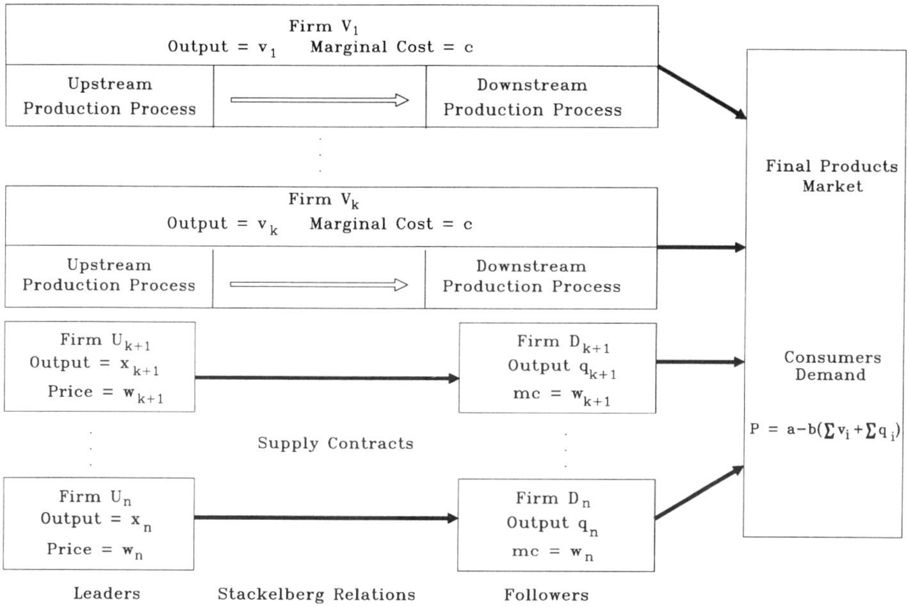

Figure 2.5. Mixed integration Game (2): Vertical Integration vs Supply Contracts

The analysis starts with the second-stage Cournot game. In the second stage of the game, two types of Cournot oligopolists compete with each other. The integrated firms choose their output quantity conditional on all other firms' output so that their marginal revenues equate their marginal costs. Firms relying on supply contracts let their marginal revenues equal the transfer price set by their suppliers. Because there are two groups of firms, each has a profit function

$$\pi_i^v = (p - c)v_i \qquad i=1,2,...k$$

$$\pi_i^d = (p - w_i)q_i \qquad i=k+1,...n$$

The first order conditions of profit maximization for these two groups of firms become

$$a - b(\sum_{j=1}^{k} v_i + \sum_{j=k+1}^{n} q_i) - bv_i = c \qquad i=1,2,...k \tag{2.7}$$

$$a - b(\sum_{j=1}^{k} v_i + \sum_{j=k+1}^{n} q_i) - bq_i = w_i \qquad i=k+1,...n \tag{2.8}$$

The solution of these simultaneous equations gives the Cournot-Nash equilibrium outputs of all firms in the second stage of the game. Note that equation (2.8) shows that these *n-k* downstream firms make their output decisions based on the transfer prices of the intermediate goods. These transfer prices are decided by their exclusive suppliers. To find the subgame perfect Nash equilibrium, we have to look at how non-integrated upstream firms make their production decisions. The derived demand for intermediate inputs can be obtained by rearranging (2.8) and replacing q_i by x_i to obtain

$$x_i = \frac{(a - w_i)}{2b} - \frac{\sum_{j=1}^{k} v_j + \sum_{j=k+1}^{n} x_j}{2} \qquad i=k+1,...n;\ i \neq j$$

These derived demand functions reflect the strategic interactions among the downstream firms.

In the first stage of the game, the *n-k* upstream firms committed to contractual relationships act to maximize their profit $\pi^u_i = (w_i - c)x_i$, $i=k+1,...n$. In order to do this they have to decide the output quantity of the intermediate goods conditional on the output of their rivals, whether vertically integrated or not. Replacing w_i by (2.8) and taking the first derivative with respect to output quantity, we have the first order conditions of profit maximization for these *n-k* firms

$$a - b(\sum_{j=1}^{k} v_i + \sum_{j=k+1}^{n} x_i) - 3bx_i - c = 0 \qquad i=k+1,...n$$

These first order conditions can be rearranged as

$$a - b\sum_{i=1}^{k} v_i - b\frac{(n-k+3)}{(n-k)}\sum_{i=k+1}^{n} x_i - c = 0$$

We can do the same for the first k equations in (2.7) and have

$$a - b\frac{(k+1)}{k}\sum_{i=1}^{k} v_i - b\sum_{i=k+1}^{n} x_1 - c = 0$$

The aggregate reaction functions of the two types of Cournot-behaved firms are then found as

$$\sum_{i=1}^{k} v_i = S - \frac{(n-k+3)}{(n-k)}\sum_{i=k+1}^{n} x_i$$

$$\sum_{i=k+1}^{n} x_i = S - \frac{(k+1)}{k}\sum_{i=1}^{k} v_i$$

where $S=(a-c)/b$. After solving these two reaction functions, we have the equilibrium output quantities for the k integrated firms and the n-k remaining firms as

$$\sum_{i=1}^{k} v_i = \frac{3kS}{(n+2k+3)} \tag{2.9}$$

$$\sum_{i=k+1}^{n} x_i = \frac{(n-k)S}{(n+2k+3)} \tag{2.10}$$

The total output of the final goods under the given degree of vertical integration is

$$Q = \frac{(n+2k)S}{(n+2k+3)} \tag{2.11}$$

It can be verified in Table 2.1 that the right-hand side of equation (2.9) is Q_C when $k=0$ and becomes Q_I when $k=n$. Moreover, because the output of final goods is a function of the number of integrated firms k, the relation between the degree of vertical integration and the equilibrium output can be found easily in this type of mixed integration game. Taking the first derivative of equation (2.9) with respect to k, we have

$$\frac{\partial Q}{\partial k} = \frac{6S}{(n+2k+3)^2} > 0$$

It is obvious that this first derivative is always larger than zero when $a>c$. The economic meaning of this result can be translated into proposition 2.4.

Proposition 2.4. *In a successive Cournot oligopoly with linear demand and fixed coefficients technology, if the vertical structure is characterized by a mixed integration with vertical integration and supply contracts, an increase in the number of vertically integrated firms increases industry output.*

This proposition can be related to the result of Greenhut and Ohta (1979), which shows that vertical integration increases the output of final products. But the difference between our result and their finding lies in the pre-integration vertical structures. By positing the pre-integration vertical structure as one of supply contracts, the Nash equilibrium output quantity differs from that of a market transactions pre-integration structure. Proposition 2.4 specifies the situation in which the change in the output quantity of the final products is caused by the pure vertical integration effect.

3.3. Mixed Integration with Full Integration and Market Transactions

This scenario describes a situation in which n downstream firms are divided into two groups: k vertically integrated firms and n-k non-integrated firms which rely on the intermediate goods market. Figure 2.6 illustrates the structure of this game.

This scenario looks similar to some of the models which appear in the literature (Greenhut and Ohta, 1979; Salinger, 1988). Without repeating others' findings, we will present our results in the light of the game theoretic framework and try to clarify some conceptual and methodological confusions in the literature.

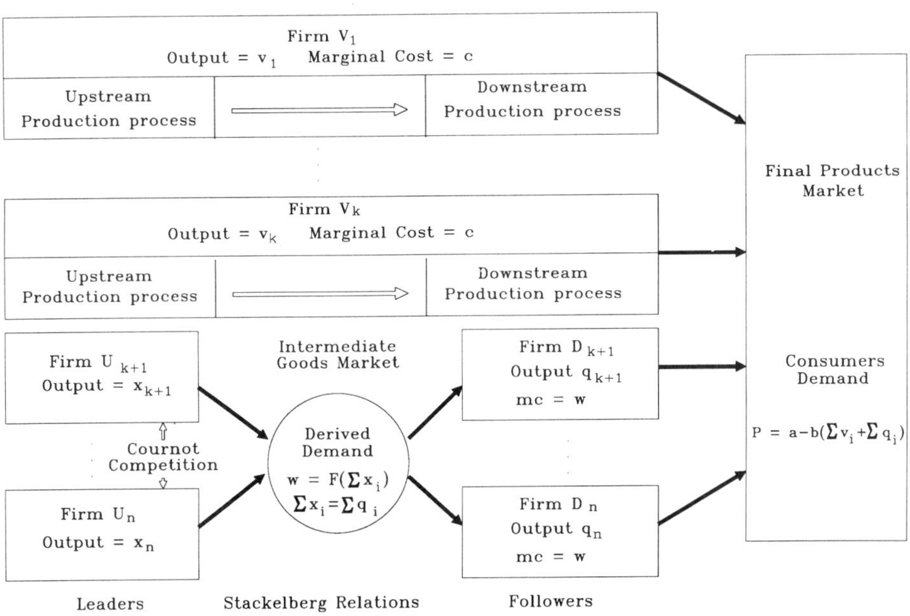

Figure 2.6. Mixed Integration Game (3): Vertical Integration vs Market transactions

The analysis starts with the second-stage Cournot game. Because there are two groups of firms, each has a profit function

$$\pi_i^v = (p - c)v_i \qquad i=1,2,...k$$

$$\pi_i^d = (p - w)q_i \qquad i=k+1,...n$$

The first order conditions of profit maximization for the integrated and non-integrated firms are

$$a - b(\sum_{j=1}^{k} v_j + \sum_{j=k+1}^{n} q_j) - 2bv_i - c = 0 \qquad i=1,2,...k;\ i \neq j$$

$$a - b(\sum_{j=1}^{k} v_j + \sum_{j=k+1}^{n} q_j) - 2bq_i - w = 0 \qquad i=k+1,...n; i \neq j$$

where c is the marginal cost of producing intermediate goods and w is the market price of the intermediate goods. Aggregating these two groups of functions and dividing them by the number of firms k and n-k respectively, we have:

$$\begin{aligned} a - b\frac{(k+1)}{k}\sum_{i=1}^{k} v_i - b\sum_{i=k+1}^{n} q_i &= c \\ a - b\sum_{i=1}^{k} v_i - b\frac{(n-k+1)}{(n-k)}\sum_{i=k+1}^{n} q_i &= w \end{aligned} \tag{2.12}$$

The equilibrium output quantity of the downstream industry depends on the price of intermediate goods, which is an exogenous variable in the second-stage game. Note that these equations serve as the inverse derived demand functions of the intermediate goods since they reflect the relationship between the intermediate input price and the demand for such inputs.

We now look at the first stage of the game. For the *n-k* non-integrated upstream firms with objective functions $\pi^u_i = (w-c)x_i$, $i=k+1,...n$, profit maximization requires

$$\frac{\partial \pi_i^u}{\partial x_i} = w + \frac{\partial w}{\partial x_i} x_i - c = 0 \qquad i=k+1,...n$$

Replacing *w* by (2.12), the first order condition for the *i*th non-integrated upstream firm can be transformed into

$$a - b\sum_{j=1}^{k} v_j - b\frac{(n-k+1)}{(n-k)} \sum_{j=k+1}^{n} x_j - 2b\frac{(n-k+1)}{(n-k)} x_i = c \qquad i=k+1,...n;\ i \neq j$$

Aggregating these first order conditions and dividing them by the number of firms *n-k*, we establish

$$a - b\sum_{i=1}^{k} v_i - b\frac{(n-k+1)^2}{(n-k)^2} \sum_{i=k+1}^{n} x_i = c \tag{2.13}$$

Using equation (2.12) and (2.13) to derive the aggregated reaction functions of the integrated firms and the non-integrated upstream firms, we obtain:

$$\sum_{i=1}^{k} v_i = \frac{k}{(k+1)}(S - \sum_{i=k+1}^{n} x_i)$$

$$\sum_{i=k+1}^{n} x_i = \frac{(n-k)^2}{(n-k+1)^2}(S - \sum_{i=1}^{k} v_i)$$

After solving the above equations simultaneously, the equilibrium output for each group of firms is found as

$$\sum_{i=1}^{k} v_i = \frac{k(2n-2k+1)S}{(k+1)(n-k+1)^2 - k(n-k)^2} \tag{2.14}$$

$$\sum_{i=k+1}^{n} x_i = \frac{(n-k)^2 S}{(k+1)(n-k+1)^2 - k(n-k)^2} \tag{2.15}$$

The total output of the final product will be the sum of equation (2.14) and (2.15), which is

$$Q = \frac{[k(n-k+1)^2 - (k-1)(n-k)^2] S}{(k+1)(n-k+1)^2 - k(n-k)^2} \tag{2.16}$$

It is easy to verify that when $k=0$, $Q=Q_C$, and when $k=n$, $Q=Q_I$ as in Table 2.1.

To investigate the effect of the degree of vertical integration on the equilibrium output and the final product price, we differentiate equation (2.16) with respect to the number of the vertically integrated firms k and have

$$\frac{\partial Q}{\partial k} = \frac{2(n-k)(n-k+1)S}{(k+1)(n-k+1)^2 - k(n-k)^2} > 0$$

We can claim, hence, that in our successive oligopoly model, the joint effect of market elimination and vertical cooperation is positive on the output quantity of final goods although the former reduces the output quantity and the latter increases it.

Proposition 2.5. *In a successive Cournot oligopoly with linear demand and fixed coefficients technology, the joint effect of market elimination and pure integration on industry output of final products is positive.*

We pointed out earlier that the economic consequence of the vertical integration process can be segregated into the market elimination effect and the vertical integration effect. When vertical integration takes place, the market for intermediate goods is gradually replaced by exclusive relations or by administration within the confines of a single firm. Concentration in the intermediate inputs market increases as more and more firms integrate vertically in a successive oligopoly, and the price of the intermediate inputs rises. The effect of market elimination on the output of final products is negative. Vertical integration, on the other hand, eliminates the double markup and lowers the effective intermediate input price for producing the final goods. This pure vertical integration effect on the equilibrium output of final goods is positive . Vertical integrations in reality are often the combination of both these effects. We show that the negative effect of market elimination is smaller than the effect of pure vertical integration. Hence, vertical integration will lead to a higher output quantity of final products. The increase in the output of final products leads to a fall in final prices and has a desirable impact on consumer welfare.

This result can be related to the results in Greenhut and Ohta (1979) and Salinger (1988). Greenhut and Ohta claim that vertical mergers always cause the price of final goods to drop. Salinger comments on their "fundamentally different conclusions" from his own by arguing the reason that Greenhut and Ohta have such results is they compare the two cases of no vertical integration and complete vertical integration. This may have ignored the effect of a vertical merger on the intermediate goods price and the non-integrated producers. Because vertical integration leads to a higher concentration in the intermediate inputs market, the price of the final products may rise after most of the firms (not all of them) integrate vertically in a model with fixed production coefficients and linear demand such as ours.

Our results do not support the findings of Salinger (1988). By carefully comparing our approach and results with his, we find that there are three reasons for the difference in outcomes. First of all, Salinger assumes that the number of firms in the two industries are not equal. And the rising prices of the intermediate inputs and the final goods occur only when the number of upstream firms is substantially smaller than that of downstream firms and when most of the upstream firms have integrated vertically. This implies that, without vertical integration, each upstream firm supplies intermediate inputs to more than one downstream firm. It is assumed in his model that vertical merger takes place between one upstream firm and one downstream firm. The nonproportional relations between the non-integrated upstream and downstream firms may be such that the concentration in the upstream industry is close to monopoly when there is still a number of downstream firms which rely on external suppliers. This unavoidably creates the horizontal merger effect in the intermediate inputs market. This type of horizontal merger effect has been characterized in Salant, Switzer and Reynolds

(1983) and elaborated lately by Farrell and Shapiro (1990). The difference here is that the horizontal merger effect is caused by vertical integration and takes place only in the intermediate goods market. It is this horizontal merger effect which causes the increase in the prices of intermediate inputs as well as final goods.

Secondly, it is true that the price of the intermediate input may rise when concentration increases in the intermediate goods market. But the input price increase can only have direct impact on the firms relying on such markets. For the vertically integrated firms, input price falls after integration. Taking the industry as a whole the effective input price will decrease as more firms become integrated; and this will contribute to the increase of the final goods and the fall of their prices, despite the increase of the intermediate inputs price for the non-integrated firms.

Finally, when Salinger derives the equilibrium in the scenario of mixed integration, he adopts a backward induction procedure and finds the Nash equilibrium outcomes under the information structure defined by Tirole (1988) as *almost perfect information.* But his explanation of the rising price after integration seems contradictory to the Nash equilibrium outcomes. According to Salinger, after some firms integrate, the residual demand curve of the non-integrated firms shifts backwards, and these non-integrated firms respond by reducing their output quantity when the goods are substitutes, which contributes to the increase in the price of the final products. Clearly, the rise in the final price happens only when the reduction in output of the non-integrated firms is larger than the increase in output of the integrated firms. But the reduction of total output of the non-integrated firms must be smaller than the increase in the total output of the integrated firms. This is one of the stability conditions of the Cournot-Nash equilibrium (Seade, 1980). Otherwise, there will be a trivial solution. Moreover, the integrated firms as a whole will respond to any reduction of the rival's output with a further increase of their output. The interaction continues until the Nash equilibrium is reached. Therefore, using the residual demand curve to explain the interactions between rational players may not be convenient. Our approach, instead, demonstrates the interactions between the rival firms explicitly.

4. PROFIT INCENTIVES AND ENDOGENEITY OF VERTICAL INDUSTRIAL STRUCTURE

In the previous sections, the equilibria under several different vertical structures in a successive oligopoly have been worked out. In these analyses, the vertical structures of oligopolistic industries are imposed exogenously, as in most existing studies on oligopolistic vertical integration (Blair and Kaserman, 1986; Perry, 1989). But what kind of vertical structure will become dominant in the underlying industry by a self-selection process of a few rational firms (players)?. In this section, we try to answer this question by looking at the relation between the firm's incentive and the vertical structure of the industry in a two-stage game framework.

To do this, we need to seek answers for the following research questions: Firstly, if all the firms, no matter whether they are upstream firms or downstream firms, rely on market transactions for their intermediate goods, do they have any profit incentive to commit themselves to contractual relations? And if *k-1* firms among each type of firms have already done so, does the *k*th firm still have such an incentive? If the answer to the first question is *yes*, then is there any profit incentive which stimulates the two firms associated by an exclusive contractual relation to integrate vertically? If *k-1* firms become vertically integrated, is the *k*th firm willing to make the move of vertical integration? The answers to these questions will help us find the vertical structure which is subgame Nash equilibrium for the adjacent industries, namely, the vertical structure under which no firm is willing to change its own vertical structure given the vertical structure(s) of all other firms.

4.1. Profit Incentive Behind a Supply Contract

Given the objective of profit maximization for all firms, the incentives for an upstream and a downstream firm to commit to a contractual relation can only be created by a higher profit after that move. Therefore, what we need to do is to compare the differences in the profits before and after two related firms make this move.

As a matter of fact, two types of comparisons can be made. The first type of comparison is based on individual rationality to see whether the profit of each individual firm becomes higher or lower after being bound by a contract. The second type of comparison is based on group rationality to compare whether the sum of the two firms' profits becomes higher or lower with a contract than without a contract.

Group rationality is satisfied if the profit of the industry increases no matter what happens to each individual firm's profit. Because individual rationality requires the increase in the profits of both the upstream firm *and* the downstream firm, it is obviously a stronger condition.

The comparison is made in the following way: First of all, the profits of the *k*th downstream firm before and after it commits itself into a contractual relation are compared when *k-1* firms have already done so (note that *k* may be equal to 1). Then, a similar comparison is made for the *k*th upstream firm. Finally, the sum of profits of those two firms with and without a supply contract are compared.

(i) Profit of the *k*th Downstream Firm

Assuming that there are *k-1* downstream firms setting up contractual relations with the same number of upstream firms, the profit of the *k*th downstream firm among *n-k+1* non-integrated firms is then expressed as

$$\pi_k^{dm} = (p - w) q_k$$

where the superscript *dm* indicates the downstream firm's vertical structure as of the market transaction type and the subscript *k* indicates it is the profit of the *k*th downstream firm. Substituting *p* by (2.1) and *w* by (2.4) and rearranging (2.6) into q_k, we have the profit of the *k*th non-integrated downstream firm expressed as

$$\pi_k^{dm} = \frac{9(n-k+1)^2 T}{[(n-k+2)^2(k+2) - (n-k+1)^2(k-1)]^2} \tag{2.17}$$

If the *k*th downstream firm commits itself to a contractual relationship with the *k*th upstream firm, its profit becomes

$$\pi_k^{dc} = (p - w_k) q_k$$

where the superscript c indicates that the kth downstream firm is committed into a contract, and w_k is the transfer price it has to pay for the intermediate input to its supplier. By using the results in (2.1), (2.4) and (2.5), the profit function becomes

$$\pi_k^{dc} = \frac{(2n-2k+1)^2 T}{[(n-k+1)^2(k+3)-(n-k)^2k]^2} \tag{2.18}$$

It is not straightforward to make the algebraic comparison between equations (2.17) and (2.18) due to the complexity of the expressions. Instead, a computer simulation is used to reveal the differences between the kth downstream firm's profits when it takes on different vertical strategies. Table 2.3 is constructed by using (2.17) and (2.18) and contains all values of the profit differences. The determinants of these differences are the horizontal market structure, represented by the total number of firms n, and the vertical structure, represented by $k-1$, the number of firms that have already set up contractual relations before the kth firm does so. The number of firms in each industry changes from 3 to 20 and the constant term, $T=(a-c)^2/b$, takes on the value of 1600.

Table 2.3. Comparison of the downstream firm's profits under market transactions and supply contracts

	n=3	4	5	6	7	8	9	10	11	12	13	14	15	16	17	18	19	20
k = 1	17.2	15.0	12.5	10.3	8.58	7.21	6.12	5.25	4.55	3.98	3.51	3.11	2.78	2.50	2.25	2.05	1.86	1.71
2	11.8	13.6	12.3	10.4	8.79	7.43	6.33	5.44	4.71	4.11	3.62	3.21	2.86	2.57	2.32	2.10	1.91	1.75
3		9.4	11.0	10.2	8.85	7.58	6.50	5.60	4.86	4.25	3.74	3.31	2.95	2.65	2.39	2.16	1.97	1.80
4			7.7	9.1	8.57	7.59	6.60	5.73	4.99	4.37	3.85	3.41	3.04	2.72	2.45	2.22	2.02	1.84
5				6.3	7.64	7.32	6.58	5.80	5.09	4.48	3.95	3.50	3.12	2.80	2.52	2.28	2.07	1.89
6					5.30	6.50	6.32	5.76	5.14	4.56	4.04	3.59	3.20	2.87	2.59	2.34	2.12	1.94
7						4.51	5.59	5.51	5.09	4.58	4.10	3.66	3.28	2.94	2.65	2.40	2.18	1.98
8							3.87	4.86	4.85	4.52	4.11	3.71	3.33	3.00	2.71	2.45	2.23	2.03
9								3.36	4.27	4.30	4.05	3.71	3.37	3.05	2.76	2.50	2.28	2.08
10									2.95	3.77	3.84	3.64	3.36	3.07	2.80	2.55	2.32	2.12
11										2.60	3.36	3.45	3.29	3.06	2.82	2.58	2.36	2.16
12											2.32	3.01	3.11	2.99	2.80	2.59	2.38	2.19
13												2.07	2.71	2.82	2.73	2.57	2.39	2.21
14													1.87	2.46	2.57	2.51	2.37	2.21
15														1.69	2.24	2.35	2.31	2.19
16															1.54	2.04	2.16	2.13
17																1.40	1.87	1.99
18																	1.29	1.72
19																		1.18

It can be clearly seen from Table 2.3, that the profit of the *k*th downstream firm is always higher when its relies on market transactions for its intermediate goods than when it is bound by exclusive supply contracts.

By recalling that the firms in each group are symmetric, we can see that the action of the *k*th firm in choosing its vertical strategy not only determines its own profits but also influences the profit of all other firms. Therefore, these profits are not only the marginal firm's profit but also the average profit for all other firms which have the same vertical structure.

This result complies with intuition. When a downstream firm relies on market transactions for intermediate goods, it can freely switch among the competing suppliers of the same goods. The competition between the upstream suppliers reduces their market power, thereby lowering the marginal cost of the downstream firms. When the firms set up exclusive contractual relationships, the downstream firms cannot turn to alternative suppliers for their inputs. The switching costs and the asymmetrically distributed market power push up the downstream firm's marginal cost, which will consequently reduce its profit.

(ii) Profit of the *k*th Upstream Firm

In contrast to the downstream firms, the exclusive relations seem to work in the upstream firms' favor. To verify this we need to investigate the differences in the upstream firms' profits under different vertical arrangements. When there are k-1 upstream firms bound by supply contracts with the *k*th firm being one of the n-k+1 firms relying on market transactions, this *k*th firm's profit will be:

$$\pi_k^{um} = (w-c)x_k$$

Substituting w and u_k by (2.4) and (2.6), the profit function becomes:

$$\pi_k^{um} = \frac{9(n-k+1)(n-k+2)T}{[(n-k+2)^2(k+2)-(n-k+1)^2(k-1)]^2} \qquad (2.19)$$

After the kth upstream firm commits itself into exclusive relations its profit function becomes

$$\pi_k^{uc} = (w_k - c)x_k$$

Using the results in (2.4) and (2.5), the profit function can be rewritten as

$$\pi_k^{uc} = \frac{2(2n-2k+1)^2 T}{[(n-k+1)^2(k+3)-(n-k)^2 k]^2} \tag{2.20}$$

The differences between $\pi^{um}{}_k$ and $\pi^{uc}{}_k$ under a variety of horizontal market structures and levels of vertical integration are the contents of Table 2.4. The negative values reveal that the kth upstream firm's profits are higher under supply contracts than they are under market transactions.

Table 2.4. Comparison of the upstream firm's profits under market transactions and supply contracts

	n=3	4	5	6	7	8	9	10	11	12	13	14	15	16	17	18	19	20
k=1	-3.13	-0.63	0.30	0.65	0.75	0.76	0.72	0.67	0.61	0.56	0.51	0.47	0.43	0.39	0.36	0.33	0.31	0.28
2	-4.51	-1.31	0.03	0.54	0.71	0.75	0.73	0.68	0.63	0.58	0.53	0.48	0.44	0.40	0.37	0.34	0.32	0.29
3		-2.19	-0.40	0.36	0.65	0.73	0.73	0.69	0.64	0.59	0.54	0.50	0.45	0.42	0.38	0.35	0.32	0.30
4			-1.02	0.08	0.53	0.69	0.72	0.70	0.66	0.61	0.56	0.51	0.47	0.43	0.39	0.36	0.33	0.31
5				-0.39	0.33	0.61	0.70	0.70	0.67	0.62	0.57	0.52	0.48	0.44	0.40	0.37	0.34	0.32
6					-0.05	0.46	0.64	0.68	0.67	0.63	0.58	0.54	0.49	0.45	0.41	0.38	0.35	0.32
7						0.15	0.52	0.64	0.66	0.63	0.59	0.55	0.50	0.46	0.42	0.39	0.36	0.33
8							0.25	0.54	0.63	0.63	0.60	0.56	0.52	0.47	0.44	0.40	0.37	0.34
9								0.31	0.54	0.60	0.59	0.56	0.52	0.48	0.45	0.41	0.38	0.35
10									0.34	0.53	0.57	0.56	0.53	0.49	0.46	0.42	0.39	0.36
11										0.35	0.51	0.54	0.53	0.50	0.46	0.43	0.40	0.37
12											0.35	0.49	0.51	0.50	0.47	0.44	0.40	0.37
13												0.34	0.47	0.48	0.47	0.44	0.41	0.38
14													0.33	0.44	0.46	0.44	0.42	0.39
15														0.32	0.42	0.43	0.42	0.39
16															0.30	0.39	0.41	0.39
17																0.29	0.37	0.38
18																	0.28	0.35
19																		0.26

Table 2.4 shows that the upstream supplier can benefit from exclusive relations only when the horizontal market structure is highly concentrated (i.e. when n is small) or when the number of firms relying on market transactions is small. When the number of firms n is larger than or equal to 8, the upstream firm's profit under market transactions is always higher than its profit under supply contracts. This result seems counter-intuitive since the exclusive supply contract can turn the downstream firm into a captive buyer. The reduction in profit of the upstream firm due to exclusive relations can only be understood through the strategic interactions between the firms. What a supply contract does for the kth upstream firm is to turn one of the downstream firms into its captive buyer. Given that the buyer is captive, the upstream firm gains market power over its buyer, which allows it to charge a higher price for the intermediate inputs in order to increase its profit. The increase in the transfer price between these two firms improves the profit margin of the upstream firm but at the same time generates an undesirable strategic interaction in the downstream industry. This strategic reaction goes against the interest of the upstream firm. The reason is that when the upstream firm increases the price of the intermediate inputs, its captive buyer then becomes a high marginal cost producer competing with all other Cournot-behaved firms in the final products market. The direct effect of the marginal cost increases leads to the decrease in the downstream firm's output quantity. All other firms respond with increases in their own outputs. The optimal response of this downstream firm is to reduce its output further. When the number of firms is small, the negative effect of strategic effect on the upstream firm's profit is dominated by the positive effect of increase in its profit margin. When the horizontal market structure is less concentrated, the strategic effect of reduction in output quantity dominates the direct effect of increase in profit margin. Therefore, it is not surprising to see that the profit of the upstream firm declines when it enters into an exclusive contractual relationship with its buyer.

This result tells us that when the horizontal market structure is less concentrated, it may not be to the advantage of an upstream firm to establish an exclusive supply relationship with its buyer, although it may benefit from such relations when the number of firms is very small or when most of the other firms have done so.

(iii) The Joint Profits of the *k*th Upstream Firm and Downstream Firm

The above comparison raises the possibility that the upstream firm and the downstream firm may have divergent interests as far as their vertical relations are concerned. While the downstream firms always prefer market transactions to supply contracts, the upstream firms benefit from supply contracts only when the number of firms is small and when side-payment between firms is not allowed. To find out whether there is a common ground to reach an agreement when a lump-sum profit transfer is allowed, we need to investigate the sum of the profits of the upstream and downstream firms together. The joint profit of the *k*th upstream and the *k*th downstream firm before and after they commit themselves into contractual relations, when *k-1* firms have already done so, can be found by adding up the profits in equations (2.17) and (2.18) as well as in (2.19) and (2.20). Table 2.5 displays the differences in the sum of these profits.

Table 2.5. Comparison of the joint profits under market transactions and supply contracts

	n=3	4	5	6	7	8	9	10	11	12	13	14	15	16	17	18	19	20
k = 1	14.1	14.4	12.8	11.0	9.33	7.96	6.84	5.92	5.17	4.54	4.02	3.58	3.21	2.89	2.62	2.38	2.17	1.99
2	7.29	12.3	12.3	11.0	9.51	8.18	7.06	6.12	5.34	4.69	4.15	3.69	3.31	2.98	2.69	2.44	2.23	2.04
3		7.23	10.6	10.5	9.49	8.32	7.23	6.30	5.51	4.84	4.28	3.81	3.41	3.06	2.77	2.51	2.29	2.09
4			6.63	9.19	9.11	8.28	7.33	6.43	5.65	4.98	4.41	3.92	3.51	3.15	2.85	2.58	2.35	2.15
5				5.93	7.98	7.93	7.28	6.50	5.76	5.10	4.52	4.03	3.60	3.24	2.92	2.65	2.41	2.20
6					5.25	6.96	6.96	6.45	5.81	5.19	4.62	4.13	3.70	3.32	3.00	2.72	2.47	2.26
7						4.65	6.12	6.15	5.74	5.22	4.69	4.21	3.78	3.40	3.07	2.79	2.54	2.32
8							4.13	5.41	5.48	5.15	4.71	4.27	3.85	3.48	3.14	2.85	2.60	2.37
9								3.68	4.81	4.90	4.64	4.27	3.89	3.53	3.21	2.91	2.65	2.42
10									3.29	4.30	4.41	4.20	3.89	3.57	3.25	2.97	2.71	2.48
11										2.95	3.87	3.99	3.82	3.56	3.28	3.01	2.75	2.52
12											2.67	3.50	3.62	3.49	3.27	3.03	2.79	2.56
13												2.42	3.18	3.31	3.20	3.02	2.80	2.59
14													2.20	2.90	3.03	2.95	2.79	2.60
15														2.01	2.65	2.78	2.72	2.58
16															1.84	2.44	2.57	2.52
17																1.69	2.25	2.38
18																	1.56	2.08
19																		1.45

The positive values mean that the sum of the profits of both the upstream and downstream firms is higher when the vertical structure is market transactions than when it is exclusive contracts. It is clear that the sum of the profits of these two types of firms is always higher under market transactions no matter what the other firms are doing.

4.2. Profit Incentive of Vertical Integration

The purpose of this section is to investigate whether the upstream and the downstream firms that are already committed to exclusive contractual relations have any incentive to integrate vertically. Since the only motivation for two firms bound by an exclusive relationship to integrate is the possible higher profit after that move, that motivation can be revealed by comparing the sum of the profits of these two merging firms and the profit of the fully integrated firm.

We assume that there are $k-1$ integrated firms ($1 \leq k < n$) and the remaining firms rely on supply contracts for the intermediate inputs. The sum of the profits of the kth upstream and the kth downstream firms relying on contracts is

$$\pi_k^c = (p - w_k)x_k + (w_k - c)x_k$$

By using equation (2.1) and the equilibrium results in (2.8) and (2.10), π^c_k can be rewritten as

$$\pi_k^c = \frac{3T}{(n + 2k + 1)^2} \tag{2.21}$$

If these two firms integrate vertically and become the kth integrated firm, by definition, their profit function becomes

$$\pi_k^i = (p - c)v_k$$

Using equations (2.1), (2.7) and (2.9), the profit of the kth integrated firm can be computed to be

$$\pi_k^i = \frac{9T}{(n+2k+3)^2} \tag{2.22}$$

We can directly compare the joint profits of the kth upstream firm and the kth downstream firm with contractual relations and the profits of the vertically integrated firm. The difference between (2.21) and (2.22) is found as follows,

$$\pi_k^c - \pi_k^i = \frac{-6(n^2+4kn+4k^2-3)}{(n+2k+1)^2(n+2k+3)^2} \tag{2.23}$$

It is a simple matter to verify that (2.23) is always negative for all n when $1<k<n$. The above expression tells us that the profit of the integrated firm is higher than those of the non-integrated firms. In other words, if the vertical industrial structure is a mixed integration characterized by vertical integration and supply contracts, two separate firms can increase their joint profits by vertical integration independent of the extent of integration in the underlying industry.

The reasons behind the increases in the integrated firms' profit are, firstly, the upstream and downstream firms bound by the contract have different objectives. Each firm tries to maximize its own profit which may or may not be consistent with joint profit maximization. The difference in their objectives prevents the two firms to follow the output strategy which maximizes the sum of their profit. But vertical integration implies that the interests of the merging firms are harmonized after vertical cooperation between them is achieved within the confines of a single firm, which leads to the increase in total profits. Secondly, as the integrated firm perceives a low marginal cost after the elimination of the markup on the price of the intermediate products, the profit of the merged firm increases, *ceteris paribus*. Thirdly, because the integrated firm becomes a lower cost producer and it tends to compete more aggressively on the final product market. The expected response from rivals with substitute products is to reduce their outputs, which may allow further increases in the output of the integrated firm. This strategic effect will have a positive impact on the integrated firm's profit. While all these benefit the integrated firms, other firms' profits become lower.

If we take the first derivative of the profit of the integrated firm in (2.22) with respect to the number of firms vertically integrated, we can find that

$$\frac{\partial \pi_k^i}{\partial k} = -\frac{36}{(n+2k+3)^3}$$

The negative sign of the first derivative tells us that when the number of integrated firms increases, the average profitability of the integrated firms will be diluted by newcomers.

4.3. Combined Impact of Market Elimination and Vertical Integration

Now, we consider a mixed integration game characterized by full vertical integration and market transactions. In this scenario, some firms rely on the intermediate inputs market for their supplies and products while other firms internalize the intermediate goods production through vertical integration. Although similar settings do appear in the literature (Greenhut and Ohta, 1979; Salinger, 1988), the issue of private incentive has not yet been looked at from the perspective of two-stage games.

Suppose there are *k-1* integrated firms with operations in both stages and there are *n-k+1* firms in each industry relying on market transactions for intermediate goods. The question is, what will be the impact on the firm's profit if one upstream firm and one downstream firm, originally relying on market transactions, integrate vertically? The combined effect of vertical integration and market elimination on the firms' profits can be found by computing the differences between the firms' profits under the two alternative vertical structures.

The sum of the profits of the *k*th non-integrated upstream and downstream firms relying on the market transactions is,

$$\pi_k^m = (p - w)q_k + (w - c)x_k$$

By using the equilibrium results in (2.15), (2.16) and the demand function for the final goods in (2.1), this joint profit function can be transformed into

$$\pi_k^m = \frac{(n-k+1)(2n-2k+3)T}{[k(n-k+2)^2-(k-1)(n-k+1)^2]^2} \tag{2.24}$$

If these two firms are fully integrated, the profit of the kth integrated firm is

$$\pi_k^i = (p-c)v_k$$

which can be transformed into (2.25) by applying equations (2.1) and (2.16)

$$\pi_k^i = \frac{(2n-2k+1)^2 T}{[(n-k+1)^2(k+1)-(n-k)^2 k]^2} \tag{2.25}$$

A computer simulation has been carried out to compare equations (2.24) and (2.25). Selected values of simulation results are included in Table 2.6.

Table 2.6. Comparison of firm's profits under vertical structures of market transactions and vertical integration

	n=3	4	5	6	7	8	9	10	11	12	13	14	15	16	17	18	19	20
k = 1	72.8	56.0	44.2	35.7	29.3	24.5	20.8	17.8	15.5	13.5	12.0	10.6	9.50	8.55	7.74	7.03	6.42	5.88
2	62.4	47.3	37.3	30.3	25.1	21.2	18.1	15.6	13.7	12.0	10.7	9.6	8.59	7.77	7.06	6.44	5.90	5.42
3		40.9	32.1	26.1	21.8	18.5	15.9	13.9	12.2	10.8	9.6	8.6	7.81	7.09	6.47	5.92	5.44	5.02
4			28.5	23.0	19.2	16.3	14.1	12.4	10.9	9.7	8.7	7.9	7.13	6.50	5.95	5.46	5.04	4.66
5				20.9	17.2	14.7	12.7	11.1	9.9	8.8	7.9	7.2	6.55	5.98	5.49	5.06	4.68	4.34
6					15.9	13.4	11.6	10.1	9.0	8.1	7.3	6.6	6.03	5.53	5.09	4.70	4.36	4.05
7						12.5	10.7	9.3	8.3	7.4	6.7	6.1	5.59	5.13	4.73	4.38	4.07	3.79
8							10.1	8.7	7.7	6.9	6.2	5.7	5.19	4.78	4.42	4.10	3.81	3.56
9								8.3	7.2	6.4	5.8	5.3	4.85	4.47	4.14	3.84	3.58	3.34
10									7.0	6.1	5.5	5.0	4.55	4.20	3.89	3.61	3.37	3.15
11										5.9	5.2	4.7	4.30	3.96	3.67	3.41	3.18	2.98
12											5.1	4.5	4.09	3.76	3.47	3.23	3.02	2.83
13												4.4	3.94	3.59	3.31	3.07	2.87	2.69
14													3.88	3.47	3.18	2.94	2.74	2.56
15														3.43	3.08	2.83	2.62	2.45
16															3.06	2.75	2.54	2.36
17																2.74	2.48	2.29
18																	2.47	2.24
19																		2.24

The values in this table are the differences in the profits of the integrated firm and the firms depending on market transactions. The positive values of these differences in profits under a variety of horizontal market structure parameters indicate that the firms' joint profits increase when they change their vertical structure from market transactions to vertical integration.

After examining the incentives in all three different mixed integration scenarios, we can establish the following proposition:

Proposition 2.6. *In a successive Cournot oligopoly with linear demand, fixed coefficients technology and constant returns to scale, vertical integration is a Nash equilibrium vertical structure.*

As has been shown, non-integrated firms have profit incentives to change their vertical structures from market transactions or supply contracts to vertical integration, no matter what is the type of vertical structure adopted by other firms, although the profit of the whole industry is lowest when the vertical structure is characterized as full vertical integration. In other words, if each firm can freely decide its vertical structure after knowing all other firms' objective functions and strategy sets, its optimal decision is to integrate vertically and it has no incentive to deviate from that point.

5. CONCLUSIONS

When comparing the three generic vertical structures in an n-firm successive Cournot oligopoly, we find that the vertical structure of full integration leads to the highest output and the lowest price for consumers and, therefore, creates the greatest social welfare. The structure of exclusive supply contracts, on the other hand, creates the double markup effect and the market elimination effect. Both of these effects reduce the equilibrium output of the final products and lead to the lowest consumer welfare. The equilibrium output quantity of the final products under market transactions falls in the middle compared with the other two cases. When the number of firms in both upstream and downstream industries increases, the horizontal market structure becomes less concentrated. The intensified competition increases the total output of final goods independent of the industry vertical structure and the relative position of output quantities under these three generic vertical industrial structures remains unchanged.

When vertical structure in the successive oligopoly is characterized by a mixed integration, i.e. some firms integrate vertically and others do not, the relations between the extent of vertical integration and the total output of the final goods in equilibrium depend on the type of mixed integration. When the vertical structure of the industry is a mixed integration with some firms relying on market transactions and others setting up supply contractual relations, the total output of final goods falls when the number of firms bound by supply contracts increases. When the vertical structure of the industry is characterized by some firms relying on market transactions for their intermediate inputs and others relying on vertical integration, the equilibrium output quantity of the final products becomes higher when more and more firms become vertically integrated.

We show that exclusive contracts may not increase the upstream firm's profits when the horizontal market structure is less concentrated. Although the upstream firm tries to increase its profits by charging a higher price of intermediate inputs for its captive buyer, the increase in its profit because of the higher profit margin may not be sufficient to compensate the losses due to the negative strategic effect in the downstream industry. The increase in the input price will be transformed into a higher marginal cost for its captive downstream firm. The optimal response of this downstream firm then is to reduce its output level conditional on the output of its rivals. The other downstream firms will all respond optimally by expanding their outputs. The magnitude of this strategic effect depends on the horizontal market structure. When the total number of firms or the number of firms relying on market transactions for their inputs is small, the upstream firms still have a profit incentive to establish contractual relations. When the number of firms increases, such an incentive soon evaporates. The exclusive contractual relations will not be desirable even for the upstream firms despite the fact that such relations increase the market power of the upstream firms over its captive buyer.

We demonstrate that the mixed integration in which some firms are integrated while others are not is not a Nash equilibrium vertical industrial structure, because the firm at the margin can always increase its profit by changing its vertical structure and become one of the vertically integrated firms in the industries characterized as such. The industrial vertical structure converges to vertical integration. Therefore, vertical integration is qualified as the Nash equilibrium vertical industrial structure under which no individual firm has any incentive to change its vertical strategy unilaterally.

Chapter 3

VERTICAL INTEGRATION IN A DIFFERENTIATED DUOPOLY

In most industries, the products of different manufacturers are rarely identical, at least in the consumer's perception. Therefore, to introduce product differentiation into our oligopolistic vertical integration model is a natural way to enrich and to extend the basic results. The purpose of this chapter is to investigate what kind of impact product differentiation may have on the equilibrium outcomes and, consequently, on the firm's vertical integration strategy, on the equilibrium industrial vertical structure and on social welfare as a whole.

This chapter is organized as follows. First, product differentiation is introduced into the successive duopoly model specified earlier. Then, the equilibrium results under different vertical settings are worked out under a two-stage Cournot game framework. The economic analysis is carried out based on the derived equilibrium results before the conclusion is provided.

1. A MODEL OF SUCCESSIVE COURNOT DUOPOLY WITH PRODUCT DIFFERENTIATION

Since vertical integration involves two sequentially related industries (or production processes), there are three possible ways to incorporate product differentiation into the model: First of all, both the final products and the intermediate goods are assumed to be differentiated; secondly, only the final products are differentiated and finally, only the intermediate goods are differentiated. We will look at a general case where the goods at both stages are differentiated and the other two cases can be easily treated as special cases.

Following Vives (1985), product differentiation is posited such that an economy consists of an oligopolistic industry and a competitive *numeraire* industry. In this oligopolistic industry, two Cournot-type firms, producing final products for consumers, have their intermediate inputs supplied by two Cournot-type upstream firms. In the final products market there is a continuum of consumers of the same type with a utility function separable and linear in the *numeraire* good. Therefore, there is no income effect on the oligopolistic sector.

PGABERYSTWYTH LLYFRGELL

The basic characteristics of the model are kept identical with the successive duopoly model with homogeneous goods as far as technology specifications, the objective of the firm, the information structure and the equilibrium concept are concerned. The game structures can be visualized by recalling the diagrams in Chapter 1. The difference emerges with the characteristics of the products when the two downstream firms produce differentiated products. As far as the preferences of the consumers are concerned, a non-address approach developed by Spence-Dixit-Stiglitz is used (Spence, 1976; Dixit and Stiglitz, 1977). This approach assumes that there are a large number of possible products in the sector or industry of interest. Product demands arise from the utility maximizing decisions of a representative consumer. This is different from the address model of Hotelling, which assumes diversity in consumers' taste while making the closeness of substitutability among goods partially an objective phenomenon. In all consumers' minds, two adjacent drugstores will be closer substitutes than two drugstores at the opposite ends of the town (Eaton and Lipsey, 1989). The non-address approach offers the advantage of allowing analysis in the value theory tradition and the use of a representative consumer.

The demand function is assumed to arise from a representative utility function $U = U(q_1,q_2)+q_0$, where q_1 and q_2 are the output quantities of two downstream duopolists respectively and q_0 is the output of the *numeraire* industry. U is assumed to be quadratic and strictly concave. In our analysis, the utility function takes the following form:

$$U(q_1,q_2) = a(q_1 + q_2) - (bq_1^2 + 2rq_1q_2 + bq_2^2)/2 \tag{3.1}$$

where $a>0$, $b>0$, $b>r$ and $b^2>r^2$. Because there is no income effect on the demand side, partial equilibrium analysis is used. By doing so, the above utility function gives rise to a linear inverse demand system:

$$\begin{aligned} p_1 &= a - q_1 - \theta q_2 \\ p_2 &= a - \theta q_1 - q_2 \end{aligned} \tag{3.2}$$

where $\theta=r/b$ is the product differentiation parameter which measures the cross-products effects. The products produced by the rival firms in the downstream industry are substitutes if $1>\theta>0$, and complements if $-1<\theta<0$. The final goods of the two downstream producers become independent if $\theta=0$ and become homogeneous when $\theta=1$.

The product differentiation for the intermediate goods is likely to involve transaction costs that prevent the easy switch between different suppliers or buyers. In other words, each upstream firm produces a kind of intermediate good which is particularly suitable only to one of the downstream firms. Switching between suppliers or buyers is costly. And because of that, the market transaction game may not be frequently observed. Therefore, the investigation is concentrated on three types of games: supply contract, mixed integration and full integration.

2. EQUILIBRIUM ANALYSIS

The purpose of this section is to carry out technical analysis. It starts with the derivation of the equilibrium outcomes under the three different vertical structure games mentioned earlier. These results will be summarized in Table 3.1 at the end of this section. The economic interpretation of the results follows in the next section.

2.1. Supply Contracts Game

Given the inverse demand system for the final product in (3.2) and the objective functions of the downstream Cournot-type duopolists

$$\pi_1^u = (p_1 - w_1)q_1$$

$$\pi_2^u = (p_2 - w_2)q_2$$

the first-order conditions of profit maximization for the downstream firms turn out to be

$$\frac{\partial \pi_1^d}{\partial q_1} = a - 2q_1 - \theta q_2 - w_1 = 0$$

$$\frac{\partial \pi_2^d}{\partial q_2} = a - \theta q_1 - 2q_2 - w_2 = 0$$

The reaction functions of the downstream Cournot duopolists with respect to their rivals' output quantities are

$$q_1 = (a - w_1 - \theta q_2)/2$$

$$q_2 = (a - w_2 - \theta q_1)/2$$

We can imagine that when the goods are substitutes ($\theta>0$), these reaction functions are downward-sloping and when the goods are complements ($\theta<0$) they become upward-sloping in the quantity space. The intercept of these two reaction functions is the Cournot-Nash equilibrium in the quantity space of final products. At equilibrium the output quantities of these two firms are

$$q_1 = \frac{a(2 - \theta) - 2w_1 + \theta w_2}{4 - \theta^2} \tag{3.3}$$

$$q_2 = \frac{a(2 - \theta) + \theta w_1 - 2w_2}{4 - \theta^2} \tag{3.4}$$

Because of the fixed proportions of the intermediate inputs, the marginal (=average) cost of the downstream firm w_i, $i=1,2$ is equivalent to the revenue which an upstream firm receives from each intermediate good sold. After certain rearrangements and letting q_i be replaced by x_i, equations (3.3) and (3.4) can be used to derive the demand system which the upstream duopolists face. Hence, the upstream firms in the first stage of the game have the derived demand system

$$w_1 = a - 2x_1 - \theta x_2$$

$$w_2 = a - \theta x_1 - 2x_2$$

Because the profit functions of the upstream firms are $\pi^u_i = (w_i - c)x_i$, $i = 1, 2$, the first order conditions of profit maximization for the upstream firms in the first stage Cournot game results in the following system of equations:

$$a - 4x_1 - \theta x_2 - c = 0$$

$$a - \theta x_1 - 4x_2 - c = 0$$

which can be transformed into the reaction functions between two upstream Cournot duopolists,

$$x_1 = \frac{a - c}{4} - \frac{\theta}{4}x_2$$

$$x_2 = \frac{a - c}{4} - \frac{\theta}{4}x_1$$

The output levels of the intermediate goods, which are the sub-game perfect equilibrium, are found at the intercept of these reaction functions as

$$x_1 = x_2 = \frac{a - c}{4 + \theta}$$

Note that when $\theta=1$ these results duplicate the outcome in Table 1.1 of Chapter 1, which can be seen as a special case with homogeneous final goods. Because quantity is chosen as the strategic variable by all firms, once the equilibrium output quantities are known, the other equilibrium results, such as market clearing prices and profits, can be found easily.

2.2. Mixed Integration Game

In this scenario, the downstream firm D_1 and the upstream firm U_1 operate independently, but firms D_2 and U_2 merge with each other and form an integrated firm V_2. So there are three players in the game, the first an integrated firm with the output level of v_2, the second a non-integrated downstream firm with the output level of q_1 and the third a non-integrated upstream firm with the output level of x_1. The demand system for the final goods becomes

$$p_1 = a - q_1 - \theta v_2$$

$$p_2 = a - \theta q_1 - v_2$$

Under the linear demand system, the integrated firm and the non-integrated downstream firm are competing with each other by using output as their strategic variable. The first order conditions of profit maximization of these two firms are

$$\frac{\partial \pi_1^d}{\partial q_1} = a - 2q_1 - \theta v_2 - w_1 = 0$$

$$\frac{\partial \pi_2^v}{\partial v_2} = a - \theta q_1 - 2v_2 - c = 0$$

These first order conditions can be transformed into the reaction functions of the downstream firm D_1 and the integrated firm V_1 as

$$q_1 = \frac{a - w_1}{2} - \frac{\theta}{2} v_2 \tag{3.5}$$

$$v_2 = \frac{a - c}{2} - \frac{\theta}{2} q_1 \tag{3.6}$$

The above equations show that the output level of the integrated firm, v_2, depends on the output of its rival q_1. The output of the non-integrated firm, q_1, depends not only on the output of its rival v_2 but also on w_1. In fact, the intermediate goods price w_1 is the transfer price determined by the output of the independent upstream firm. This output must satisfy the individual rationality of the non-integrated upstream firm. Knowing that the average (= marginal) cost of firm D_1 is equal to the revenue for each intermediate good of firm U_1, equation (3.5) can be transformed into

$$w_1 = a - 2x_1 - \theta v_2$$

and the profit function of the upstream firm U_1 becomes

$$\pi_1^u = (a - 2x_1 - \theta v_2 - c)\, x_1$$

This profit function is maximized when its first derivative satisfies the following condition

$$a - 4x_1 - \theta v_2 - c = 0$$

The above equation can be transformed into the reaction function of the upstream firm U_1 in (3.7). It shows that the equilibrium output of firm U_1 cannot be obtained unless the output of the integrated firm is known,

$$x_1 = \frac{a-c}{4} - \frac{\theta}{4}v_2 \tag{3.7}$$

The reaction function of the integrated firm can be found by modifying equation (3.6) to be

$$v_2 = \frac{a-c}{2} - \frac{\theta}{2}x_1 \tag{3.8}$$

The subgame perfect Nash equilibrium output quantities are found by solving (3.7) and (3.8) simultaneously and we obtain

$$x_1 = \frac{(2-\theta)(a-c)}{8-\theta^2}$$

$$v_2 = \frac{(4-\theta)(a-c)}{8-\theta^2}$$

After knowing x_1, v_2, and the intermediate goods price w_1, the final product prices p_1 and p_2 can be found accordingly, as can the profits of individual firms.

2.3. Full Vertical Integration Game

In this scenario, the two-stage game degenerates into an ordinary differentiated Cournot duopoly and the Nash equilibrium outcomes are straightforward by finding the intercept of the reaction functions of the integrated firms V_1 and V_2, which can be derived from the first order conditions of profit maximization:

$$a - 2v_1 - \theta v_2 - c = 0$$

$$a - \theta v_1 - 2v_2 - c = 0$$

The equilibrium output quantities of the vertically integrated firms are

$$v_1 = v_2 = \frac{a - c}{2 + \theta}$$

Based on the equilibrium output quantities derived above, the other equilibrium results can be easily worked out. Table 3.1 summarizes the key equilibrium results such as the output quantities, the prices of the intermediate goods as well as the final products and profits under the three alternative vertical structures.

3. PRODUCT DIFFERENTIATION AND EQUILIBRIUM VERTICAL STRUCTURE

The equilibrium results are summarized in Table 3.1, which provide us with opportunities to examine further the impact of product differentiation on the equilibrium output, the profitability of the individual firms as well as of the industry and social welfare.

Before starting the formal analysis, we should be aware that the product differentiation parameter θ lies in the range $-1<\theta \leq 1$. This includes the extreme case of two independent successive monopolies ($\theta=0$) and the case of a successive duopoly with homogeneous goods ($\theta=1$). As has been indicated earlier, when θ is greater than zero, the final goods of the rival producers are substitutes; otherwise, they are complements.

Table 3.1. Equilibrium Results for a Differentiated Successive Cournot Duopoly

<table>
<tr><th>Eq. results</th><th>Supply contracts</th><th>Mixed integration</th><th>Full integration</th></tr>
<tr><td>q_1</td><td>$\frac{S}{4+\theta}$</td><td>$\frac{(2-\theta)S}{8-\theta^2}$</td><td>$\frac{S}{2-\theta}$</td></tr>
<tr><td>q_2</td><td>$\frac{S}{4+\theta}$</td><td>$\frac{(4-\theta)S}{8-\theta^2}$</td><td>$\frac{S}{2+\theta}$</td></tr>
<tr><td>p_1</td><td>$c+\frac{3S}{4+\theta}$</td><td>$c+\frac{3(2-\theta)S}{8-\theta^2}$</td><td>$c+\frac{S}{2+\theta}$</td></tr>
<tr><td>p_2</td><td>$c+\frac{3S}{4+\theta}$</td><td>$c+\frac{(4-\theta)S}{8-\theta^2}$</td><td>$c+\frac{S}{2+\theta}$</td></tr>
<tr><td>w_1</td><td>$c+\frac{2S}{4+\theta}$</td><td>$c+\frac{2(2-\theta)S}{8-\theta^2}$</td><td>$c$</td></tr>
<tr><td>w_2</td><td>$c+\frac{2S}{4+\theta}$</td><td>c</td><td>c</td></tr>
<tr><td>π_1^u</td><td>$\frac{2T}{(4+\theta)^2}$</td><td>$\frac{2(2-\theta)^2 T}{(8-\theta^2)^2}$</td><td rowspan="2">$\frac{T}{(2+\theta)^2}$</td></tr>
<tr><td>π_1^d</td><td>$\frac{T}{(4+\theta)^2}$</td><td>$\frac{(2-\theta)^2 T}{(8-\theta^2)^2}$</td></tr>
<tr><td>π_2^u</td><td>$\frac{2T}{(4+\theta)^2}$</td><td rowspan="2">$\frac{(4-\theta)^2 T}{(8-\theta^2)^2}$</td><td rowspan="2">$\frac{T}{(2+\theta)^2}$</td></tr>
<tr><td>π_2^d</td><td>$\frac{T}{(4+\theta)^2}$</td></tr>
<tr><td>Π</td><td>$\frac{6T}{(4+\theta)^2}$</td><td>$\frac{4(7-5\theta+\theta^2)T}{(8-\theta^2)^2}$</td><td>$\frac{2T}{(2+\theta)^2}$</td></tr>
<tr><td>*Consumer surplus*</td><td>$\frac{(1+\theta)T}{(4+\theta)^2}$</td><td>$\frac{(10+2\theta-5\theta^2+\theta^3)T}{(8-\theta^2)^2}$</td><td>$\frac{(1+\theta)T}{(2+\theta)^2}$</td></tr>
<tr><td>*Social welfare*</td><td>$\frac{(7+\theta)T}{(4+\theta)^2}$</td><td>$\frac{(38-18\theta-\theta^2+\theta^3)T}{(8-\theta^2)^2}$</td><td>$\frac{(3+\theta)T}{(2+\theta)^2}$</td></tr>
</table>

* $S = (a-c)$, $T = (a-c)^2$

3.1. Dominant Strategy and Nash Equilibrium Vertical Structure

In the successive duopoly setting, the profits of the firms depend on their own vertical structure as well as on the vertical structure of their rivals. Under the given information structure of *almost perfect information* and in the absence of uncertainty, a rational player tries to determine his vertical structure based on his payoff function while taking into account his rival's payoff function and the strategy set. Because the strategy set of each firm consists of supply contracts and vertical integration, a payoff matrix can be constructed by using the equilibrium results in Table 3.1. The common numerator $T=(a-c)^2$ is omitted. To make the comparison meaningful, the firms' payoffs under the supply contracts are the sums of the profits of the downstream and the upstream firms bound by supply contracts. The payoff of the vertically integrated firm is the profit of the merged firm.

		Firm 2's Strategy	
		Contract	Integration
Firm 1's Strategy	Contract	$\frac{3}{(4+\theta)^2}$; $\frac{3}{(4-\theta)^2}$	$\frac{3(2-\theta)^2}{(8-\theta^2)^2}$; $\frac{(4-\theta)^2}{(8-\theta^2)^2}$
	Integration	$\frac{(4-\theta)^2}{(8-\theta^2)^2}$; $\frac{3(2-\theta)^2}{(8-\theta^2)^2}$	$\frac{1}{(2+\theta)^2}$; $\frac{1}{(2+\theta)^2}$

Figure 3.1. Payoff Matrix of a Differentiated Duopolist

This matrix shows the payoffs of the players in four possible strategy combinations. Given that the firms' payoffs depend on the product differentiation parameter, it is not immediately clear what the Nash equilibrium vertical structure will be. To find out whether there exists a pure strategy Nash equilibrium, we need to compare the payoffs of each firm in these strategy combinations. Because the strategy set consists of two possible strategies, supply contracts and vertical integration, we use two superscripts, *c* and *i* to denote the possible strategies of the firms. The first letter denotes the strategy chosen by Firm 1 and the second letter denotes the strategy chosen by Firm 2. Noting the symmetry between the two firms, we only need to compare the payoffs of firm 1 in Figure 3.1. The results of this comparison are reflected in the following expressions

$$\pi_1^{ii} - \pi_1^{ci} = \frac{2(8+4\theta^2-\theta^4)T}{(2+\theta)^2(8-\theta^2)^2} \tag{3.9}$$

$$\pi_1^{ic} - \pi_1^{cc} = \frac{2(32+8\theta^2-\theta^4)T}{(4+\theta)^2(8-\theta^2)^2} \tag{3.10}$$

Equation (3.9) shows the difference in Firm 1's payoffs between the strategies of vertical integration and supply contracts, given the fact that its rival has already chosen the strategy of vertical integration. It is clear that when $-1<\theta<1$, equation (3.9) is always positive. In other words, Firm 1's payoff is higher when it chooses vertical integration than when it chooses supply contracts. Equation (3.10) compares the same firm's payoffs when it integrates and when it does not integrate under the condition that its rival chooses the supply contracts instead. The comparison result shows that Firm 1's payoff is higher when it becomes vertically integrated than when it is not integrated. The result of the comparison shows that no matter what the rival firm does, vertical integration always provides Firm 1 with higher payoffs than the alternative strategy of supply contracts. By definition, vertical integration becomes the dominant strategy for each player. It becomes clear that vertical integration is the Nash equilibrium vertical structure of the game.

After knowing that vertical integration is the dominant strategy for all players independent of the level of product differentiation, we may still want to know what impact product differentiation may have on the firms' payoffs. To reveal such relations, Figure 3.2 is constructed. In this figure, the horizontal axis is the product differentiation parameter θ which indicates the nature and level of product differentiation. When θ is larger than zero, the final goods are substitutes, otherwise, they are complements. When θ approaches *1*, the products are more homogeneous, and the products are highly differentiated when θ approaches *0*. The vertical axis indicates the payoffs of the firm, which are functions of the product differentiation parameter θ. Besides the payoffs under the two symmetric strategies of vertical integration and supply contracts, there are two possibilities of mixed integration strategies. *Mix(c)* means the firm itself follows the supply contracts strategy while its rival chooses the vertical integration strategy, and *Mix(i)* represents the scenario where the firm integrates vertically and its rival does not.

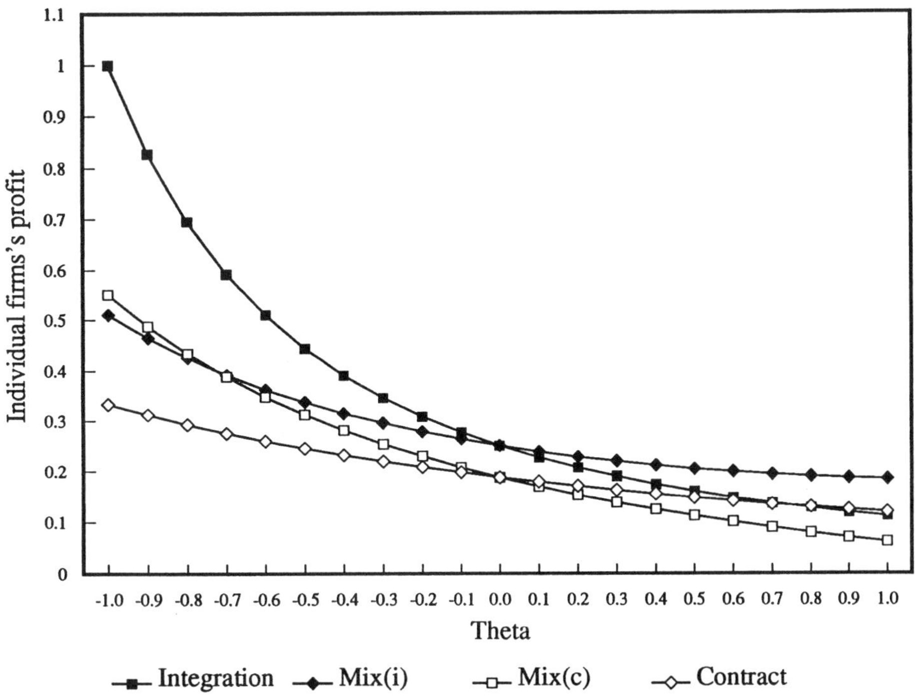

Figure 3.2. Individual Firm's Profits under Alternative Vertical Structures

We first look at the point θ=*0*. This is the extreme point of product differentiation which eliminates any strategic interaction between the rival firms. The firms can decide their vertical strategy independent of the type of vertical structure their rivals choose. The game becomes two separate successive monopolies. What is shown here is consistent with the well known result that the joint profit of two merged firms is larger than the sum of the profits of two merging firms in the case of a successive monopoly with fixed coefficients technology.

When $-1<\theta<0$, the final products of competing producers are complements, and vertical integration is obviously the dominant strategy for each firm to follow. Therefore, it is also the Nash equilibrium vertical structure of the industry. At that equilibrium point, the profit of the industry is the greatest.

When $0<\theta<0.73$, the final products of rival producers become substitutes. In this scenario, if its rival is not vertically integrated, the vertically integrated firm V_1 will have the highest profit. On the other hand, because of the markup over marginal cost of the intermediate inputs, the supply contract is the worst strategy possible for any firm facing a vertically integrated competitor. Rational players can see through it and try to integrate vertically.

When $0.73<\theta<1$, the firm's profit under supply contracts becomes higher than that under vertical integration. The intuition behind this is that when θ is close to 1, the products become less differentiated and the competition between rival products becomes increasingly intense. In this case, the firms' profits are higher in the case of supply contracts than in vertical integration. The exclusive contracts reduce the degree of competition by raising the perceived marginal costs of the final product producers. But each individual firm has incentive to integrate vertically once it knows that its rivals have chosen supply contracts, hence the supply contracts cannot be the Nash equilibrium vertical structure.

We may conclude that full vertical integration is a Nash-equilibrium vertical structure for the complete range of the product differentiation parameter under investigation although the supply contracts and the mixed integration may lead individual firms to higher profits.

3.2. Level of Product Differentiation and Industrial Profitability

The profits of the industry under the three different vertical structures is the sum of individual firms' profits and is denoted by Π. The profits under the three alternative vertical structures are, as shown in Table 3.2, the functions of the product differentiation parameter θ. Table 3.2 also includes the comparative statics of the total profits of all firms under the three vertical structures. We want to know the comparative profitability under these vertical structures and, particularly, how the level of product differentiation may influence the profitability of the industry.

Table 3.2. Industrial Profitability and Impact of Product Differentiation

Vertical structure	Supply contracts	Mixed integration	Full integration
Π	$\frac{6T}{(4+\theta)^2}$	$\frac{4(7-5\theta+\theta^2)T}{(8-\theta^2)^2}$	$\frac{2T}{(2+\theta)^2}$
$\frac{\partial\Pi}{\partial\theta}$	$\frac{-12T}{(4+\theta)^3}$	$\frac{-4(40-44\theta+15\theta^2-2\theta^3)T}{(8-\theta^2)^3}$	$\frac{-4T629}{(2+\theta)^3}$

After comparing the profitability under these vertical structures, we establish the following relations

$$\Pi^i = \frac{2T}{(2-\theta)^2} \geq \frac{6T}{(4+\theta)^2} = \Pi^c \quad \textit{if} \quad -1<\theta\leq 0.73$$

In Chapter 1, we have shown that when the final goods are homogeneous, vertical integration yields the lowest profit for the industry. Since vertical integration is the dominant strategy for each firm, individual rationality keeps the profit of the industry as well as of each individual firm at their lowest levels. Therefore, the outcome of the vertical integration game is similar to the outcome of the *prisoners' dilemma* game. The result in (3.11) shows that when the level of product differentiation is high or when the final products are complements, the profitability of the industry characterized as full integration is the highest. The *prisoners' dilemma* type of problem does not appear.

This result can be related to, but is different from, the findings reported by Bonanno and Vickers (1989). They argue, using a Bertrand duopoly model, that vertical integration will hurt the interests of competing firms by reducing the possibility of cooperative behavior. Our result shows that vertical disintegration (which can be interpreted as adopting supply contracts in our model) may or may not increase the firm's profit depending on the degree of product differentiation. This result is also different from Lin (1988), who states that the quantity competition between downstream firms will lead to a noncooperative outcome like in the *prisoners' dilemma* type of game. Namely, the profits of the integrated firms and the industry become lower after all firms become vertically integrated. Our result shows that the noncooperative outcome is not the only equilibrium outcome in the vertical integration game. When final products are substantially differentiated, vertical integration can increase the firm's profits as well. In other words, individual rationality and group rationality become consistent when the final products are complements or are highly differentiated substitutes.

The comparative statics results are all negative when in the relevant range of the product differentiation parameter θ. This means that the sum of firms' profits in these three vertical structures declines as the final goods become less differentiated. When the level of product differentiation is low and the final products are fairly close substitutes, the competition between the rival firms becomes stronger, which leads to lower profits for the firms as well as for the industry.

3.3. Welfare Implications of Vertical Structure in a Differentiated Successive Duopoly

To answer the question of whether vertical integration is socially desirable, we need to look at the comparative levels of social welfare under different vertical structures. Table 3.3 reports the levels of static social welfare (consumer surplus + producer surplus) and the results of comparative statics under the three vertical structures.

Table 3.3. Comparative Levels of Social Welfare

Vertical structure	Supply contracts	Mixed integration	Full integration
Social welfare	$\frac{(7+\theta)T}{(4+\theta)^2}$	$\frac{(38-18\theta-\theta^2+\theta^3)T}{(8-\theta^2)^2}$	$\frac{(3+\theta)T}{(2+\theta)^2}$
$\frac{\partial W}{\partial \theta}$	$\frac{-(10+\theta)}{(4+\theta)^3}$	$\frac{-(144-136\theta+30\theta^2+2\theta^3-\theta^4)}{(8-\theta^2)^3}$	$\frac{-(4+\theta)}{(2+\theta)^3}$

The comparison among the levels of social welfare shows that social welfare under the vertical integration game is always larger than the social welfare under the mixed integration game, while the latter is always higher than that under the supply contracts game. This relationship is independent of the degree of product differentiation. Similar to the successive monopoly, vertical integration under successive oligopoly improves social welfare.

The results of comparative statics show that when the degree of product differentiation decreases, social welfare decreases. The speed of decline is fastest when the vertical structure of the industry is characterized as vertical integration. Although the output quantity of the industry increases and the equilibrium prices decrease, consumer surplus declines as goods become less differentiated. The reason is that the preference of the consumer is characterized such that the variety is viewed as positive in welfare terms, and consumer surplus becomes higher when the goods are highly differentiated, *ceteris paribus*. The decline in the profitability of the industry as the goods become more homogeneous leads to the increase in social welfare.

4. CONCLUSIONS

The introduction of product differentiation into a successive duopoly provides some new insights. The profits of merging firms and the whole industry are not always the highest under full vertical integration. When the final goods are substitutes and when degree of the product differentiation is low, vertical integration results in lower profits for the merging firms than what would be obtained under the vertical structure of supply contracts. It is because the level of competition between the rival firms with less differentiated products makes the cooperation less likely, and that dampens their profitability. But when the products are highly differentiated, direct competition is of less concern for the rival firms, and economic efficiency can be increased by eliminating the double marginalization in the intermediate goods market. Therefore, the relative profitability of vertical integration changes when the level of product differentiation varies. When the final goods are complements, vertical integration becomes the vertical structure which produces the highest profit for the merging firms and for the industry as a whole. This is because, first of all, vertically integrated firms enjoy a lower marginal cost and produce more output than otherwise. Secondly, because the final goods are complements, an increase in one firm's output reinforces the output increase of the other firm(s) by shifting its demand curve outwards. This increases the firm's profits and improves social welfare.

Our results show that when the level of product differentiation is low, the vertical integration game turns out to be a *prisoners' dilemma*. All the firms in equilibrium have the structure of vertical integration although this will lower all firms' profits. This is because the structure of vertical integration is the Nash equilibrium vertical structure and full vertical integration is the dominant strategy for each individual firm. But when the final goods are highly differentiated or when the products become complements, the *prisoners' dilemma* situation is avoided. The profits of the firms are higher under the structure of vertical integration than under any other vertical structure and vertical integration is in the individual firm's interest as well as in the interest of the whole industry. The implication for corporate strategy is that the effort to increase product differentiation may be highly rewarding if it can lead to the avoidance of a *prisoners' dilemma*.

It has also been demonstrated that any attempt of the individual firm to deviate from vertical integration or to reduce the cooperation between vertically related firms not only lowers the profitability of the firms but also harms the public interest by reducing social welfare. The combination of profit and consumer's surplus is highest under vertical integration because of the relatively high industrial output quantity and the lower price of the final products. Moreover, the welfare-maximizing structure of the full vertical integration is guaranteed by the private incentive of individual firms since it is a self-enforcing vertical structure by rational firms.

Chapter 4

VERTICAL INTEGRATION IN A SUCCESSIVE OLIGOPOLY WITH VARIABLE PROPORTIONS OF INPUTS

1. INTRODUCTION

In the previous chapters, the issues of vertical integration have been investigated from several aspects under the assumption that the technology is characterized by fixed proportions of inputs. This assumption is a good approximation for a number of industry sectors and for relations between manufacturers and distributors (retailers). It is important to note that substitutions among production factors exist in many other industries, and policy implications of vertical integration derived from models characterized by fixed coefficients technology may not be applicable when substitution among input factors is possible. For instance, although it is generally accepted by economists that vertical integration lowers the prices of the final goods and improves social welfare when technology is characterized by fixed proportions of inputs, the impact of substitutability among the intermediate inputs on market equilibrium and social welfare still remains controversial. Part of the controversy is caused by the mix-up in the effects of vertical merger and horizontal merger (Waterson, 1982), which leads to the conclusion that the price path of the final products depends on the elasticity of substitution. This has been corrected recently by Abiru (1988), who shows that vertical integration cannot increase the price of the final products even when the elasticity of substitution is low.

Still, several questions remain to be answered, such as what key factors lead to the decline in the price of the final goods after vertical integration, what types of strategic interactions take place among the firms in adjacent industries, and what is the effect of pure vertical integration. In reality, industrial vertical structures may take different forms when vertical integration actually takes place. We know that the impact of vertical integration depends on the pre-integration status of the industry with fixed input proportions, but it is not clear what kind of impact input substitutability may have on equilibrium outcomes among the alternative vertical structures of market transactions, supply contracts or full integration.

This chapter should be read as a natural extension of the previous chapters. The vertical relations between two industries are the focus of the analysis. By exploring a successive Cournot duopoly model using a production function with constant elasticity of substitution, we will assess the impact of substitutability among the intermediate inputs on the equilibrium output level of the final goods, the derived demand elasticity, the intermediate as well as final goods' prices. More specifically, we shall investigate the extent of the market elimination effect and the pure integration effect under conditions of input substitutability. The structure of this chapter is as follows: Initially, the successive duopoly model is introduced to incorporate the substitutability of the input factors. Then, equilibrium results are derived with emphasis on the derived demand elasticity for intermediate inputs under the three alternative industrial vertical structures. Finally, the impacts of the market elimination and pure integration effects on the equilibria are highlighted.

2. A BASIC FRAMEWORK

We consider three vertically related industries. The downstream industry uses two inputs α and β to produce homogeneous final products for consumers. The horizontal market structure of the downstream industry is an oligopoly. Input factor α is supplied by an oligopolistic industry and input factor β is produced in a perfectly competitive industry.

The firms in each industry are assumed to be symmetric. We further assume that there are two Cournot-behaved firms in the downstream industry and two Cournot-behaved firms in the upstream industry characterized by oligopolistic competition.

The final products are assumed to be homogeneous. The demand function for the final products, with constant price elasticity, is assumed to be:

$$p = (q_1 + q_2)^{-\frac{1}{\varepsilon}} \tag{4.1}$$

where p is the market price of the final products, q_i is the output of the ith downstream firm, and ε is the constant price elasticity of demand, $|\varepsilon| > 1$[13]. Note that the demand structure is different from that used in the previous chapters, for the following reasons. First, a demand function with constant elasticity makes mathematical analysis manageable. Second, given the fact that the constant elasticity demand function has been widely used in vertical integration models with variable proportions of inputs, the results derived in this chapter can be compared with those in the literature.

The technology of production is characterized by a constant elasticity substitution (CES) production function with constant returns to scale:

$$q_i(\alpha,\beta) = [\gamma\alpha_i^{(\sigma-1)/\sigma} + (1-\gamma)\beta_i^{(\sigma-1)/\sigma}]^{\sigma/(\sigma-1)} \qquad i=1,2 \tag{4.2}$$

where σ $(1>\sigma>0)$ is the elasticity of substitution between the intermediate inputs α and β; α_i denotes the quantity of the intermediate input α supplied to the ith downstream firm and β_i is intermediate input β supplied to the same firm from a competitive market. γ $(0<\gamma<1)$ is the distributive parameter. The efficiency parameter is normalized to 1. This function is twice differentiable when σ is not equal to 1.

The CES production function offers the advantage of generality because it includes some well known production functions, such as the linear, Cobb-Douglas and Leontief production functions as its special cases[14]. The results derived under a CES production function should be relevant for a wide range of technologies.

Each downstream firm is assumed to be an efficient producer and the cost function corresponding to the production function in (4.2) can be written as

$$C_i(w_\alpha,w_\beta) = [\gamma^\sigma w_{\alpha i}{}^{1-\sigma} + (1-\gamma)^\sigma w_\beta{}^{1-\sigma}]^{(1-\sigma)^{-1}} q_i \qquad i=1,2 \tag{4.3}$$

where w_α and w_β are the prices of the two intermediate inputs. Because of constant returns to scale, we can write the marginal cost function as

[13] This is a transformation of a general constant elasticity demand function $(q_1+q_2).p^\varepsilon=Z$ where $Z>0$ by selecting a proper unit so $Z=1$.

[14] See Varian (1984, p.30).

$$mc_i(w_\alpha,w_\beta) = \left(\gamma^\sigma w_{\alpha_i}{}^{1-\sigma} + (1 - \gamma)^\sigma w_\beta{}^{1-\sigma}\right)^{1/(1-\sigma)} \qquad i=1,2 \qquad (4.4)$$

Equation (4.4) is also the average cost function, because of the assumption of constant returns to scale. The upstream firms are assumed to employ technology with constant returns to scale that generates marginal cost to be equal to c.

A Stackelberg-type *leader-follower* relationship exists between the downstream firms and the upstream oligopolists. In other words, the upstream firms have first-mover advantages and can decide the output of the intermediate input, anticipating the interactions among the downstream firms. One of the differences between the fixed inputs proportions model and the variable inputs proportions model is that when substitutability exists the downstream firms have to make two decisions in order to maximize their profit. First, they have to decide how much final product to produce, conditional on their conjecture about their rivals' actions. Second, they have to decide how to produce that product, conditional on the given input prices. The upstream firms only need to decide how much intermediate good α to produce, conditional on their buyers' optimal responses and on the price of the substituting input factor β.

The underlying game is described as follows. When the game starts, the upstream firms decide their outputs of intermediate input by considering the reaction of and interactions between the downstream firms (the input prices are pre-determined at the market clearing conditions). Then, the downstream firms compete as Cournot duopolists in the final goods market. The equilibrium outputs, prices and profits are then determined accordingly. As in the previous chapters, three vertical structures, i.e. market transactions, supply contracts and full vertical integration, are posited. Subgame perfect Nash equilibrium is the equilibrium concept.

3. EQUILIBRIUM ANALYSIS

In this section a set of equilibrium outcomes will be worked out when the vertical relations between the firms in adjacent industries take the alternative forms. To ensure that the equilibrium derived below is sub-game perfect, the analysis is carried out via backward induction. More specifically, we look at the equilibrium conditions in the downstream industry (second-stage) first. Based on the equilibrium outcomes in the second stage, the equilibrium results in the upstream industry are derived. The focus is on the derived demand elasticity for the following reasons. First of all, the derived demand elasticity reflects the structure and the behavior of the players in the downstream industry. Under the assumption of almost perfect information, the upstream oligopolists are assumed to be able to observe the interactions between the downstream firms. Once the upstream oligopolists know the derived demand they have all the information needed for decision-making. Secondly, the derived demand elasticity facing each upstream firm depends on the ways the transactions of the intermediate inputs are realized. This allows us to compare how changes in the vertical structure influence the equilibrium outcomes. Finally, the methods used in the previous chapters to derive the subgame perfect equilibrium become inconvenient when multiple inputs and substitutability are introduced. Therefore, instead of comparing the equilibrium output quantities or prices directly, we are going to compare the derived demand elasticities for the intermediate input. By so doing, additional insights on the economic impacts of vertical structures can be obtained.

3.1. Equilibrium under Market Transactions Game

In this section the equilibrium outcomes are investigated under the two-stage game theoretic framework when the vertical structure between two adjacent oligopolistic industries is characterized by market transactions. This means that all firms can choose the buyers and suppliers in the intermediate inputs market freely and there is a uniform input price for input α in the inputs market.

In the downstream industry, the Cournot duopolists choose their output quantity conditional on their rival's output in order to maximize their own profits. The first order conditions of profit maximization are

$$\frac{d\pi_i}{dq_i} = p + q_i\frac{dp}{dq_i} - mc_i = 0 \qquad i=1,2$$

The above first order conditions can be easily rearranged as

$$\frac{(p-mc)}{p} = \frac{1}{2}\frac{(q_1+q_2)}{p}\frac{dp}{d(q_1+q_2)} = \frac{1}{2\varepsilon} \tag{4.5}$$

The first order conditions can then be written alternatively as (4.6),

$$p = \frac{1}{1 - (2\varepsilon)^{-1}} mc \tag{4.6}$$

Equation (4.6) shows that under the assumption of a constant elasticity demand function and a finite number of firms, the market clearing price of the Cournot-Nash game is a linear function of the firms' marginal costs. Once the marginal costs are known, the market clearing price of the final product can be found easily.

From (4.4), we know that the marginal costs of the downstream firms depend on intermediate input prices and the substitution parameter. The comparative levels of the prices of different inputs determine the proportions of the various inputs used. For the competitively supplied input factor β, price is assumed to be constant. But the price of the production factor α is the equilibrium outcome of the Cournot-Nash game in the upstream industry. In addition, this price depends on market conditions and behavior of firms in both the downstream and upstream industries. The responses of the downstream firms towards input price changes are reflected in the derived demand elasticity. Therefore, the expression and the properties of the derived demand elasticity of the downstream industry have to be worked out.

In the perfect competition case, as is well known, the derived demand elasticity for any input depends on the demand elasticity of the final products, on the elasticity of substitution among the production factors and on the shares of those factors in the production costs (Allen, 1938). In the case of an oligopoly, the derived demand elasticity may also be influenced by the market structure, and the beliefs and the behavior of firms. Allen's result has been extended to the case of oligopoly by Waterson (1982), who shows that in an oligopolistic industry which uses only two types of inputs, the industry's derived demand elasticity for an input factor α, e_a, is the weighted average of the demand elasticity for the final products ε and the elasticity of substitution between two production factors σ,

$$e_\alpha = k_\alpha \varepsilon + (1 - k_\alpha)\sigma \tag{4.7}$$

where the weight k_α is the share of input α in the total factor payments,

$$k_\alpha = \frac{w_\alpha \alpha}{C(w_\alpha, w_\beta)}$$

C is the total cost of the final products and $w_\alpha > 0$ is the price of input α. Because ε and σ are constants and determined exogenously in our model, the exact expression for the weight, k_α, is the only item that needs to be known before further analysis can be performed.

To find k_α, Shephard's lemma and the condition of the linearly homogeneity of the production function are used. By Shephard's lemma (the derivative property), the amount of an input factor employed to produce a certain quantity of final goods is the first derivative of the total cost function with respect to the price of that input w_α:

$$\alpha = \frac{\partial C(w_\alpha, w_\beta)}{\partial w_\alpha}$$

Therefore, the weight in the elasticity of derived demand can be written as

$$k_\alpha = \frac{w_\alpha}{C(w_\alpha, w_\beta)} \frac{\partial C(w_\alpha, w_\beta)}{\partial w_\alpha} ,$$

which is the elasticity of total cost with respect to w_α. By using the property of a linearly homogeneous production function, we can transform k_α into the form of the marginal cost function of the downstream firm:

$$k_\alpha = \frac{w_\alpha}{mc(w_\alpha, w_\beta)} \frac{\partial mc(w_\alpha, w_\beta)}{\partial w_\alpha} ,$$

which is the elasticity of marginal cost with respect to w_α. Substituting mc in (4.4) into the above equation, we have k_α as

$$k_{\alpha} = \frac{\gamma^{\sigma} w_{\beta}^{\sigma-1}}{(1-\sigma)[(1-\gamma)^{\sigma} w_{\alpha}^{\sigma-1} + \gamma^{\sigma} w_{\beta}^{\sigma-1}]}$$

Once k_{α} is known, it is easy to derive the elasticity of derived demand e_{α}.

$$e_{\alpha} = \frac{(\varepsilon+\sigma)\gamma^{\sigma} w_{\beta}^{\sigma-1} + \sigma(1-\sigma)(1-\gamma)^{\sigma} w_{\alpha}^{\sigma-1}}{(1-\sigma)[(1-\gamma)^{\sigma} w_{\alpha}^{\sigma-1} + \gamma^{\sigma} w_{\beta}^{\sigma-1}]} \tag{4.8}$$

It should be pointed out that e_{α} in (4.8) is no longer a constant but a function of the input prices w_{α} and w_{β} and the exogenously determined parameters. Because of this, the analytical advantage of constant demand elasticity for final products is lost when we analyze the intermediate goods market. The derived demand elasticity e_{α} provides the upstream oligopolists with all the relevant information on the demand side for their decision-making. In the upstream industry, the payoff functions of the Cournot-behaved duopolists are

$$\pi_i^u = (w_{\alpha} - c)\alpha_i \qquad i=1,2$$

The maximization of the payoff function of the *i*th upstream firm requires the first derivative of its payoff function to become zero

$$\frac{\partial \pi_i^u}{\partial \alpha_i} = w_{\alpha} + \alpha_i \frac{\partial w_{\alpha}}{\partial \alpha_i} - c = 0 \qquad i=1,2$$

The above first order condition can be easily transformed to become

$$\frac{w_{\alpha} - c}{w_{\alpha}} = \frac{1}{2}\frac{\alpha}{w_{\alpha}}\frac{\partial w_{\alpha}}{\partial \alpha} = \frac{1}{2e_{\alpha}} \tag{4.9}$$

which means that the profit margin for the upstream firms at equilibrium is the inverse of twice the elasticity of the derived demand for intermediate inputs.

Substituting e_α as defined in (4.8) into equation (4.9), the market clearing price w_α under the given parameters can be found by solving the following equation

$$w_\alpha = \frac{(2\sigma + 1)(1 - \gamma)^\sigma w_\alpha^{\sigma - 1} + (4\sigma + 1)(\varepsilon - \sigma)\gamma^\sigma w_\beta^{\sigma - 1}}{2\sigma(1 - \gamma)^\sigma w_\alpha^{\sigma - 1} + 4\sigma(\varepsilon - \sigma)\gamma^\sigma w_\beta^{\sigma - 1}} c \tag{4.10}$$

where w_β, the price of the competitively supplied intermediate input β, is determined exogenously.

Note that the sub-game perfect intermediate input price w_α in (4.10) is written in its implicit form and is the function of several exogenously determined parameters. Although it is not possible to find an explicit solution for w_α, it can be shown that such a solution exists. Once the unique sub-game perfect equilibrium price for the intermediate input w_α^* is known, other equilibrium results are easy to obtain.

Market transactions are just one possibility of institutional arrangement to complete the transactions of goods between the adjacent production processes. Under this type of vertical structure, market imperfection exists within each industry, but no vertical restraints exist between different industries.

3.2. Equilibrium under Supply Contracts Game

When the vertical relations between the upstream and downstream firms are governed by supply contracts, there is also market imperfection between the two adjacent industries[15]. A supply contract, like other types of vertical restraints, changes the direction and magnitude of competition forces in the intermediate goods and final products markets, thereby influencing the equilibrium outcomes of the game. In the supply contract game, there are two essential incentives which motivate an upstream

---

[15] A similar effect may be caused by market imperfections due to the narrowly defined transaction costs, such as transport and dealing expenses.

firm to deviate from the equilibrium reached in the market transactions game. First of all, an upstream firm has an incentive to increase its output under the conjecture that the increase in output will be translated into a lower intermediate input price for its customer. Consequently, the corresponding downstream firm will compete more aggressively because it enjoys a lower marginal cost *vis à vis* its competitors and demands more input factor from its supplier. In addition to this, the downstream firm may substitute input factor β by input factor α. Secondly, this upstream firm may have an incentive to reduce its output of intermediate inputs simply because the exclusive supply contracts eliminate direct competition between the rival upstream firms. Which of these two forces will play a dominant role can only be seen after further analysis. In this section, we will derive the equilibrium outcomes under the assumption that the vertical structure between two industries is a supply contractual relationship. By doing this, we can gain additional insights regarding the impact of vertical structures on the equilibrium when substitutability between intermediate inputs exists.

The analysis starts from the second stage of the game (downstream industry). The first order condition of profit maximization requires the perceived marginal profit function of each Cournot-behaved firm to become zero. In other words, the firm's marginal revenue must be equal to its marginal cost,

$$p + q_i \frac{dp}{dq_i} = mc_i(w_{\alpha_i}, w_\beta), \qquad i=1,2$$

where mc_i is defined in (4.4). The marginal costs with subscript i reflect the fact that the vertical structure is supply contracts and the individual downstream firm buys its inputs α from different suppliers. This type of vertical arrangement allows the prices of intermediate input α to differ among the downstream firms. After some rearrangements, we have the following equation:

$$p(1 - \frac{s_i}{\varepsilon}) = mc_i(w_{\alpha_i}, w_\beta)$$

where $s_i=q_i/Q$ stands for the share of the ith downstream firm's output in the total output of the entire downstream industry. If we let $m_i = (1 - s_i/\varepsilon)$, the above equation can be rewritten as

$$mc_i(w_{\alpha_i}, w_\beta) = pm_i \tag{4.11}$$

For an efficient producer using the two intermediate inputs α and β, its marginal cost should be equal to the ratio of the factor prices and the marginal products of all input factors. Therefore, the following equation must be satisfied:

$$mc_i(w_{\alpha i}, w_\beta) = \frac{w_{\alpha i}}{q_{\alpha i}} = \frac{w_\beta}{q_\beta} \tag{4.12}$$

where q_α and q_β denote the marginal products of the input factors α and β respectively. Combining (4.11) and (4.12), the first order condition of profit maximization with respect to the inputs employment becomes the following system:

$$\begin{aligned} p \cdot m_i \cdot q_{\alpha i} &= w_{\alpha_i} \\ p \cdot m_i \cdot q_\beta &= w_\beta \end{aligned} \tag{4.13}$$

We have already shown that the output of the downstream firm depends critically on the intermediate input price $w_{\alpha i}$. The input price of the factor α, $w_{\alpha i}$, is determined by the *i*th upstream firm's decision over what should be the output of this input. This decision can only be made based on the perceived derived demand elasticity for this input. This is the reason why we have to know what the derived demand elasticity is. The formula of the derived demand elasticity in (4.10), which is used under the vertical structure of market transactions, cannot be applied here because contractual relations change the perception of the upstream oligopolists. What upstream duopolists face in a supply contracts game is not the derived demand elasticity of the industry, but the individual derived demand for each upstream firm. A new formula which reflects the changes of the vertical structure, market conditions and the behavior of downstream firms has to be worked out.

By differentiating equations in (4.13) with respect to the input price $w_{\alpha i}$ at the point which satisfies the Nash equilibrium condition in the downstream industry, we can define the total effect of a small change of input price $w_{\alpha i}$ on the downstream firm's production decision as follows

$$\mu \frac{\partial \alpha_i}{\partial w_{\alpha_i}} + \phi \frac{\partial \beta_i}{\partial w_{\alpha_i}} = 1 \tag{4.14}$$

$$\phi \frac{\partial \alpha_i}{\partial w_{\alpha_i}} + \nu \frac{\partial \beta_i}{\partial w_{\alpha_i}} = 0 \tag{4.15}$$

where

$$\mu = \frac{\partial (pm_i q_{\alpha_i})}{\partial \alpha_i}$$

$$\nu = \frac{\partial (pm_i q_{\beta_i})}{\partial \beta_i}$$

$$\phi = \frac{\partial (pm_i q_{\alpha_i})}{\partial \beta_i} = \frac{\partial (pm_i q_{\beta_i})}{\partial \alpha_i}$$

Rewriting the above system by using the definitions:

$$e_{\alpha_i} = -\frac{w_{\alpha_i}}{\alpha_i} \frac{\partial \alpha_i}{\partial w_{\alpha_i}} \qquad \textit{and} \qquad e_{\beta_i} = \frac{w_{\alpha_i}}{\beta_i} \frac{\partial \beta_i}{\partial w_{\alpha_i}}$$

we have

$$-\mu(\frac{\alpha_1}{w_{\alpha_i}})e_{\alpha_i} + \phi(\frac{\beta_1}{w_\beta})e_{\beta_i} = 1 \tag{4.16}$$

$$-\phi(\frac{\alpha_1}{w_{\alpha_i}})e_{\alpha_i} + \nu(\frac{\beta_1}{w_\beta})e_{\beta_i} = 0 \tag{4.17}$$

The explicit expression of the derived demand elasticity $e_{\alpha i}$ can be found by solving (4.16) and (4.17). It is

$$e_{\alpha_i} = -\frac{w_\alpha \nu}{\alpha_i(\mu\nu - \phi^2)} \tag{4.18}$$

This derived demand elasticity can then be written as a weighted index of the final demand elasticity and the elasticity of substitution after some mathematical manipulations[16]. The actual expression of the derived demand elasticity for the intermediate input factor α becomes

$$e_{\alpha_i} = \varepsilon \frac{w_{\alpha_i}\alpha_i}{pq_i s_i(m_i + 1 - s_i)} + \sigma \frac{pq_i m_i - w_{\alpha_i}\alpha_i}{pq_i m_i} \tag{4.19}$$

It can be verified that this derived demand elasticity is different from the derived demand elasticity defined in (4.10). This expression provides the derived demand elasticity of one Cournot-type downstream firm with respect to the price changes of the intermediate input α.

Once the derived demand elasticity is known, it will be straightforward to determine the equilibrium output quantities and prices of the profit maximizing upstream firms by applying the following rule:

$$\frac{w_{\alpha_i} - c}{w_{\alpha_i}} = \frac{1}{e_{\alpha_i}} \qquad i=1,2 \tag{4.20}$$

where $e_{\alpha I}$ is the elasticity of the derived demand of the ith downstream Cournot duopolist who is committed to a supply contract. It says that the price-cost margin of the upstream oligopolist must be equal to the reciprocal of the derived demand elasticity $e_{\alpha i}$.

---

[16] See Appendix 4.1. for derivation.

3.3. Equilibrium under the Full Vertical Integration Game

Under the full vertical integration game, the prices of both intermediate inputs are set equal to their marginal costs. The equilibrium results, therefore, are governed by the following equation:

$$p\left(1 - \frac{s_i}{\varepsilon}\right) = mc_i(c, w_\beta) \tag{4.21}$$

By using equation (4.4) and assuming symmetry among all the firms, the equilibrium price of the final goods, p, can be found, as can industry output.

4. PRE-INTEGRATION VERTICAL STRUCTURES AND THE CONSEQUENCE OF VERTICAL INTEGRATION

In this section we are going to show that, with the presence of substitution among intermediate inputs, the impact of vertical integration can be separated into a market elimination effect and a pure vertical integration effect. By so doing, the results derived in the previous chapters can be extended to the case of variable proportions of inputs. Moreover, it will also allow us to extend the findings of Abiru (1988); thereby the economic consequences and welfare implications of vertical integration can be correctly assessed.

4.1. The Significance of the Market Elimination Effect

Due to the complexity in the mathematical expressions of the equilibrium outcomes, the direct comparison between the explicit solutions under supply contracts and that under market transactions is impractical. Because the output decisions of oligopolists depend on, among other things, their perceived elasticity of demand, it will not be difficult for us to infer the equilibrium output quantities if we know the derived demand elasticities under the alternative vertical structures. The logic goes like this.

If the derived demand elasticity under one type of vertical structure is higher than that under another, the equilibrium intermediate input price must be lower. If the derived demand elasticities are the same for all the possible scenarios under the comparison, the equilibrium outputs of intermediate inputs as well as final goods cannot be different. The two vertical structures under investigation are market transactions and supply contracts. If the perceived elasticities of derived demand are identical under these two alternative vertical structures, the upstream firms have no incentive to change the intermediate input price. After comparing the elasticity of derived demand under the market transactions game, e_α , and the elasticity of derived demand the individual upstream firms perceived under the supply contracts game, $e_{\alpha i}$, we have the following proposition.

Proposition 4.1. *In a successive duopoly with a constant elasticity demand and with a constant elasticity of substitution among intermediate inputs, the derived demand elasticity perceived by upstream firms is higher if the vertical relations between the downstream firms and the upstream firms are governed by supply contracts than if they are governed by market transactions.*

Proof. To proof Proposition 4.1, we compare the two derived demand elasticities e_α and the derived demand elasticity $e_{\alpha i}$. From the expression of the elasticity of derived demand in (4.7), we know that such an elasticity in the market transactions game is the weighted average of the elasticity of demand and the elasticity of substitution and the weight is the share of the input factor α in the total cost function. In the case of the supply contracts game, by using (4.19) and noting that $m_i=(1-s_i/\varepsilon)$, we can rewrite the derived demand elasticity for the *i*th upstream firm's output as

$$e_{\alpha_i} = \varepsilon \frac{w_{\alpha_i} \alpha_i}{C_i A_i} + \sigma \left(1 - \frac{w_{\alpha_i} \alpha_i}{C_i}\right) \qquad (4.22)$$

where

$$A_i = s_i \left(1 + \frac{1 - s_i}{m_i}\right)$$

Comparing the two expressions of elasticity of derived demand for intermediate inputs in (4.7) and (4.22), we can see that the difference between the two lies in the weight of the elasticity of the final demand. In the market transactions game, it is clear that the denominator of the weight term is the total cost function of the final products. In the supply contracts game, the denominator depends on the total cost function, A_i, which is a function of output shares of the ith downstream firm in the total industrial output and the demand elasticity of the final products. When A_i is equal to 1, we can immediately infer that the upstream firms face an identical elasticity of the derived demand no matter whether the vertical structure is market transactions or supply contracts. Otherwise the elasticity of the derived demand in supply contracts game will be higher (or lower than that in the market transactions game when A_i is smaller (or larger) that 1, *ceteris paribus*. Because of the assumption of symmetry in the model and the duopolistic horizontal market structure, at equilibrium the market share of the ith downstream firm will be equal to one half of the whole market, or $s_i = 0.5$. Therefore, we can establish the following relationship.

$$0.75 < A_i = s_i + \frac{\varepsilon s_i(1 - s_i)}{\varepsilon - s_i}) < 1 \tag{4.23}$$

Using (4.23) and noting (4.7) and (4.22), we have established the following inequality,

$$2e_\alpha > e_{\alpha i} > e_\alpha \tag{4.24}$$

This means that the elasticity of the derived demand in the supply contracts game is higher than that in the market transactions game, but it is less than two times of the elasticity of the derived demand in the market transactions game. Q.E.D.

The result of Proposition 4.1 makes it clear that exclusive contractual relations *per se* do not lead to a higher input price. Facing a more elastic demand for intermediate input, the upstream firms can only act to have a lower intermediate input price to maximize their profits. The intuition behind this is as follows. In the market transactions game, the increase in the intermediate goods price will push up the marginal costs of all downstream firms, and the strategic interactions between the downstream firms are absent. In the supply contracts game, when an upstream firm acts to increase its input price, only the marginal cost of its own buyer increases. The increase in the downstream firm's marginal cost not only cause the direct effect of reducing output of the final goods, but also allow its rival in the downstream industry to become more aggressive. It is this strategic effect which determines the higher derived demand elasticity of intermediate inputs.

One of the advantages of using the derived demand elasticity to analyze equilibrium input prices under different vertical structures is that it allows us to separate the competition effect from the strategic effect due to changes in the vertical relations. To illustrate this point, we are going to show that the equilibrium intermediate input price in the supply contracts game is higher than that in the market transactions game despite the fact that the upstream firms involved in supply contractual relations face a more elastic derived demand. In order to do this, we need to compare the price-cost margins with the property of subgame perfectness under the two different vertical structures.

In the supply contracts game, the vertical relationship between the supplier and buyer is exclusive, the upstream firm in fact behaves like a monopolist. We know that the price-cost margin is equal to the inverse of the demand elasticity the monopolist faces when it acts to maximize the profit. The price-cost margin of the upstream firm in the supply contracts game is determined in the same way as in (4.20). In the market transactions game, the upstream firms have to compete against one another in the intermediate inputs market. When the horizontal market structure in the intermediate inputs market is a duopoly, we know from (4.9) that the price-cost margin at equilibrium in such a market is equal to the inverse of twice the derived demand elasticity. Under the assumption that marginal cost for the upstream firms is equal to a constant c and by considering the condition that the derived demand elasticity in the market transactions game is always larger than one half of the derived demand elasticity in the supply contracts game, it is clear that the price-cost margin in the market transactions game is smaller than that in the supply contracts game. This result is restated in Proposition 4.2.

Proposition 4.2. *In a successive duopoly with a constant elasticity demand and with a constant elasticity of substitution among intermediate inputs, the price of the intermediate inputs supplied by upstream firms is higher if the vertical relation between the downstream and upstream firms is governed by supply contracts than if it is governed by market transactions.*

Combining the results of Propositions 4.1 and 4.2, we see clearly what kinds of consequences the strategic effect and the competition effect may cause. Exclusive contractual relations increase the elasticity of the derived demand because of the strategic effect in the downstream firm and, at the same time, eliminate the competition in the intermediate inputs market.

Because of the higher input price of one of the two inputs for the downstream firms, exclusive contractual relations will lead to a higher price of the final products compared to the market transaction game.

The difference in the derived demand elasticities between the vertical structures of market transactions and supply contracts confirms our suspicion that Abiru (1988) mixes two different effects on the price of the final product. He separates the horizontal merger effect from the vertical integration effect by analyzing a successive oligopoly with variable proportions of inputs instead of a monopolistic supplier. But he does not notice that there are several possibilities to carry out transactions with intermediate inputs in a successive oligopoly, as he only looks at market transactions and full vertical integration. We have shown that the changes in the output quantity (price) of final goods are caused by two distinct forces: the market elimination effect, which is reflected by the change from market transactions to a supply contracts relationship, and the *pure* vertical integration effect, which is represented by the integration of the firms relying on contracts. The former is caused by differences in the vertical structure game setting before vertical integration takes place and the latter occurs when the relation between two sequential production stages changes from supply contracts to vertical integration.

4.2. The Pure Effect of Vertical Integration

After vertical integration, the markup on the intermediate inputs is completely eliminated, so the marginal cost function for an integrated firm becomes

$$mc_i(c,w_\beta) = (\gamma^\sigma c^{1-\sigma} + (1-\gamma)^\sigma w_\beta^{1-\sigma})^{\frac{1}{1-\sigma}} \qquad i=1,2 \tag{4.25}$$

Comparing equations (4.25) and (4.4) allows us to make the following proposition about the equilibrium prices of final products under vertical integration and contracts.

Proposition 4.3. *In a successive Cournot duopoly with a constant elasticity of demand and a constant elasticity of substitution, the equilibrium output of the final product increases when the vertical structure between adjacent industries changes from supply contracts to vertical integration.*

Proof: Because the price of the intermediate input must be larger than or equal to its marginal cost, $w_{\alpha i} \geq c$, in order to let the profit maximizing upstream firm produce, and because a property of the cost function implies that the unit cost must monotonously decrease when the price of one of the input factors falls when all others are the same, $\partial AC/\partial w_i < 0$, we have

$$mc(c,w_\beta) < mc_i(w_{\alpha_i},w_\beta)$$

by noting that marginal cost is equal to average cost.

When c replaces w_α in the cost function of the integrated firm, the downstream firms perceive a lower marginal cost. They tend to produce more before reaching a new equilibrium. Therefore the price for the final product, p, must fall after integration and the output quantity will increase. Intuitively speaking, the improvement in social welfare, the fall in price and the increase in output, are due to gains in economic efficiency, which, in turn, is caused by the elimination of mark-ups after integration.

5. CONCLUSIONS

In this chapter we continued to investigate the impact of vertical integration in an oligopolistic setting with a focus on the relations between the subgame perfect Nash equilibrium and the possibility of substitution among intermediate inputs. Our results show that the substitutability of intermediate inputs, represented by a CES production function in the downstream industry, does not change the basic conclusion which states that vertical integration is welfare-enhancing because the output quantity of the final goods increases and the final price falls.

After considering the three generic vertical structures of market transactions, supply contracts and full integration, we derived and compared the formulae of the derived demand elasticity for the intermediate inputs. We found that the derived demand of the downstream firms is more elastic under supply contracts than under market transactions. The reason is that the strategic interactions among the Cournot-behaved downstream firms increases the elasticity of the demand for intermediate inputs. In the market transactions game, the increase in the intermediate goods price will push up the marginal costs of all downstream firms, and the strategic interactions between the downstream firms are absent. In the supply contracts game, when an upstream firm acts to increase its input price, only the marginal cost of its own buyer increases. The increases in the downstream firm's marginal costs not only cause the direct effect of reducing output of the final goods, but also allow its rival in the downstream industry to become more aggressive. It is this strategic effect which determines the higher derived demand elasticity of intermediate inputs. Although the upstream firms face a more elastic derived demand for intermediate inputs they still have a higher profit margin than under market transaction game. It is because the price-cost margin is negatively related to the number of firms which compete directly in the intermediate goods market. The supply contractual relations eliminate direct competition among the upstream firms, which increases the price-cost margin.

Our results show that the impact on the equilibrium results are clearly visible. Substitution between a competitively supplied input and the input supplied by upstream oligopolists reduces the market power of the upstream oligopolists. Still, contractual relations, which are often observed, reduce the output of the final goods by eliminating the intermediate inputs market which is essential for market transactions.

Our results can be related to the recent work of Abiru (1988) who investigated the impact of vertical integration on the prices of the final products with substitutability among inputs. We improved Abiru's results by considering three alternative game settings. We demonstrated that the vertical integration effect investigated by Abiru can be further segregated into the market elimination effect and the pure vertical integration effect. Although Abiru separated the effects of the horizontal and the vertical mergers with the possibility of substitutions among inputs, he did not consider issues of pre-integration vertical structures. We demonstrated that there are differences in pre-integration vertical structures and these differences have important impact on the equilibrium outcomes.

These results may have important policy implications for assessing the economic and welfare impacts of vertical integration. Many studies, including ours, show that in successive oligopolistic industries the output of the final product increases and the price decreases after vertical integration, no matter whether the technology is characterized as fixed or variable proportions of inputs. Our findings tell us that the merits of vertical integration depend largely on the vertical structures before vertical integration takes place. We show that although the overall effect of vertical integration on social welfare is always positive, the improvement in social welfare may not be as substantial under market transactions compared as it is under supply contracts. If other factors which often accompany vertical integration, e.g. transaction costs, agency problems, coordination costs, etc., which are absent from our analysis, are taken into consideration, over(under)-valuation of social welfare improvement due to vertical integration is a realistic danger if not enough attention is paid to the differences in the pre-integration vertical structures.

Appendix 4.1. Derivation of the Derived Demand Elasticity in the Supply Contracts Game

Expansion of μ in (4.4) leads to:

$$\mu = m_i(p q_{\alpha\alpha} + x_{\alpha_i}^2 \frac{dp}{dq_i}) - \frac{p q_{\alpha_i}^2}{\varepsilon Q}(1 - s_i)$$

where $q_{\alpha\alpha}$ denotes the partial derivative of the marginal product function of the input factor α and Q is the total output of the final products in the downstream industry.

Twice differentiating the homogenous of degree one production function $q(\alpha,\beta)$ with respect to input factor α leads to[17]

$$q_{\alpha\alpha}\alpha + q_{\alpha\beta}\beta = 0$$

Recalling the definition of the direct elasticity of substitution as

$$\sigma = \frac{q_\alpha q_\beta}{q q_{\alpha\beta}}$$

we have the following equation:

$$q_{\alpha\alpha} = \frac{\beta_i}{\alpha_i} q_{\alpha\beta} = \frac{\beta_i}{\alpha_i} \frac{q_{\alpha_i} q_{\beta_i}}{q_i \sigma}$$

Because the marginal products of the input factors α and β can be written as

[17] See Varian (1984 p.330).

$$q_{\alpha_i} = \frac{w_{\alpha_i}}{pm_i} \qquad \textit{and} \qquad q_{\beta_i} = \frac{w_\beta}{pm_i}$$

μ may appear as

$$\mu = \frac{w_{\alpha_i} w_\beta \beta_i}{m_i \sigma p q_i \alpha_i} - \frac{w_{\alpha_i}^2}{m_i \varepsilon p Q} - \frac{w_{\alpha_1}^2}{m_i^2 \varepsilon p Q}(1 - s_i)$$

Similarly, for ν in (4.14) and (4.15) we have

$$\nu = m_i(p q_{\beta\beta} + q_{\beta_i}^2 \frac{dp}{dq_i}) - \frac{p q_{\beta_i}^2}{\varepsilon Q}(1 - s_i)$$

Because of

$$q_{\beta\beta} = -\frac{\alpha_i}{\beta_i} q_{ab} = -\frac{\alpha_i}{\beta_i}\frac{q_{\beta_i} q_{\beta_i}}{q_i \sigma}$$

ν can be transformed to:

$$\nu = \frac{w_{\alpha_i} w_\beta \alpha_i}{m_i \sigma p q_i \beta_i} - \frac{w_\beta^2}{m_i \varepsilon p Q} - \frac{w_\beta^2}{m_i^2 \varepsilon p Q}(1 - s_i)$$

For ϕ in (4.15), we have:

$$\phi = m_i(p q_{\alpha\beta} + q_{\alpha_i} q_{\beta_i} \frac{p}{\varepsilon Q}) - \frac{p q_{\alpha_i} q_{\beta_i}}{\varepsilon Q}(1 - s_i)$$

and it can be transformed into

$$\phi = \frac{w_{\alpha_i} w_\beta}{m_i p \sigma} - \frac{w_{\alpha_i} w_\beta}{m_i p \varepsilon Q} - \frac{w_{\alpha_i} w_\beta}{m_i^2 p \varepsilon \beta_i}(1 - s_i)$$

Substituting μ, ν and ϕ into equation (4.18), the elasticity of the derived demand can be written as

$$e_{\alpha_i} = \frac{\varepsilon m_i w_{\alpha_i} \alpha_i + \sigma s_i (m_i + 1 - s_i)(p q_i m_i - w_{\alpha_i} \alpha_i)}{m_i s_i p q_i (m_i + 1 - s_i)}$$

or alternatively as:

$$e_{\alpha_i} = \varepsilon \frac{w_{\alpha_i} \alpha_i}{p q_i s_i (m_i + 1 - s_i)} + \sigma \frac{(p q_i m_i - w_{\alpha_i} \alpha_i)}{p q_i m_i}$$

which appears in the text as (4.19).

PART II

OLIGOPOLISTIC VERTICAL INTEGRATION WITH ASYMMETRIC OBJECTIVES

Chapter 5

VERTICAL INTEGRATION IN A SUCCESSIVE OLIGOPOLY WITH ASYMMETRIC OBJECTIVES

1. INTRODUCTION

The main purpose of this chapter is to analyze the economic consequences of asymmetric firm objectives in a successive oligopoly, particularly the impact of objective asymmetry on the vertical relations between the firms in two adjacent industries. The scarcity of studies on the issue and recent developments in Eastern Europe and some other economies provide justifications for such analysis. Objective asymmetry originates in mixed oligopolistic markets. In such markets there are at least one private firm and one public firm. Private firms, in this context, are profit maximizers. Public firms behave differently. Different assumptions are made about the public firm's objectives. The most common is that a public firm maximizes social welfare (consumer surplus and producer surplus). We will examine the situation in which private and public firms compete in one of the two sequentially related industries. This allows us to investigate how asymmetric objectives affect the vertical relations between the firms and how the equilibrium outcome changes under alternative vertical structures. These issues will be studied by investigating the interactions between public firms and private firms in vertically related industries. The implications for public policy will be addressed after the economic rationales of using public firms to control successive oligopoly are provided.

This chapter consists of 4 sections. In the next section, a model of successive oligopoly with asymmetric objectives is posited and three scenarios are specified in the context of vertical integration. The equilibrium outcomes under various game settings are derived and analyzed in section 3. Section 4 summarizes the major findings and discusses their economic significance.

2. A MODEL OF MIXED SUCCESSIVE OLIGOPOLY

It has been recognized that the advantage as well as the challenge of modelling an oligopoly in the game theoretic framework is that a whole range of possible solution concepts can be employed depending on the types of interactions between economic agents, the information structure and the conjectural variations of the players. A simple model of a mixed successive duopoly is posited first in which two sequentially related industries are considered. Under this particular framework, three game scenarios which differ in their information structure and in the behavior of the players will be discussed. These scenarios are designed to facilitate the discussion of equilibria under various types of interactions between public and private firms.

Suppose there are two sequentially related industries, e.g. the computer hardware industry and the semiconductor industry. The downstream industry consists of two firms D_1 and D_2 producing differentiated final products for consumers while the upstream industry produces the intermediate inputs. We assume that there are two firms in the upstream industry U_1 and U_2, each supplying the intermediate inputs to a specific downstream firm. This implies that the intermediate inputs for final products are not acquired in the intermediate inputs market, but through contractual relations between suppliers and buyers. The possibility of switching between suppliers or buyers is excluded. An alternative vertical structure is vertical integration in which both upstream firms decide to merge with the downstream firms, or *vice versa*. When one downstream firm decides to integrate vertically with an upstream firm, it is a mixed integration.

A mixed duopoly is postulated in the downstream industry: there is one public firm and one private firm, providing similar products and competing in the final goods market. The concept of a *public firm* is used to describe an economic institution which provides goods or services to society and whose assets are owned by public agencies. The public firm operates in the interest of the public and pursues the objective of social welfare maximization rather than profit maximization. The public firm is assumed to compete with its privately-owned rival whose objective is profit maximization. Because of asymmetric information and monitoring costs, the government agencies and the management of the public firm may behave differently from the designed objective of the public firm. However, the discussions of the control mechanism in the principal-agent framework are not the focus of this study[18].

---

[18] The possibility of pursuing objectives other than social welfare by public enterprises or their managers is discussed extensively in Bös (1989).

A mixed duopoly can be created via three different approaches. First of all, one of the private firms operating in an oligopolistic market may be nationalized by the government. Alternatively, the government may create a new public firm in an industry that has been a monopoly. Privatization may create mixed oligopolies in sectors which have high barriers to entry[19]. We consider these three approaches as being equally possible. Since issues such as entry and exit of public firms are not the focus of this analysis, these three approaches do not make any difference in the equilibrium results.

Asymmetry in objectives can also be introduced in the upstream industry since there are cases where public and private firms compete to provide intermediate inputs, such as the coal and petroleum industries in the U.K. The equilibrium outcome under such a setting is less interesting. It is difficult to imagine a different strategy for this upstream public firm other than setting the intermediate input price equal to its marginal cost, which produces the same result as in vertical integration.

The structure of the basic model which will be subsequently analyzed is depicted in Figure 5.1.

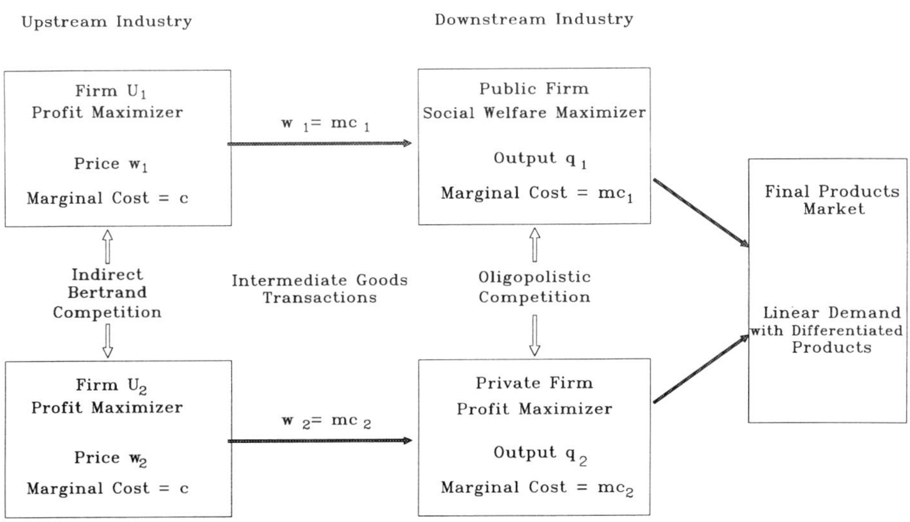

Figure 5.1. Structure of a Mixed Successive Duopoly

---

[19] Privatization in Britain, Chile and Poland, for example, may lead to different types of mixed markets (Vickers and Yarrow, 1991; Bös, 1991)

The demand for final products is represented by a linear inverse demand system

$$p_i = a - q_i - \theta q_j \qquad i=1,2;\ i \neq j \tag{5.1}$$

where p_i stands for the price of the final products produced by firm D_i and q_i represents the output of downstream firm D_i. The product differentiation parameter θ is larger than zero and smaller than 1. When θ approaches 1, the products of rival firms are close substitutes and when θ approaches zero, these products become highly differentiated goods. The parameter a is positive. The utility function of a representative consumer from which the above demand system arises takes the following expression:

$$U(q_1,q_2) = a(q_1 + q_2) - (q_1^2 + 2\theta q_1 q_2 + q_2^2)/2 \tag{5.2}$$

The relation between the utility function and the demand system can be understood by making an analogy with production theory. We can think of the representative consumer producing utility by consuming products q_1 and q_2 as inputs. This consumer is maximizing his profit (consumer surplus) with a technology represented by $U(q_1, q_2)$. Therefore, the demand system arising from such maximization will have the property of an input demand system (Vives, 1985)

$$\frac{\partial CS(q_1, q_2)}{\partial q_i} = p_i(q_1, q_2) \qquad i=1,2$$

where CS stands for consumer surplus.

The technology of the downstream industry displays constant returns to scale. The production of final goods may require several inputs, and the assumption of the fixed proportions of inputs allows us to normalize them as one input. In order to avoid unnecessary complication of analysis, we assume that there is no specific cost in the downstream production process. The assumption of symmetry in cost and demand is made to simplify the analysis. It is further assumed that the entry of new firms into both industries is blocked.

The payoff functions of the profit-maximizing upstream firms are

$$\pi_i^u = (w_i - c)q_i \quad i=1,2 \tag{5.3}$$

where w_1 and w_2 are the intermediate input prices charged to the public firm and the private firm in the downstream industry respectively.

The payoff function of the downstream private firm is its individual profit, denoted by π_2^d,

$$\pi_2^d = (p - w_2)q_2 \tag{5.4}$$

The payoff function of the downstream public firm is *social welfare* defined as the equally weighted sum of consumer surplus and the downstream firms' producer surplus

$$W = CS + \pi_1^d + \pi_2^d$$

Since the representative consumer maximizes his surplus, $U(q_1,q_2) - (p_1q_1+p_2q_2)$, and the downstream firm's producer surplus is $p_iq_i - w_iq_i$, $i=1,2$, the payoff function can be written alternatively as

$$W(q_1, q_2) = a(q_1 + q_2) - (q_1^2 + 2\theta q_1 q_2 + q_2^2)/2 - (q_1 w_1 + q_2 w_2) \tag{5.5}$$

The payoff function of the public firm defined in (5.5) can be interpreted as the downstream public firm facing a non-negative profit constraint and acting to maximize a general welfare function which is expressed as

$$W = (1-\lambda)(CS + \pi_1^d + \pi_2^d) + \lambda(\pi_1^u + \pi_2^u) \tag{5.6}$$

λ, $0 \leq \lambda < 1$, is the parameter which allows consumer surplus and profits of private firms to take on different weights in the social welfare function. When λ is zero, the upstream firms' profits are excluded from welfare calculation. When λ is greater than zero but less than 1, the profits of the upstream firms become part of social welfare, its actual weight depending on λ.

It can be shown that when the Cournot-behaved public firm faces a non-negative profit constraint and acts to maximize the payoff function as in (5.6), the weight of the upstream supplier's profit in the payoff function, λ, will become zero. The intuition behind is as follows. For a given intermediate price w_1, the non-negative profit constraint is equivalent to $p_1 \geq w_1$. The public firm facing such constraint acts to maximize its payoff functions in (5.6). The constraint becomes binding when the final price equals its marginal cost. In other words, marginal cost pricing is the best the public firm can do. When the public firm acts to maximize social welfare in (5.5) without facing the non-negative profit restraint and the upstream firm does not take on any weight in its objective, the upstream firm's profit is considered to be part of the marginal costs by the downstream public firm, and it will act to let $p_1 = mc_1$. We can see that the equilibrium output quantities of the public firm are the same under these two alternative payoff functions. Given the fact that government agencies often put the non-negative profit as one of the operational objectives of public enterprises and considering the convenience of using the payoff function in (5.5) in our analysis, we assume that the public firm uses payoff function as expressed in (5.5).

Another interpretation of the payoff function defined in (5.5) is that it reflects the fact that these upstream firms may be multinational enterprises whose profits are not part of the social welfare of the host country.

The concept of *gross benefit* will be used to define the equally weighted sum of consumer surplus and all firms' producer surplus (Bergström and Varian, 1985). The word *gross benefit* is used to reflect the fact that although the upstream firms' producer surplus is treated as costs from the viewpoint of the downstream firm, the upstream firms' producer surplus may become part of social welfare when the two industries are within one economy. In the literature of multinational enterprises, national economic welfare and global welfare are often used in the similar context (Caves, 1982). When intermediate inputs are imported, the profits of foreign suppliers cannot be counted as part of the national economic welfare, but as part of the global welfare. Gross benefit can be written as

$$G(q_1, q_2) = a(q_1 + q_2) - (q_1^2 + 2\theta q_1 q_2 + q_2^2)/2 - (q_1 + q_2)c \tag{5.7}$$

where c is the marginal cost to produce the intermediate input. When the upstream and downstream firms integrate vertically, $w_1 = w_2 = c$, then gross benefit equals social welfare.

In the following analysis, we posit three game scenarios in the downstream industry.

Scenario 1: Cournot-competition. In this scenario, the public and private firms have symmetric conjectural variations but asymmetric objectives. The downstream public firm, constrained by the information structure and the strategy set, tries to maximize economic welfare and the downstream and upstream private firms try to maximize their profits.

Scenario 2: Stackelberg competition where the public firm acts as a Stackelberg leader and the private firm acts as a Stackelberg follower. In this scenario, the public firm enjoys the first-mover advantage. The public firm, knowing the reaction function of the private firm, acts to maximize economic welfare. After knowing the output of the public firm, the private firm, as a passive player, chooses its output level accordingly to maximize its own profit.

Scenario 3: Stackelberg competition where the private firm acts as a Stackelberg leader and the public firm acts as a Stackelberg follower. In this scenario, the roles of the public firm and the private firm are reversed. The public firm will stick to a pre-determined decision rule to maximize economic welfare, such as the marginal cost pricing rule after the private firm has decided upon its output. The private firm makes its output decision as a first mover, based on the conjectures of the public firm's reaction function.

A Stackelberg equilibrium differs from Cournot equilibrium in the sense that one firm chooses its strategic variable first: the players move sequentially. Moreover, when the leader moves, he knows exactly how the *follower* will react to his choice, so he picks the point on the follower's reaction curve that maximizes his own payoff. It should be clear that both Stackelberg and Cournot equilibria are (subgame perfect) Nash equilibria but in different games. The only difference between these two types of games lies in the timing of the players' moves (Shapiro, 1989).

In a mixed successive duopoly, four types of vertical structures are posited.

(a) *Supply contracts.* This is the scenario where all intermediate inputs transactions are carried out through exclusive contracts and each firm tries to maximize its individual payoff.

(b) *Backward integration by the public firm.* In this scenario the downstream public firm integrates with its supplier, but the relations among the remaining private firms are governed by supply contracts for intermediate inputs.

(c) *Backward integration by the private firm.* This setting reverses the vertical structure of the public and private firms where the public firm relies on an independent supplier for its inputs and its private competitor is a vertically integrated firm.

(d) *Full vertical integration.* When both the public firm and private firm in the downstream industry integrate backwards, they are said to have full vertical integration.

Combinations of the various game settings and vertical structures result in 12 scenarios which are subjects of analyses. These scenarios are summarized in Table 5.1.

Table 5.1. Structures of Equilibrium Analysis

1.a.	Cournot game with supply contracts	2.a.	Stackelberg game with public firm as leader and with contracts	3.a.	Stackelberg game with private firm as leader and with contracts
1.b.	Cournot game with an integrated public firm	2.b.	Stackelberg game with an integrated public firm as leader	3.b.	Stackelberg game with private firm as leader and with an integrated public firm
1.c.	Cournot game with integrated private firm	2.c.	Stackelberg game with public firm as leader and with an integrated private firm	3.c.	Stackelberg game with an integrated private firm as leader
1.d.	Cournot game with full integration	2.d.	Stackelberg game with public firm as leader and with full integration	3.d.	Stackelberg game with private firm as leader and with full integration

When the game starts, the upstream firms at the first stage of the game decide the prices of intermediate inputs. At the second stage, the downstream firms compete in quantities in the final products market after the intermediate input prices are known. Through interactions among the firms in the final products market, the equilibrium output quantities and other equilibrium outcomes are determined. These equilibrium outcomes obviously depend on the type of downstream game and the vertical structure of the industry.

3. EQUILIBRIUM ANALYSIS

In this section, we will derive the Nash equilibrium outcomes systematically under the various game settings specified in the previous section, e.g. output quantities and prices of final products, firms' profits and level of social welfare. To ensure perfectness of the Nash equilibrium results in the two-stage game, a backward solution procedure is adopted.

3.1. Mixed Successive Duopoly with Downstream Cournot Game

In this scenario, the public and private firms in the downstream industry act as Cournot players and they compete over quantity to maximize their individual payoffs. Although these firms have different payoff functions, the conjectural variations of the firms are symmetric. The downstream firms make simultaneous moves.

3.1.a. Equilibrium Outcomes with Supply Contracts

A supply contractual relation implies that the public firm and the private firm purchase their intermediate inputs through their exclusive suppliers at fixed prices before they begin production. After knowing the input prices, the public firm acts to maximize its payoff, which is the social welfare, by choosing its output based on its conjecture as to the output of its private rival. Mathematically, this requires the first-order condition of maximizing social welfare defined in (5.5) to be satisfied. This condition is

$$\frac{\partial W}{\partial q_1} = a - q_1 - \theta q_2 - w_1 = 0 \tag{5.8}$$

The above first-order condition establishes the implicit reaction function of the public firm with respect to the output of the private firm in the downstream industry. We can rewrite the first-order condition in such a way that the output of the public firm which maximizes social welfare is expressed as the function of the output of its private competitor q_2 and the exogenously determined marginal costs w_1. That is

$$q_1 = a - \theta q_2 - w_1 \tag{5.9}$$

Similarly, for the private firm, its profit maximization requires

$$\frac{\partial \pi_2^d}{\partial q_2} = a - \theta q_1 - 2q_2 - w_2 = 0$$

The corresponding reaction function of the private firm becomes

$$q_2 = (a - \theta q_1 - w_2)/2 \tag{5.10}$$

The intersection of the two reaction functions in (5.9) and (5.10) is the Nash equilibrium from which no firm has any incentive to deviate unilaterally. The uniqueness of the equilibrium is guaranteed by the linear demand function and the assumption of constant marginal cost. The equilibrium outputs of the two downstream firms are found to be

$$q_1 = \frac{a(2-\theta) - 2w_1 + \theta w_2}{2-\theta^2} \tag{5.11}$$

$$q_2 = \frac{a(1-\theta) + \theta w_1 - w_2}{2-\theta^2} \tag{5.12}$$

Note that the equilibrium outputs depend on the marginal costs of the downstream firms. An increase in the rival's marginal cost increases the firm's equilibrium output when their products are substitutes. The magnitude of change depends on how closely products are related. An increase in the firm's own marginal cost will always reduce its output level, but the impact on output is twice as large for the public firm as it is for the private firm.

When the final goods are perfect substitutes, the output of the downstream private firm depends critically on the difference between the intermediate input prices, w_1 and w_2. The private firm's output is positive only when the public firm's marginal cost is higher than that of the private firm.

At the first stage of the game, the two upstream firms act to maximize their payoffs by competing indirectly in the intermediate input prices. Competition takes place via the derived demand function for the intermediate inputs, which, in turn, depend on the interactions between the downstream firms. These interactions between the downstream firms are reflected in the equilibrium outputs q_i in the downstream industry. When we substitute the derived demand for the intermediate inputs in the payoff functions of the upstream firms, the upstream firms' objective functions defined in (5.3) can be expanded as

$$\pi_1^u = \frac{(w_1 - c)[a(2-\theta) - 2w_1 + \theta w_2]}{2-\theta^2}$$

$$\pi_2^u = \frac{(w_2 - c)[a(1-\theta) + \theta w_1 - w_2]}{2-\theta^2}$$

Since the upstream firms use the intermediate inputs prices as their strategic variables, a Bertrand-Nash solution is derived. The first-order conditions for profit maximization with respect to w_1 and w_2 are

$$\frac{\partial \pi_1^u}{\partial w_1} = a(2-\theta) + 2c - 4w_1 + \theta w_2 = 0$$

$$\frac{\partial \pi_2^u}{\partial w_2} = a(1-\theta) + c + \theta w_1 - 2w_2 = 0$$

The solution of these simultaneous equations provides the subgame perfect equilibrium intermediate input prices, which are

$$w_1 = c + \frac{4-\theta-\theta^2}{8-\theta^2}S \qquad (5.13)$$

$$w_2 = c + \frac{4-2\theta-\theta^2}{8-\theta^2}S \qquad (5.14)$$

where $S=(a-c)$. It is clear that w_1 is always higher than w_2. The economic significance of the input price differences will be explored further in the next section.

The equilibrium outputs of the final products are found by substituting w_1 and w_2 into (5.11) and (5.12), which gives

$$q_1 = \frac{2(4-\theta-\theta^2)S}{(2-\theta^2)(8-\theta^2)} \qquad (5.15)$$

$$q_2 = \frac{(4-2\theta-\theta^2)S}{(2-\theta^2)(8-\theta^2)} \qquad (5.16)$$

The market clearing prices of final products can be found by substituting (5.15) and (5.16) into the linear demand system defined in (5.1). These prices of final products are

$$p_1 = c + \frac{4-\theta-\theta^2}{8-\theta^2}S \tag{5.17}$$

$$p_2 = c + \frac{12-2\theta-7\theta^2+\theta^4}{(2-\theta^2)(8-\theta^2)}S \tag{5.18}$$

Combining equations (5.13) and (5.14), we can rewrite the prices of the final goods as the expressions of the prices of the intermediate inputs. They are

$$p_1 = w_1$$

$$p_2 = w_2 + \frac{4+2\theta-\theta^2-2\theta^3}{(2-\theta^2)(8-\theta^2)}$$

The price of the final goods produced by the public firm is equal to its marginal cost w_1. It means that the public firm should continue its production until the price equals its marginal cost[20]. Because of this, the profit of the public firm becomes zero

$$\pi_1^d = 0 \tag{5.19}$$

Since $a>c$, the profit of the private firm in the downstream industry is found as

$$\pi_2^d = \frac{(4-2\theta-\theta^2)^2 T}{(2-\theta^2)^2(8-\theta^2)^2} > 0 \tag{5.20}$$

where $T=(a-c)^2$. The upstream firms' profits are

[20] Notice that this rule is different conceptually from the marginal cost pricing principle which implicitly assumes that price is used as the firm's strategic variable, though in this scenario the result turns out to be the same.

$$\pi_1^u = \frac{2(4-\theta-\theta^2)^2 T}{(2-\theta^2)(8-\theta^2)^2} > 0 \tag{5.21}$$

$$\pi_2^u = \frac{(4-2\theta-\theta^2)^2 T}{(2-\theta^2)(8-\theta^2)^2} > 0 \tag{5.22}$$

Social welfare can be found as

$$W = \frac{(2+\theta)^2(28-32\theta+3\theta^2+4\theta^3)T}{2(2-\theta^2)^2(8-\theta^2)^2}$$

and gross benefit is found as

$$G = \frac{(304-144\theta-256\theta^2+92\theta^3+67\theta^4-12\theta^5-6\theta^6)T}{2(2-\theta^2)^2(8-\theta^2)^2}$$

3.1.b. Equilibrium Results with Backward Integration by the Public Firm

When the public firm integrates backward and the private firm in the downstream industry is still non-integrated, the vertical structure of this successive duopoly becomes asymmetric. As we already know, the equilibrium prices of the intermediate inputs differ if the downstream firms pursue asymmetric objectives. The welfare maximizing firm tends to pay more than the profit maximizing firm for similar inputs. The consequence of these input price differences provides the public firm with an incentive to integrate backward in order to eliminate what might be considered as *unfair pricing* practice from intermediate input producers. The change in the public firm's vertical structure results in a change in its perceived marginal cost. The public firm's marginal cost becomes c after the mark-up over its intermediate input is eliminated. The Nash equilibrium output levels of the public and private firms change accordingly following the changes in the vertical structure of the public firm. The Nash equilibrium output of the final products under the new condition become

$$q_1 = \frac{2(a-c) - \theta(a-w_2)}{2-\theta^2} \tag{5.23}$$

$$q_2 = \frac{(a-w_2)-(a-c)\theta}{2-\theta^2} \tag{5.24}$$

We notice that q_1 and q_2 depend on the intermediate input price w_2, which is decided by the non-integrated upstream firm. This upstream firm will react optimally to the changes in the public firm's vertical structure by adjusting its input price. After substituting q_2 in (5.24) into its profit function $\pi^u_2 = (w_2-c)q_2$, the upstream firm's payoff function becomes

$$\pi^u_2 = (w_2-c)\frac{(a-w_2)-(a-c)\theta}{2-\theta^2}$$

The intermediate input price w_2, which maximizes the upstream firm's profit, is

$$w_2 = c + \frac{1-\theta}{2}S \tag{5.25}$$

After knowing the equilibrium price of the intermediate inputs, the subgame perfect Nash equilibrium output quantities of the downstream firms can be computed by substituting (5.25) into (5.23) and (5.24) and this results in

$$q_1 = \frac{(4-\theta-\theta^2)S}{2(2-\theta^2)} \tag{5.26}$$

$$q_2 = \frac{(1-\theta)S}{2(2-\theta^2)} \tag{5.27}$$

The market clearing prices of the final products are

$$p_1 = c$$

$$p_2 = c + \frac{(3+3\theta-\theta^2-\theta^3)S}{2(2-\theta^2)}$$

Note that the final goods price of the public firm is equal to c, the cost of producing the intermediate input. This is because it is already a vertically integrated firm. The final good price of the private firm can also be written in terms of deviations from its marginal cost w_2

$$p_2 = w_2 + \frac{(1-\theta)S}{2(2-\theta^2)}$$

The profitability of the integrated public firm and those of the non-integrated private firms are

$$\pi_1^v = 0 \tag{5.28}$$

$$\pi_2^d = \frac{(1-\theta)^2 T}{4(2-\theta^2)^2} \tag{5.29}$$

$$\pi_2^u = \frac{(1-\theta)^2 T}{4(2-\theta^2)} \tag{5.30}$$

Social welfare and gross benefit are

$$W = \frac{(19 - 6\theta - 14\theta^2 + 2\theta^3 + 3\theta^4)T}{8(2 - \theta^2)^2}$$

$$G = \frac{(23 - 14\theta - 12\theta^2 + 6\theta^3 + \theta^4)T}{8(2 - \theta^2)^2}$$

3.1.c. Equilibrium Results with Backward Integration by the Private Firm

Unlike the previous scenario, the private downstream firm may integrate backward with its supplier while the public firm remains non-integrated. As in a successive monopoly, private firms have an incentive to integrate vertically if the outputs of public firms remain unchanged. Facing the residual demand curve, the downstream private firm's marginal cost after integration is c. The equilibrium in this case may not be as clear cut as in the successive monopoly not only because the public firm will respond to changes in the output level of the private firm, but also because the non-integrated upstream firm will react optimally to changes in the vertical structure of the industry. By adapting the Nash equilibrium in the downstream industry expressed in (5.11) and (5.12), the equilibrium outputs of the final products can be written as

$$q_1 = \frac{2a - (a-c)\theta - 2w_1}{2 - \theta^2} \tag{5.31}$$

$$q_2 = \frac{a - c - \theta(a - w_1)}{2 - \theta^2} \tag{5.32}$$

In the process of finding the second stage Nash equilibrium, the intermediate input price w_1 is treated as an exogenous variable. To ensure the subgame perfectness of the equilibrium, we need to know the intermediate input price w_1 which satisfies the individual rationality of the non-integrated upstream firm. By using the expression for the second stage Nash equilibrium output as the perceived derived demand function of the independent supplier we can write the payoff function of the non-integrated upstream firm as

$$\pi_1^u = (w_1 - c)\,\frac{2(a - w_1) - \theta(a - c)}{2 - \theta^2}$$

The non-integrated upstream firm acts to maximize its profit by setting the intermediate input price. This price is

$$w_1 = c + \frac{2 - \theta}{4} S \tag{5.33}$$

By substituting w_1 into equations (5.31) and (5.32), we have the subgame perfect Nash equilibrium output quantities at the second stage of the game as

$$q_1 = \frac{(2 - \theta) S}{2(2 - \theta^2)} \tag{5.34}$$

$$q_2 = \frac{(4 - 2\theta - \theta^2) S}{4(2 - \theta^2)} \tag{5.35}$$

The market clearing prices for the final products under the given equilibrium output quantities are easily found as

$$p_1 = c + \frac{2 - \theta}{4} S$$

$$p_2 = c + \frac{4 - 2\theta - \theta^2}{4(2 - \theta^2)} S$$

The profit of the public firm becomes

$$\pi_1^d = 0 \tag{5.36}$$

and the profit of its intermediate input supplier is

$$\pi_1^u = \frac{(2-\theta)^2 T}{8(2-\theta^2)} \tag{5.37}$$

The profit of the integrated private firm is found as

$$\pi_2^v = \frac{(4-2\theta-\theta^2)^2 T}{16(2-\theta^2)^2} \tag{5.38}$$

Social welfare and gross benefit are

$$W = \frac{(64-32\theta-40\theta^2+12\theta^3+7\theta^4)T}{32(2-\theta^2)^2}$$

$$G = \frac{(96-64r-48\theta^2+28\theta^3+3\theta^4)T}{32(2-\theta^2)^2}$$

3.1.d. Equilibrium Results Under Full Vertical Integration

When both the downstream public and private firms are integrated backwards, a case of full vertical integration occurs. The perceived marginal costs for both private and public firms fall to c and the two-stage game degenerates into a one-stage Nash game. By substituting c into w_1 and w_2 in equations (5.11) and (5.12), the equilibrium outputs of two integrated firms are found as

$$q_1 = \frac{(2-\theta)S}{2-\theta^2} \tag{5.39}$$

$$q_2 = \frac{(1-\theta)S}{2-\theta^2} \tag{5.40}$$

The market clearing prices of the final products are

$$p_1 = c$$

$$p_2 = c + \frac{(1-\theta)S}{2-\theta^2}$$

while profits of two integrated firms are

$$\pi_1^v = 0 \tag{5.41}$$

$$\pi_2^v = \frac{(1-\theta)^2 T}{(2-\theta^2)^2} \tag{5.42}$$

Social welfare and gross benefit become identical under full integration

$$W = G = \frac{(7-6\theta-2\theta^2+2\theta^3)T}{2(2-\theta^2)^2}$$

Since vertical integration eliminates the mark-up on intermediate inputs, or $w_1 = w_2 = c$, the difference between economic welfare and gross benefits, that is equal to the upstream producers' surplus, disappears.

3.2 Mixed Successive Duopoly with Downstream Stackelberg Game when Public Firm Acts as Leader

Although there is apparently no consensus among economists on the economic roles of the state-owned enterprises in a mixed economy, state-owned enterprises are in a position which is unique compared to private firms. In the literature of regulation and public enterprises, public firms are often granted a dominant position, as the second-best pricing theory implicitly assumes (Bös, 1989). Public firms are willing and able, under certain circumstances, to influence the conduct of the private firms operating in the market characterized by imperfect competition. This relation implies a downstream Stackelberg game with the private firm acting as a Stackelberg *follower* while the public firm plays the role of a Stackelberg *leader*. The downstream private firm responds passively to the moves of the public firm. For any given output of the public firm, it tries to maximize its profit by changing its own output. Knowing the behavior of its private rival, the public firm acts as a Stackelberg *leader* and chooses its output to maximize economic welfare. This means that the reaction function of the private firm is incorporated into the payoff function of the public firm. The equilibrium point in the second-stage game is decided by the public firm along the reaction function of the follower.

3.2.a. Equilibrium Results under a Supply Contracts Game

In the downstream Stackelberg game, the public firm, acting as the leader, is able to pre-commit its output by correctly anticipating the reaction of its private rival. We know that the Stackelberg follower will respond optimally after knowing the output of the leader and that the pattern of its reaction is reflected in its reaction function. When the public firm decides its output level, it has to know the reaction function of the private firm. To find the reaction of the private firm, we set the first derivative of the private firm's profit function with respect to its output equal to zero,

$$\frac{\partial \pi_2^d}{\partial q_2} = a - \theta q_1 - 2q_2 - w_2 = 0$$

The corresponding reaction function of the downstream private firm toward the output of its public rival becomes

$$q_2 = (a - \theta q_1 - w_2)/2 \tag{5.43}$$

We can simply substitute the reaction function in (5.43) into the payoff function of the downstream public firm defined in (5.5). The payoff function of the public firm then becomes

$$W(q_1) = [3a^2 - 6aw_2 + 3w_2^2 + 8(a - w_1)q_1 - 6(a - w_2)\theta q_1 - (4 - 3\theta)q_2^2]/8 \tag{5.44}$$

We take the first derivative of equation (5.44) with respect to q_1 and let the derivative function equal zero, and the output of the public firm which maximizes its payoff is found as

$$q_1 = \frac{4a - 3a\theta - 4w_1 + 3\theta w_2}{4 - 3\theta^2} \tag{5.45}$$

The equilibrium output of the private firm is determined by substituting q_1 in (5.45) into the reaction function of the private firm in (5.43). This gives

$$q_2 = \frac{2a(1 - \theta) + 2\theta w_1 - 2w_2}{4 - 3\theta^2} \tag{5.46}$$

Because q_2 in (5.46) is on the reaction curve of the private firm, it is the equilibrium output of the private firm , which has no incentive to deviate unilaterally from this output level.

This equilibrium in the downstream industry depends on the firms' marginal costs, w_1 and w_2, which are determined by the upstream firms. These intermediate input prices should maximize the profits of the upstream firms under given vertical structures of the industry and market conditions. By using (5.45) and (5.46) as the derived demand functions of the intermediate inputs, the payoff functions of the upstream firms can be transformed into

$$\pi_1^u = \frac{(4a - 3a\theta - 4w_1 + 3\theta w_2)(w_1 - c)}{4 - 3\theta^2}$$

$$\pi_2^2 = \frac{[2a(1 - \theta) + 2\theta w_1 - 2w_2](w_2 - c)}{4 - 3\theta^2}$$

To find the Bertrand-Nash equilibrium input prices, we derive the first order conditions of profit maximization of these upstream firms,

$$\frac{\partial \pi_1^u}{\partial w_1} = 4(a + c) - 3a\theta - 8w_1 + 3\theta w_2 = 0$$

$$\frac{\partial \pi_2^u}{\partial w_2} = a + c - a\theta + \theta w_1 - 2w_2 = 0$$

The solutions of these two simultaneous equations are the intermediate input prices which satisfy the individual rationality of the upstream firms. They are the Bertrand game equilibrium input prices in the first stage.

$$w_1 = c + \frac{8 - 3\theta - 3\theta^2}{16 - 3\theta^2} S \tag{5.47}$$

$$w_2 = c + \frac{8 - 4\theta - 3\theta^2}{16 - 3\theta^2} S \tag{5.48}$$

To find the subgame perfect output levels for downstream firms, we substitute (5.47) and (5.48) into (5.45) and (5.46) respectively, which gives

$$q_1 = \frac{4(8-3\theta-3\theta^2)S}{(16-3\theta^2)(4-3\theta^2)} \tag{5.49}$$

$$q_2 = \frac{2(8-4\theta-3\theta^2)S}{(16-3\theta^2)(4-3\theta^2)} \tag{5.50}$$

The market clearing prices of the final products, expressed as deviations of the cost of intermediate inputs c, are

$$p_1 = c + \frac{32-4\theta-40\theta^2+6\theta^3+9\theta^4}{(4-3\theta^2)(16-3\theta^2)}S \tag{5.51}$$

$$p_2 = c + \frac{3(2-\theta^2)(8-4\theta-3\theta^2)}{(4-3\theta^2)(16-3\theta^2)}S \tag{5.52}$$

The prices of the final products can also be written in terms of the variation of the marginal costs of the downstream firms, which are

$$p_1 = w_1 + \frac{(8-4\theta-3\theta^2)\theta}{(4-3\theta^2)(16-3\theta^2)}S$$

$$p_2 = w_2 + \frac{16-8\theta-18\theta^2+12\theta^3+9\theta^4+9\theta^5}{(4-3\theta^2)(16-3\theta^2)}S$$

The profits of the participants are

$$\pi_1^d = \frac{4\theta(8-3\theta-3\theta^2)(8-4\theta-3\theta^2)T}{(4-3\theta^2)(16-3\theta^2)} \tag{5.53}$$

$$\pi_2^d = \frac{4(8-4\theta-3\theta^2)^2 T}{(4-3\theta^2)^2(16-3\theta^2)^2} \tag{5.54}$$

$$\pi_1^u = \frac{4(8-3\theta-3\theta^2)^2 T}{(4-3\theta^2)(16-3\theta^2)^2} \tag{5.55}$$

$$\pi_2^u = \frac{4(8-4\theta-3\theta^2)^2 T}{(4-3\theta^2)^2(16-3\theta^2)} \tag{5.56}$$

It should be noted that the profit of the public firm is no longer zero. The public firm deviates from the marginal pricing rule in order to maximize social welfare. Social welfare and gross benefit can be found as

$$W = \frac{(448-252\theta^2-72\theta^3)T}{2(4-3\theta^2)(16-3\theta^2)^2}$$

$$G = \frac{(1216-640\theta-692\theta^2+168\theta^3+108\theta^4)T}{2(4-3\theta^2)(16-3\theta^2)^2}$$

3.2.b. Equilibrium Results With Backward Integration by the Public Firm

In this scenario, the downstream public firm, acting as a Stackelberg leader, integrates with its supplier and the downstream private firm, as a Stackelberg follower, continues to purchase its intermediate inputs from an independent supplier. After the public firm integrates, the markup on its intermediate input is eliminated and its perceived marginal cost w_1 becomes c. The equilibrium outputs of the public and private firms under the new vertical structure will adjust accordingly.

By substituting w_1 with c in (5.45) and (5.56), the equilibrium outputs of the final goods can be found as

$$q_1 = \frac{(a-c)[4(a-c)-3a\theta+3\theta w_2]}{4-3\theta^2} \qquad (5.57)$$

$$q_2 = \frac{2a(1-\theta)-2w_2}{4-3\theta^2} \qquad (5.58)$$

The upstream firm, which supplies the intermediate input to the downstream private firm, has an incentive to change its intermediate input price w_2, because the derived demand function it faces has changed after the public firm integrates vertically. Its payoff function, $\pi^u{}_2 = (w_2-c)q_2$, can be written as

$$\pi_2^u = \frac{(w_2-c)[2a(1-\theta)-2w_2]}{4-3\theta^2}$$

By taking the first derivative with respect to the input price, the intermediate input price w_2 which maximizes the payoff function of the non-integrated upstream firm is

$$w_2 = c + \frac{1-0}{2}S \qquad (5.59)$$

Substituting w_2 in (5.59) into (5.57) and (5.58), the subgame perfect equilibrium outputs of the final products are found as

$$q_1 = \frac{(8-3\theta-3\theta^2)S}{2(4-3\theta^2)} \qquad (5.60)$$

$$q_2 = \frac{(1-\theta)S}{(4-3\theta^2)} \qquad (5.61)$$

while the profit of the integrated public firm is again found to be non-zero unless the products of the two downstream firms are independent

$$\pi_1^v = \frac{\theta(1-\theta)(8-3\theta-3\theta^2)T}{4(4-3\theta^2)^2} \tag{5.62}$$

The profits of the non-integrated private firm and its supplier can be derived as

$$\pi_2^d = \frac{(1-\theta)^2 T}{(4-3\theta^2)^2} \tag{5.63}$$

$$\pi_2^u = \frac{(1-\theta)^2 T}{2(4-3\theta^2)} \tag{5.64}$$

Social welfare is found as

$$W = \frac{(19-6\theta-9\theta^2)T}{8(4-3\theta^2)}$$

and the gross benefit is

$$G = \frac{(23-14\theta-5\theta^2)T}{8(4-3\theta^2)^2}$$

3.2.c. Equilibrium Results with Backward Integration by the Private Firm

In this scenario, the public firm, acting as a Stackelberg leader, is non-integrated. Instead, the downstream private firm is integrated vertically with its supplier. Following vertical integration, the private firm's perceived marginal cost w_2 becomes c. The equilibrium outcomes of a Stackelberg duopoly in the downstream industry expressed in (5.45) and (5.46) can be transformed into the equilibrium outputs under the new vertical structure by replacing w_2 with c in those two equations, which gives the equilibrium output quantities as

$$q_1 = \frac{a(4-3\theta)-4w_1+3\theta c}{4-3\theta^2} \tag{5.65}$$

$$q_2 = \frac{2a(1-\theta)+2\theta w_1-2c}{4-3\theta^2} \tag{5.66}$$

To find the value of w_1 which satisfies the individual rationality of the non-integrated upstream firm, we rewrite the upstream firm's payoff function as

$$\pi_1^u = \frac{(w_1-c)[4a-3\theta(a-c)-4w_1]}{4-3\theta^2}$$

Maximization of the upstream firm's profit requires its first derivative to be equal to zero

$$\frac{\partial \pi_1^u}{\partial w_1} = 4(a+c)-3\theta(a-c)-8w_1=0$$

The equilibrium intermediate input price with the property of subgame perfectness turns out to be

$$w_1 = c + \frac{4-3\theta}{8}S \tag{5.67}$$

After the subgame perfect equilibrium intermediate input price w_1 is known, the public firm acts to maximize its payoff function while taking into account the reaction of its private rival. It chooses its output quantity as

$$q_1 = \frac{(4 - 3\theta)S}{2(4 - 3\theta^2)} \tag{5.68}$$

The optimal reaction of the integrated private firm after knowing the public firm's output can be found by substituting q_1 in (5.68) into its reaction function defined in (5.43) and noting $w_2 = c$. The equilibrium output for this private firm turns out to be

$$q_2 = \frac{(8 - 4\theta - 3\theta^2)S}{4(4 - 3\theta^2)} \tag{5.69}$$

The profits of the public firm, its upstream supplier and the integrated private firm can be found as

$$\pi_1^d = \frac{\theta(8 - 4\theta - 3\theta^2)(4 - 3\theta)T}{16(4 - 3\theta^2)^2} \tag{5.70}$$

$$\pi_1^u = \frac{(4 - 3\theta)^2 T}{16(4 - 3r^2)} \tag{5.71}$$

$$\pi_2^v = \frac{(8 - 4\theta - 3\theta^2)^2 T}{16(4 - 3\theta^2)^2} \tag{5.72}$$

Social welfare and gross benefit are

$$W = \frac{(64 - 24\theta - 27\theta^2)T}{32(4 - 3\theta^2)}$$

$$G = \frac{3(32 - 24\theta - 3\theta^2)T}{32(4 - 3\theta^2)}$$

3.2.d. Equilibrium Results with Full Vertical Integration

In this scenario, both the downstream firms are integrated. The two-stage game degenerates into an ordinary Stackelberg game with both firms' marginal costs equal to c. Hence, the equilibrium outputs can be found easily by replacing w_1 and w_2 with c in equations (5.45) and (5.46), which leads to

$$q_1 = \frac{(4 - 3\theta)S}{4 - 3\theta^2}$$

$$q_2 = \frac{2(1 - \theta)S}{4 - 3\theta^2}$$

The profits of the two integrated firms can be found as

$$\pi_1^v = \frac{\theta(1 - \theta)(4 - 3\theta)T}{(4 - 3\theta^2)^2} \tag{5.73}$$

$$\pi_2^v = \frac{4(1 - \theta)^2 T}{(4 - 3\theta^2)^2} \tag{5.74}$$

Social welfare, which is equal to gross benefit, is

$$W = G = \frac{(7 - 6\theta)^2 T}{2(4 - 3\theta^2)}$$

3.3. Mixed Successive Duopoly with Downstream Stackelberg Game when Private Firm Acts as Leader

In this section, the competition in the downstream industry is a Stackelberg duopoly, but the roles of the two firms are reversed. The public firm becomes the Stackelberg follower and the private firm plays the role of a Stackelberg leader. The private firm tries to maximize its profits by taking into account the reactions of the public firm.

In the regulatory context, it is frequently assumed (not unreasonably) that the public firm plays a leading role and private firms have no other choice but to follow the moves of the public firm. This assumption imposes a strong requirement for information. To control an oligopoly, the requirement for information about private firms' operations is very strong. Information concerning the cost functions and the reaction functions of private firms may often be private.

By directly participating in the industry via a public firm, the government is in a better position to assess the operation of private firms, but the public firm at the leadership position still requires more information about the conduct of the private firms than in the case where the public firm plays a role of follower. As an alternative, the public firm may be instructed to follow some type of decision rule, such as marginal cost pricing, if that can result in an improvement of economic welfare. Marginal cost pricing is relative easy to implement in practice, since it does not require the public firm to possess information concerning the reaction function of the private firm. Therefore, this scenario should not be seen as a simple manipulation of a Stackelberg game, but as a correspondence to a more sophisticated interpretation of the marginal cost pricing rule which is often used by public firms. Hence, without apology, we can start analyzing the mixed Stackelberg duopoly with a private firm as the leader.

3.3.a. Equilibrium Results under a Supply Contracts Game

In this scenario, the public firm, acting as a Stackelberg follower, and the private firm, as a Stackelberg leader, both rely on external suppliers for their intermediate inputs.

When the private firm acts to maximize its own profit, it has to take into account the reactions of the public firm. This reaction is reflected in the public firm's reaction function which describes the optimal response of the public firm with respect to the output of the private rival. This reaction function is found as

$$q_1 = a - \theta q_2 - w_1 \tag{5.75}$$

Substituting the public firm's reaction function into the profit function of the private firm, the payoff of the private downstream firm as Stackelberg leader becomes

$$\pi_2^d = [a - \theta(a - \theta q_2 - w_1) - q_2 - w_2]\, q_2$$

The first order condition of profit maximization turns out to be

$$\frac{\partial \pi_2^d}{\partial q_2} = a(1-\theta) - 2(1-\theta^2)q^2 + \theta w_1 - w_2 = 0$$

The equilibrium output of the private firm becomes a function of its own marginal cost w_2 and the marginal cost of the public firm w_1

$$q_2 = \frac{a(1-\theta) + \theta w_1 - w_2}{2(1-\theta^2)} \tag{5.76}$$

Substituting equation (5.76) into the public firm's reaction function in (5.75) yields the equilibrium output of the public firm

$$q_1 = \frac{2a - a\theta(1+\theta) - (2-\theta^2)w_1 + \theta w_2}{2(1-\theta^2)} \tag{5.77}$$

Because the vertical structure is characterized as a supply contract and the upstream firms have price setting power, equations (5.76) and (5.77) can be seen as derived demand functions from the viewpoint of the two upstream firms. The intermediate input prices, which are Bertrand equilibria in the first stage of the game, are worked out by using these derived demand functions. We can write the payoff functions of the upstream firms as

$$\pi_1^u = \frac{[2a - a\theta(1+\theta) - (2-\theta^2)w_1 + \theta w_2](w_1 - c)}{2(1-\theta^2)}$$

$$\pi_2^u = \frac{[a(1-\theta) + \theta w_1 - w_2](w_2 - c)}{2(1-\theta^2)}$$

By taking the first derivatives with respect to w_1 and w_2, the first order conditions of profit maximization are found as

$$\frac{\partial \pi_1^u}{\partial w_1} = a(1-\theta)(2-\theta) - 2(2-\theta^2)w_1 + \theta w_2 + (2-\theta^2)c = 0$$

$$\frac{\partial \pi_2^u}{\partial w_2} = a(1-\theta) + \theta w_1 - 2w_2 + c = 0$$

The solutions of these two simultaneous equations provide the Bertrand-Nash equilibrium intermediate input prices. They are

$$w_1 = c + \frac{4-\theta-3\theta^2}{8-5\theta^2}S \tag{5.78}$$

$$w_2 = c + \frac{(2-\theta)(2-\theta-2\theta^2)}{8-5\theta^2}S \tag{5.79}$$

Substituting w_1 and w_2 into equations (5.76) and (5.77), we can find the output quantities of the two downstream firms as

$$q_1 = \frac{(4+3\theta)(2-\theta^2)S}{2(1+\theta)(8-5\theta^2)} \tag{5.80}$$

$$q_2 = \frac{(4+2\theta-\theta^2)S}{2(1+\theta)(8-5\theta^2)} \tag{5.81}$$

The prices of the final products of the public and private firms are found as

$$p_1 = c + \frac{(1-\theta)(4+3\theta)}{8-5\theta^2}S \tag{5.82}$$

$$p_2 = c + \frac{3(1-\theta)(4+2\theta-\theta^2)}{2(8-5\theta^2)}S \tag{5.83}$$

The profits of the public and private firms in the downstream industry are derived as

$$\pi_1^d = 0 \tag{5.84}$$

$$\pi_2^d = \frac{(4+2\theta-\theta^2)^2(1-\theta)T}{4(1+\theta)(8-5\theta^2)^2} \tag{5.85}$$

Profits of the two upstream firms are

$$\pi_1^u = \frac{(1-\theta)(4+3\theta)^2(2-\theta^2)^2T}{2(1+\theta)(8-5\theta^2)^2} \tag{5.86}$$

$$\pi_2^u = \frac{(1-\theta)(4+2\theta-\theta^2)^2T}{2(1+\theta)(8-5\theta^2)^2} \tag{5.87}$$

Social welfare and gross benefit can be found accordingly as

$$W = \frac{(112 + 96\theta - 88\theta^2 - 76\theta^3 + 15\theta^4 + 13\theta^5)T}{8(1+\theta)(8-5\theta^2)^2}$$

$$G = \frac{(304 + 160\theta - 352\theta^2 - 180\theta^3 - 95\theta^4 + 45\theta^5)T}{8(1+\theta)(8-5\theta^2)^2}$$

3.3.b. Equilibrium Results with Backward Integration by the Public Firm

When the downstream public firm integrates backward and the downstream private firm continues to rely on its independent supplier for its intermediate inputs, the public firm's perceived marginal cost w_1 is reduced to c. The new equilibrium outputs can be found by substituting w_1 by c in (5.76) and (5.77), yielding

$$q_1 = a - c - \frac{\theta(a - a\theta + c\theta - w_2)}{2(1-\theta^2)} \tag{5.88}$$

$$q_2 = \frac{a(1-\theta) + \theta c - w_2}{2(1-\theta^2)} \tag{5.89}$$

To find the Nash equilibrium intermediate input price, w_2, which is subgame perfect, we have to know w_2 which maximizes the non-integrated upstream firm's payoff function. Substituting (5.88) into this firm's profit function leads to

$$\pi_2^u = \frac{(a - a\theta + \theta c - w_2)(w_2 - c)}{2(1-\theta^2)}$$

The intermediate price w_2, which maximizes profit of the upstream firm is found as

$$w_2 = c + \frac{1-\theta}{2}S \tag{5.90}$$

Substituting w_2 in (5.90) back into equations (5.88) and (5.89), the subgame perfect Nash equilibrium outputs of the final products are found as

$$q_1 = \frac{(4+3\theta)S}{4(1+\theta)} \tag{5.91}$$

$$q_2 = \frac{S}{4(1+\theta)} \tag{5.92}$$

The profits of individual firms are found as

$$\pi_1^v = 0$$

$$\pi_2^d = \frac{(1-\theta)T}{16(1+\theta)}$$

$$\pi_2^u = \frac{(1-\theta)T}{8(1+\theta)}$$

Social welfare and gross benefit are found as

$$W = \frac{(19+13\theta)T}{32(1+\theta)}$$

$$G = \frac{(23 + 9\theta)T}{32(1 + \theta)}$$

3.3.c. Equilibrium Results With Backward Integration by the Private Firm

In this scenario, the downstream public firm remains non-integrated and its private rival, acting as a Stackelberg leader, integrates backward with an upstream firm. To know the equilibrium at the downstream industry after vertical integration of the private firm, the equilibrium outputs of Stackelberg follower and leader expressed in (5.76) and (5.77) can be modified by replacing w_2 with c. The new equilibrium outputs of the downstream industry Stackelberg game are

$$q_1 = \frac{(a - w_1)(2 - \theta^2) - (a - c)\theta}{2(1 - \theta^2)} \tag{5.93}$$

$$q_2 = \frac{a - c - a\theta - \theta w_1}{2(1 - \theta^2)} \tag{5.94}$$

The supplier of the public firm is able to observe the equilibrium in the downstream industry and acts to maximize its own profit which can be written as the function

$$\pi_1^u = \frac{[(a - w_1)(2 - \theta^2) - (a - c)\theta](w_1 - c)}{2(1 - \theta^2)}$$

Profit maximization requires the first order condition

$$\frac{\partial \pi_1^u}{\partial w_1} = (a + c - 2w_1)(2 - \theta^2) - (a - c)\theta = 0$$

be satisfied.

The intermediate input price which satisfies the individual rationality of the upstream firm is found to be

$$w_1 = c + \frac{2-\theta-\theta^2}{2(2-\theta^2)}S \tag{5.95}$$

Knowing the marginal cost and reaction function of its public rival, the private firm will choose its output to maximize its own profit. The public firm will, consequently, decide its output under the given output of the private firm to maximize economic welfare. The subgame perfect Nash equilibrium outputs for the two firms are found by substituting (5.95) into (5.93) and (5.94). They are

$$q_1 = \frac{(2+\theta^2)S}{4(1-\theta^2)} \tag{5.96}$$

$$q_2 = \frac{(4+2\theta-\theta^2)S}{4(1+\theta)(2-\theta^2)} \tag{5.97}$$

The profit of the public firm is found to be zero

$$\pi_1^d = 0 \tag{5.98}$$

The profits of the public firm's supplier and the vertically integrated private firm are found as

$$\pi_1^u = \frac{(1-\theta)(2+\theta)^2 T}{8(1+\theta)(2-\theta^2)} \tag{5.99}$$

$$\pi_2^v = \frac{(1-\theta)(4+2\theta-\theta^2)^2 T}{16(1+\theta)(2-\theta^2)^2} \tag{5.100}$$

Social welfare and gross benefit are found as

$$W = \frac{(64+32\theta-56\theta^2-20\theta^3-11\theta^4+\theta^5)T}{32(1+\theta)(2-\theta^2)^2}$$

$$G = \frac{(96+32\theta-96\theta^2-28\theta^3+23\theta^4+5\theta^5)T}{32(1+\theta)(2-\theta^2)^2}$$

3.3.d. Equilibrium Results under Full Vertical Integration

When both the downstream public firm and the downstream private firm are integrated, the perceived marginal costs of both firms become c. The game degenerates into a simple Stackelberg duopoly with the private firm acting as the leader. The equilibrium output quantities can easily be found after replacing w_i by c in equations (5.26) and (5.27). This leads to

$$q_1 = \frac{(2+\theta)S}{2(1+\theta)}$$

$$q_2 = \frac{S}{2(1+\theta)}$$

The profit of the public firm is obviously equal to zero

$$\pi_1^v = 0$$

and the profit for the private firm is

$$\pi_2^v = \frac{(1-\theta)T}{4(1+\theta)}$$

Economic welfare as well as gross benefit will be

$$W = G = \frac{(7+\theta)T}{8(1+\theta)}$$

The equilibrium results derived will be used in discussions in the next section, in which the economic meaning of these results will become clearer. To facilitate the discussion, these analytical results will be organized in a number of tables and figures closely related to the propositions established below.

4. MAJOR FINDINGS

The equilibrium results in the previous section constitute the basis for discussion of several normative and positive issues related to public enterprises. These issues range from regulating the successive oligopoly to the vertical integration strategy of the corporation. The discussions are carried out around following questions: Why do marginal costs differ between public and private firms? What is the value of first-mover advantage in a mixed successive oligopoly? Is there an optimal rule of regulating successive oligopoly by public enterprises? What can a public firm do to control such an oligopoly? What is the equilibrium vertical structure in a successive oligopoly with asymmetric objectives? By addressing these issues in the game theoretic framework of a mixed successive oligopoly, some new insights are obtained.

4.1. Cost Difference Between the Public Firm and the Private Firm

One of the criticisms levelled against public enterprises is that these enterprises are economically inefficient. For example, they typically pay much more for their inputs than private firms. These inputs may include labor, intermediate goods and other resources. These claims are well supported by casual observations of industrial reality and empirical studies. For instance, in a survey of studies which have sought to compare cost levels in public and private production in a number of countries including the U.S., Germany, Canada and Australia in various types of production activities, Borcherding, Pommerehne and Schneider (1982) find that the majority of public firms show higher cost levels than private enterprises carrying on comparable activities. Some recent empirical evidences do not directly compare cost levels of public and private firms, although indirect indicators show that public firms perform worse than their private counterparts[21]. Partly for this reason, some economists build their models by assuming that public firms pay a premium over their inputs compared to private firms (Cremer, Marchand and Thisse, 1989).

A number of well developed theories are readily available to explain this phenomenon. One explanation is that X-inefficiency is the major cause as public firms are, to a certain extent, under the protection of the government and shielded from genuine competition, therefore public firms are less motivated to produce efficiently (Leibenstein, 1966). Also, because also the property rights of public firms are only vaguely specified, the principal-agent problem can be more serious in public firms than in private ones (Jensen and Meckling, 1976). And finally it may be that a number of non-market failures will emerge when the government wants to eliminate market failures by directly intervening in the market through public firms (Wolf, 1979).

All of these theories are well established and convincing. But it can be shown through our simple successive duopoly model that the downstream public firm still pays more than the private firm in equilibrium when the possibility of all those inefficiencies are excluded. The explanation is that, under the vertical structure of supply contract, the difference between the marginal costs of the downstream firms, that depend on the intermediate input prices, is caused by asymmetric objectives

[21] Public firms are found to be typically less efficient than private firms in oligopolistic industries. In natural monopolies, the results are quite ambiguous. Most of the empirical studies use efficiency measures other than the cost levels due to technical and practical difficulties. See e.g. Boardman and Vining (1989) and Yarrow (1986).

between the public and private firm in the downstream industry. This endogenously determined cost difference is likely to be sustained if the firms in the downstream industry consistently pursue different objectives.

Proposition 5.1. *In a mixed successive duopoly with linear demand and constant returns to scale, the marginal costs of the downstream public firm are higher than those of the private firm if they rely on supply contracts for intermediate inputs. Moreover, their marginal cost difference increase as their products becomes less differentiated.*

Proposition 5.1. is proved by comparing the subgame perfect equilibrium intermediate input prices w_1 and w_2 in all three alternative game settings. Table 5.2 contains the items which need to be compared.

The comparison among these intermediate input prices shows that $w_1>w_2$ since $a>c$, where a is the intercept of the linear demand curve and c is the marginal cost of producing the intermediate input. Recalling that the input prices are equal to the marginal costs of the downstream firm, we can also show that the first derivative of the marginal cost difference with respect to the product differentiation parameter θ is always positive. This means the differences between the marginal costs of the public and private firms become larger when the final products are less differentiated.

The intuition behind this price difference can be understood with the assistance of Figure 5.2. Figure 5.2, which illustrates the interactions between and among firms in the two adjacent industries, is constructed by using the Cournot game with homogeneous goods, although the scenarios under Stackelberg games can be adapted easily. Because the downstream firms use quantity as their strategic variable in both the Cournot game and Stackelberg game, the firms' reaction curves are depicted in the quantity space.

Suppose the downstream public firm behaves exactly like the private firm initially and chooses profit maximization as its payoff function. Then the two-stage duopoly becomes symmetric. In equilibrium, the upstream firms charge exactly the same intermediate input price for public and private firms alike. The firms in the downstream industry consequently have identical marginal costs. The Cournot-Nash equilibrium with symmetric objectives is identified at the intersection of their reaction curves at point A in Figure 5.2.

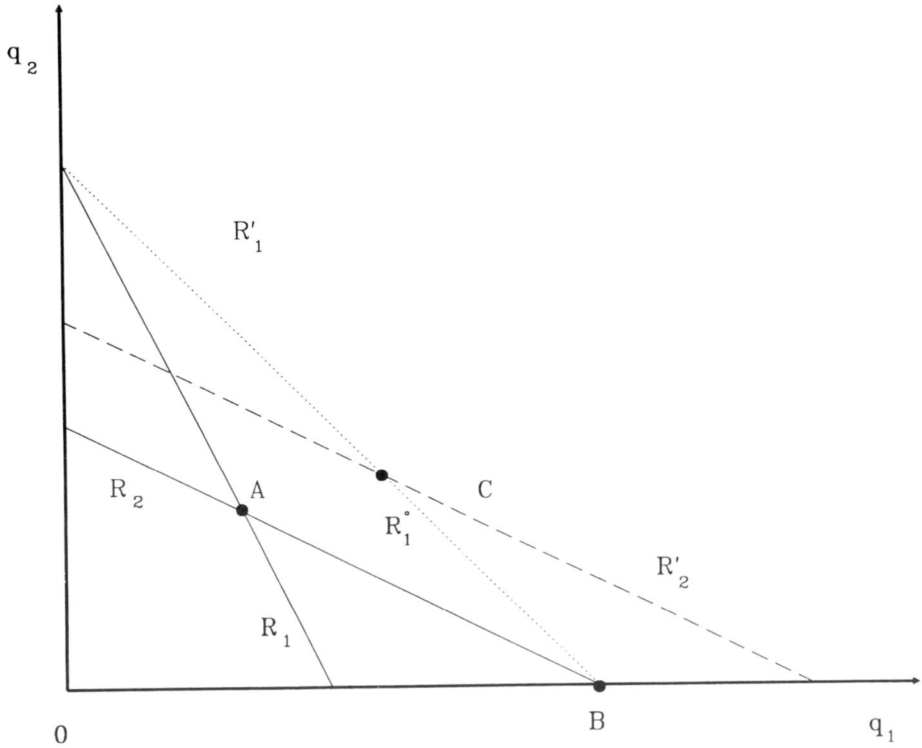

Fig. 5.2 The Reaction Functions in a Mixed Duopoly

No one is willing to deviate unilaterally from this point, and the two symmetric firms divide the final product market equally.

Now, suppose that the government instructs the public firm to pursue the objective of welfare maximization. If the public firm believes that the output quantity of its private rival will remain unchanged (Cournot-type conjectural variation), for any given output of the private firm, the public firm is expected to increase its output such that the price of the final products equals its marginal cost. The private firm has to do a similar mental exercise and to figure out what may happen after its rival becomes a welfare maximizing public firm. Obviously, after the increase in the public firm's output, the price of the final products falls to zero. The optimal response of the private firm is to reduce its own output. Under the Cournot conjecture, the public firm will maintain its output level. The action of the private firm reduces the industrial output,

Table 5.2. Comparison of the Subgame Perfect Nash Equilibrium Input Prices Between Public and Private Firms.

Game Settings	Input price of public firm	Input price of private firm	Differences in input prices
Cournot Game	$c+\frac{(4-\theta-\theta^2)S}{8-\theta^2}$ (5.13)*	$c+\frac{(4-2\theta-\theta^2)S}{8-\theta^2}$ (5.14)*	$\frac{\theta S}{8-\theta^2}$
Stackelberg game with public firm as leader	$c+\frac{(8-3\theta-3\theta^2)S}{16-3\theta^2}$ (5.47)*	$c+\frac{(8-4\theta-3\theta^2)S}{16-3\theta^2}$ (5.48)*	$\frac{\theta S}{16-3\theta^2}$
Stackelberg with private firm as leader	$c+\frac{(4-\theta-3\theta^2)S}{8-5\theta^2}$ (5.78)*	$c+\frac{(2-\theta)(2-\theta-2\theta^2)S}{8-5\theta^2}$ (5.79)*	$\frac{\theta(1-\theta^2)S}{8-5\theta^2}$

* The numbers in brackets indicate the equations where they can be found.

thereby raising the final good price above the marginal cost of the private firm. It generates a positive profit for the private firm. But with the objective of welfare maximization, the public firm's reaction towards the private firm's move is to produce extra output that exactly matches the quantity reduction of the private firm. This interaction process continues until the private firm's output diminishes to zero. In fact, these moves and counter-moves do not actually take place, as the rational players are able to figure out the equilibrium before the game starts and choose the outputs required by the Nash equilibrium.

It is shown in Figure 5.2 that the intersection of the reaction functions of the two downstream firms with asymmetric objectives but with symmetric marginal costs is point B at the border. Note that the reaction function of the downstream public firm R_1 simply turns around and changes its slope after the introduction of asymmetry in the firms' objective functions. This change is different from the shift caused by the changes in the demand and/or cost conditions. The new reaction function of the public firm becomes R_1'. The economic interpretation of the public firm's reaction curve is that the public firm's objective is to maximize social welfare which requires the output of the public firm $q_1 = Q^*-q_2$ where Q^* is the welfare maximizing output quantity. In other words, the public firm will produce the competitive level of the output which satisfies market needs. Subsequently, the private firm ceases production. The equilibrium market structure then becomes a public firm monopoly.

Now let us look at the first stage of the game (upstream industry). Given that the information structure is *almost perfect*, upstream firms know exactly how the interactions between the downstream firms will take place. Because the upstream firms have market power to set the intermediate input prices, they have the power to influence the equilibrium outcomes in the downstream industry by changing the input price.

The profit maximizing upstream firms will set the prices of the intermediate goods at such level that their own profits can be maximized by taking into account the reactions of and interactions between the downstream firms. The downstream private firm's supplier obviously has incentive to lower its intermediate input price given the presence of the public firm in the downstream industry. The demand for its intermediate goods would become zero if it charged the same price as the supplier to the public firm does. This reduces the perceived marginal cost of the private firm in the downstream industry and creates a marginal cost difference. This difference leads to a positive output of the downstream private firm and a positive profit for its supplier as well. The difference between the intermediate input prices remains simply because prices for the intermediate goods cannot be equal in equilibrium from the viewpoint of the private firm's supplier. The upstream firm can always increase its profit by undercutting its price against its rival.

Figure 5.2 illustrates the sub-game perfect equilibrium in output space. The reaction curve of the downstream private firm R_2 moves to the up and right direction and becomes R_2'. The reaction function of the public firm moves in the same direction and becomes R_1''. The equilibrium moves from point *B* on the border to point *C*. The new equilibrium is illustrated by the intercept of R_1'' and R_2'. The output of the private firm becomes positive and industrial output is higher than that in the Cournot game with symmetric objectives.

When final products are differentiated, the public firm's monopoly may not be the equilibrium market structure even when the two downstream firms have identical marginal costs and therefore the border solution, that would be obtained with equal input price, may not happen. But the basic insights will not change although the shape of the reaction functions are slightly different as will be shown next.

After knowing that the marginal costs between the public firm and the private firm will differ so long as they pursue different objectives, the question now is whether their costs are higher than those under a successive duopoly where firms have symmetric objectives of profit maximization. To answer this question, we need to look at the first stage game more closely and compare the sub-game perfect Nash equilibrium input prices when the downstream firms have symmetric and asymmetric objectives. We have the following proposition:

Proposition 5.2. *The input prices for the public firm and the private firm are lower when the downstream industry is a mixed duopoly than under a duopoly with symmetric profit maximization.*

To understand Proposition 5.2, we first look at the equilibrium under a successive duopoly with symmetric objectives of profit maximization. Since the upstream firms are competing over input prices through their downstream buyers, they act as Bertrand-behaved players. The input prices are clearly strategic complements because the final products are perfect substitutes (Bulow *et al.*, 1985). We use Figure 5.3 to depict the upward-sloping reaction curves of both the public firm's supplier and the private firm's supplier in the space of the input prices.

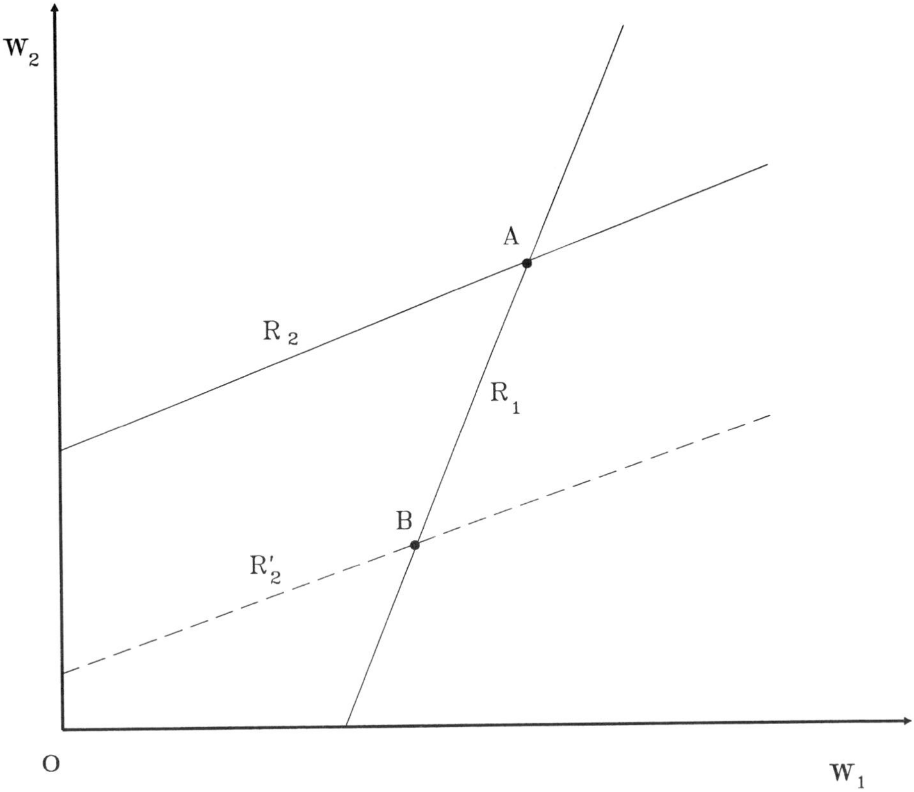

Figure 5.3. Equilibrium Input Prices under Symmetric and Asymmetric Objectives

For any w_2, there is an input price w_1 which represents the best response of the public firm's supplier after it takes into account the equilibrium in the second stage game and the input price charged by its indirect rival. The reaction curve R_1 depicts the best response of the public firm's supplier and the optimal input price charged for public firm w_1 conditional on the input price w_2 set by its upstream rival. The reaction function of the private firm's supplier is represented by R_2. The symmetric equilibrium at point *A* gives the input prices w_1 and w_2 which no supplier is willing to deviate from unilaterally. Therefore it is a Nash equilibrium.

When the public firm acts as a welfare maximizer, it will act in such a way so as to let the price of the final product equal its marginal cost. Here we need the result of the property of invariance of the input price in the successive monopoly literature. It has been shown that in a successive monopoly, the input price charged by the monopolistic supplier is independent of the market structure in the final products market under the condition of linear demand and constant marginal costs (Greenhut and Ohta, 1976). In other words, the upstream firm will charge the same price for the inputs whether the downstream industry is characterized as perfect competition, where price equals marginal cost, or monopoly, where marginal revenue equals marginal cost.

When the public firm acts to maximize profit, its marginal revenue equals its marginal cost and when it acts to maximize social welfare, price equals its marginal cost. By combining the property of invariance of the input in the successive monopoly and the exclusive relationship between the public firm and its supplier, we know the input price charged by the public firm's supplier will be the same whether the public firm chooses to let the price equal its marginal cost or to let the marginal revenue equal its marginal cost so long as the private firm's supplier does not change its input price. Hence, R_1 remains unchanged when the public firm changes from being a profit maximizer to being a welfare maximizer.

It is interesting to note that the reaction curve of the private firm's supplier will shift downwards to R_2' after the public firm changes its objective. This is because, as Proposition 1 indicates, the input price of the private firm must be lower than that of the public firm. The intercept of this reaction curve on the vertical axis is at the origin. Because of the strategic complementarity property of the input prices, which is represented by the upward-sloping reaction curves, the shift of the reaction function of the private firm's suppliers from R_2 to R_2' will elicit a response from its rival. The new equilibrium for input prices is reached at point B where the input prices for both the public firm and the private firm become lower than those under the symmetric objective of profit maximization. Therefore, after the downstream public firm changes its objective, both upstream firms have an incentive to reduce their prices on the intermediate inputs. The indirect competition over prices of the intermediate goods reaches an equilibrium when no firm has any incentive to change its price again given the price of the intermediate input of its rival.

The analysis for the two kinds of Stackelberg games tells us that the difference between the intermediate input prices does not disappear although the information structure and roles of the firms in the Stackelberg game differ from those in the Cournot game.

As has just been shown, both firms pay less for their inputs and produce more final goods when the public firm, with the objective of welfare maximization, is introduced into the downstream industry to control a successive duopoly. The introduction of a welfare maximizing public firm in the downstream industry increases the economic welfare not only by increasing the output of the final goods, but also by reducing the market power of the upstream oligopolists. Both downstream firms' marginal costs become lower with objective asymmetry than without objective asymmetry, although the difference in their marginal costs remains.

We have to be very careful when using this result to explain the cost difference between the public firm and the private firm in general because of the various negative elements related to public firms, such as agency problems, X-inefficiency, nonmarket failures, etc. These negative elements accompanying the public firm may have a dominant impact on deciding the relative economic efficiency of the firms.

4.2. First-Mover and Second-Mover Advantages

It is well known that, compared with symmetric Cournot players, the Stackelberg leader is the first-mover and it may use this advantage to improve its payoff if all players are profit maximizers and if the strategic variables are strategic substitutes. In the Stackelberg game with quantity competition, the leader benefits from the first-mover advantage (Shapiro, 1989)[22]. It is not clear whether the above conclusion still holds when one player acts to maximize social welfare and the other acts to maximize its own profit. A player's preference for one role or another depends on the levels of its payoffs and any changes in the payoff functions of the players have important impacts on the equilibrium results. Three questions can be raised here. First, can the public firm improve social welfare by acting as a Stackelberg leader when the second-stage game changes from a Cournot game to a Stackelberg game? Secondly, what kind of impact the public firm's leadership may have on private firms' profits? Thirdly, does social welfare deteriorate and private firms' profits increase when the role of Stackelberg leader and follower changes between the welfare maximizing public firm and the profit maximizing private firm? The following proposition provides the answer for the first question.

---

[22] When the reaction functions of the two identical players are upwards sloping (e.g. strategic complements), each firm may prefer the other to be a leader (Dowrick, 1986). When firms facing unequal capacity constraints, the larger firm may prefer to act as a price leader and the small firm prefers to be follower (Deneckere and Kovenock, 1992).

Proposition 5.3. *If the public firm acts as the Stackelberg leader and the private firm as the Stackelberg follower, social welfare is strictly higher than that if both firms act as Cournot-type players.*

Proof: We need three steps to prove proposition 5.3. Step 1: The payoff of the downstream public firm as a Stackelberg leader must be at least as high as it would be as a Cournot player. In Stackelberg game, the information structure is such that the leader knows the follower's reaction function which specifies the output of the follower for each possible output of the Stackelberg leader. This would allow the leader to choose the output level on the follower's reaction curve, which is its most-favored point. Given the fact that the payoff of the leader is social welfare, clearly then, the welfare must be at least as high as in a Cournot game in which no firms have any informational and dynamic advantages.

Step 2: The subgame perfect equilibrium intermediate input prices w_1 and w_2, are lower in a Stackelberg game than in a Cournot game. To find out the differences between the intermediate input prices (which are the marginal costs of the downstream firms) under the two alternative game settings, comparisons are made between the subgame perfect equilibrium input prices. Table 5.3 summarizes the results of this comparison. It can be easily verified that the differences between the intermediate prices under these two game settings are positive under the conditions specified in the model, namely, all parameters are positive since $a-c>0$, $1>\theta>0$.

Step 3: Noting the social welfare function defined in (5.5), we have $\partial W/\partial w_1<0$; $\partial W/\partial w_2<0$. Therefore, the reduction in input prices must unambiguously increase social welfare. Q.E.D.

The intuition behind this proposition is as follows. The level of social welfare never decreases when the public firm acts as a Stackelberg leader compared with that when it acts as a Cournot player. The reduction in the firms' marginal costs causes an unambiguous increase in social welfare because the welfare function is a decreasing function of the downstream firm's marginal costs. Therefore, economic welfare must increase after the downstream public firm changes its behavior from Cournot-type to Stackelberg leader.

Table 5.3. Comparison of Marginal Costs of Downstream Firms

Game Settings	Public firm's marginal costs	Private firm's marginal costs
Cournot Game (1)	$c + \dfrac{(4-\theta-\theta^2)S}{8-\theta^2}$ (5.13)*	$c + \dfrac{(4-2\theta-\theta^2)S}{8-\theta^2}$ (5.14)*
Stackelberg game with public firm as leader (2)	$c + \dfrac{(8-3\theta-3\theta^2)S}{16-3\theta^2}$ (5.47)*	$c + \dfrac{(8-4\theta-3\theta^2)S}{16-3\theta^2}$ (5.48)*
Differences (1) - (2)	$\dfrac{2\theta^2(2+\theta)S}{(8-\theta^2)(16-3\theta^2)}$	$\dfrac{2\theta^2(2+\theta)S}{(8-\theta^2)(16-3\theta^2)}$

* the numbers in brackets indicate the equations where they can be found

We can see that in the successive duopoly model, in addition to the first-mover advantages a Stackelberg leader may have in a one-stage game, the public firm imposes a positive externality on input producers, which is also welfare enhancing.

In a one-stage Stackelberg game with symmetric objectives, a Stackelberg follower tends to be worse-off compared with a Cournot player. That relation is re-examined in our model with asymmetric objectives. This leads to the following proposition:

Proposition 5.4. *In a successive duopoly with linear demand and constant returns to scale, the private downstream firm's profit is higher (lower) if it acts as a Stackelberg follower than as a Cournot player when the level of product differentiation is high (low).*

Proposition 5.4 describes the relative profit levels of the downstream private firm when the private and public firm behave as Cournot players, moving simultaneously and when the private firm acts as follower in a Stackelberg game. This proposition can be proved by comparing the payoffs of the downstream private firms in these two alternative game settings in (5.20) and (5.54) respectively.

$$\pi_2^{dC} = \frac{(4-2\theta-\theta^2)^2}{(2-\theta^2)^2(8-\theta^2)^2} \geq \pi_2^{dF} = \frac{4(8-4\theta-3\theta^2)^2}{(4-3\theta^2)(16-3\theta^2)^2} \qquad \textit{if } \theta \geq 0.91$$

where the superscripts C stands for Cournot and F for Stackelberg follower. The direct comparison shows that when the final goods of the public and private producers are very goods substitutes ($\theta>0.91$), the private firm may be worse-off by acting as a Stackelberg follower. If the level of product differentiation is high ($\theta<0.91$), the sign of the difference in the private firm's profits between it acting as a Cournot player and as a Stackelberg follower is negative. This means that the payoff of the downstream private firm is higher when it acts as a Stackelberg follower than when it acts as a Cournot player.

The intuition behind the relative magnitude of the downstream private firm's payoffs can be contributed to the asymmetry in the firms' objectives. As Proposition 5.1 has established, the asymmetry in objectives creates the difference in marginal costs of the downstream firms and the private firm is the more efficient producer (with a lower marginal cost) than its public counterpart.

When taking this into account, the public firm will produce less output when acting as a Stackelberg leader than as a Cournot player in the hope that the reduction in its output can stimulate the downstream private firm to produce more output than otherwise. Therefore, the public firm can gain more in its payoff by cutting output. Secondly, the lower the level of product differentiation, the stronger the strategic impact of a public firm's move would be, and the less the necessity for a public firm's output reduction. The way that the private firm can benefit from the position of the Stackelberg follower depends on the balance of the direct effect and the strategic effect. As a consequence, the downstream private firm may improve its payoff by acting as a Stackelberg follower than by acting as a Cournot player when the level of the product differentiation is high.

The next question which is still unanswered is whether the private downstream firm can gain by acting as the first mover if the players have asymmetric objectives.

Proposition 5.5. *In a successive duopoly with linear demand and constant returns to scale, the downstream private firm prefers being a Stackelberg follower to being a Stackelberg leader when the final products are highly differentiated.*

The verification of proposition 5.5 is established by direct comparison of the profits of the private firm in equilibrium expressed in (5.54) and (5.85) in these two types of games.

$$\pi_2^{dF} = \frac{4(8-4\theta-3\theta^2)^2}{(4-3\theta^2)(16-3\theta^2)^2} \geq \pi_2^{dL} = \frac{(1-\theta)(4+2\theta-\theta^2)^2}{4(1+\theta)(8-5\theta^2)^2} \qquad \textit{if } \theta \leq 0.77$$

The results of the comparison show that when product differentiation is high, that is the product differentiation parameter θ is less than 0.77, the private firm is better-off by acting as a Stackelberg follower than as a Stackelberg leader.

An interesting insight from these propositions is that a *win-win* solution may emerge in which both the public firm and the private firm in the downstream industry are better-off. This insight can be better understood with the aid of Figure 5.4.

In Figure 5.4, one set of iso-profit curves are replaced by a family of iso-welfare curves. The middle of the circles is the maximum economic welfare attainable under given market and technology conditions and constant intermediate input prices. Point *A* is the tangent of the iso-welfare curve on the reaction curve of the private firm, which indicates the equilibrium of the Stackelberg game when the downstream public firm acts as the leader and the downstream private firm plays the role of the follower. Point *N* is the intersection of these two firms' reaction curves, which indicates a Cournot-Nash equilibrium point. It is clear that the payoffs of both players are higher at point *A* than at point *N*.

When the roles of the two firms are reversed, the private firm has the first-mover *advantage* and can choose an output at the tangent of its iso-profit curve on the reaction function of the public firm, as indicated by point B in Figure 3. But acting as the first mover, the downstream private firm cannot expect the public firm to restrain its output to stimulate the private firm to increase the output. The only rational response of the public firm towards a given output of the private firm is to choose its output level so that the price of the final products equals its marginal cost.

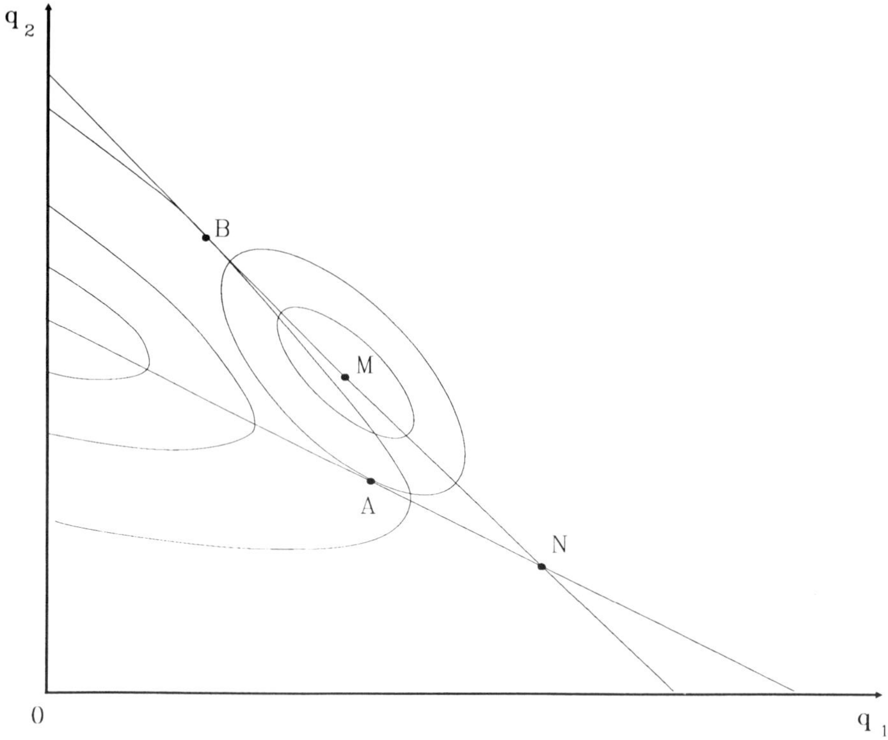

Figure 5.4. Equilibria in Stackelberg game with asymmetric objectives

Although the private firm can gain by its first-mover advantage, the negative impact of losing the strategic benefit may be so strong that it outweighs the first-mover advantage.

Moreover, the change in the roles between the downstream firms with asymmetric objectives has important implications for the upstream firms. The increase in the output of the downstream private firm reduces the elasticity of the derived demand for intermediate inputs. Therefore, the upstream firm with price setting power would increase its price for intermediate inputs. This will push up the marginal cost of the private firm and let the whole family of the iso-profit curves move downwards. Moreover, the increase in the output of the downstream private firm is matched by the reduction in the output of the public firm along its reaction curve. That will change the perception of its supplier and force it to reduce its intermediate input price, thereby pushing the reaction curve of the public firm upwards. Both of these actions influence the equilibrium outcomes in the downstream industry and both of these moves reduce the profitability of the private firms. In equilibrium, the payoff of the private firm may be lower than that when it acts as a Stackelberg follower. As illustrated in Figure 5.4, point B is at the lower level of the iso-profit curve than point A.

Our results show that, in contrast to common belief, the first mover in the quantity space may not necessarily enjoy an unchallenged benefit. In a mixed successive duopoly, the private downstream firm may be hurt if it has to move first under the conditions that the players in the downstream game pursue different objectives. Instead, as a Stackelberg follower, it may improve its payoffs due to *second-mover advantages*.

The weakness of the Stackelberg model lies in the randomness of the roles of leader and follower. The roles of leader and follower are often determined arbitrarily without theoretical justification. It has been observed that, for instance, in the French automobile industry, state-owned auto-makers and private firms co-exist, each enjoying its own unique strategic position. What has been demonstrated here may shed some light on these kinds of equilibria.

This result can also be related to the study of Beato and Mas-Colell (1984) who look for the conditions, in a one-stage mixed duopoly, under which the marginal cost price rule is the best simple rule for the public firm. We analyze the impact on the private incentive of asymmetric objectives after the roles of players change in a Stackelberg game and show in a successive mixed duopoly that the downstream private firm may not like to be in the position of a Stackelberg leader. Therefore, it may not be simple for the public firm to follow the marginal cost pricing rule. If both firms do not like the role of Stackelberg leader, it is likely that a Cournot solution may prevail, which may lead to an inefficient outcome.

4.3. Optimal Decision Rule of Public Firm in Mixed Successive Duopoly[23]

The question we may ask now is that, can a simple decision rule be found which allows the public firm to maximize economic welfare? Earlier literature on using public

---

[23] The term *optimal* is used here in the sense of the second-best (see e.g. Baumol and Bradford, 1970).

firms as an instrument to regulate an oligopoly is in the spirit of the second best. It is assumed implicitly that the public firm takes into account the reaction of the oligopolists and that the private firms respond passively to the decisions of the public firm (Rees, 1984). Recent studies have noticed that the public firm's decision should depend on the types of conjectural variations of the public and private firms. But the role of the public firm is still limited as either a Nash player or a Stackelberg leader (De Fraja and Delbono, 1989).

Given the fact that the private firms are often well established in an industry, it may be reasonable to assume that these firms are in the position of being first-movers. In other words, they may act as Stackelberg leaders if they find that it is in their interest. If the strategy sets of both the public and private firms consist of being a leader or a follower, we can imagine a *choosing the role* game in its strategic form as depicted in Figure 5.5.

If a simple mixed oligopoly can be thought of as a one-stage game and a mixed successive oligopoly can be characterized as a two-stage game, we can think of Figure 5.5 as depicting the third stage *choosing the role* game in a three-stage game. In this three-stage game, a public firm and a private firm choose their roles as either a leader or a follower before the upstream firms set the input prices.

		Downstream Private Firm	
		Leader	Follower
Downstream Public Firm	Leader	Disequilibrium	Stackelberg game with public firm as leader Price > Marginal cost
	Follower	Stackelberg game with private firm as leader Price = Marginal cost	Cournot Game Price = Marginal cost

Figure 5.5. Strategy Matrix of Choosing the Role Game

Casual empiricism indicates that there is no universal decision rule which could be used by the public firm. The optimal decision largely depends on the specific role each firm plays. Therefore, the following proposition is established.

Proposition 5.6. *In a mixed successive duopoly with constant returns to scale and linear demand, the downstream public firm should set its output such that the price is higher than its marginal cost when it acts as a Stackelberg leader and it should not do so when it acts as a Cournot-type player or a Stackelberg follower.*

The proof of Proposition 5.6. is provided by examining the price-cost margins of the public firms. The prices of final product prices and marginal costs of the public firm under three alternative game settings are summarized in Table 5.4.

It is found that when both the downstream public and private firms engage in Cournot competition or when they engage in Stackelberg competition with the public firm as a follower, the price of the public firm is equal to its marginal cost. When the public firm acts as a Stackelberg leader, its price is higher than its marginal cost and the welfare maximizing public firm earns a positive profit.

This outcome seems contradictory with the intuition that under the assumption of constant returns to scale a public firm could always increase economic welfare by a small triangle if it increases its output marginally when price is higher than its marginal cost.

The intuition behind this is strikingly simple. Because the marginal cost of the downstream private firm is lower than that of the downstream public firm, as established in Proposition 1, the small welfare loss of the triangle caused by the difference between the final product price and the marginal cost of the public firm can be sufficiently compensated by the increase in economic welfare caused by the increase in the output of a more efficient private producer. Thus the total welfare may be higher than otherwise when the public firm charges a higher price for its final products than its marginal cost.

This can be seen more clearly if we take a close look at the strategic interactions between the firms in two industries. In the downstream industry, any adjustment of the strategic variable of the public firm would elicit, in addition to the direct effect on its payoff functions, a reaction from its private counterpart. This reaction imposes the strategic effect on the public firm's payoff function.

Table 5.4. Price Cost Margin of the Downstream Public Firm

Game Settings	Prices of the final products	Marginal costs	Margins
Cournot Game	$c + \frac{(4-\theta-\theta^2)S}{8-\theta^2}$ (5.17)*	$c + \frac{(4-\theta-\theta^2)S}{8-\theta^2}$ (5.13)*	Zero
Stackelberg game with public firm as leader	$c + \frac{(32-4\theta-40\theta^2+6\theta^3+9\theta^4)S}{(4-3\theta^2)(16-3\theta^2)}$ (5.51)*	$c + \frac{(8-3\theta-3\theta^2)S}{16-3\theta^2}$ (5.47)*	Positive
Stackelberg with private firm as leader	$c + \frac{(1-\theta)(4-3\theta)S}{8-5\theta^2}$ (5.82)*	$c + \frac{(4-\theta-3\theta^2)S}{8-5\theta^2}$ (5.78)*	Zero

* The numbers in the brackets are the equation numbers

Technically speaking, the complete effect on the public firm's payoff function can be expressed in terms of a total derivative and the maximization of the public firm's objective function requires that its total derivative function equals zero,

$$\frac{dW}{dq_1} = \frac{\partial W}{\partial q_1} + \frac{\partial W}{\partial q_2}\frac{\partial q_2}{\partial q_1} = 0 \qquad (5.99)$$

where W is social welfare defined in (5.5). The first term on the right-hand side is the direct (static) effect of a small change of the strategic variable q_1 on the level of economic welfare and the second term reflects the indirect (strategic) effect.

What we will do next is to check whether the marginal cost pricing rule satisfies the first order condition of economic welfare maximization in all three game settings by noting that the marginal-cost pricing requires that the first term on the right-hand side is zero. This means that we can check whether or not the second term on the right-hand side of the equation (5.99) is zero.

In a Cournot game, the conjectural variation of the public firm is known as $\partial q_2/\partial q_1=0$. The above condition is naturally satisfied.

In a Stackelberg game with the private firm acting as a leader, the private firm needs to know the decision rule of the public firm. It is not difficult to figure out the decision rule of the public firm. In this game the private firm acts as a Stackelberg leader and must choose its output first. Once the output of the private firm is known, the optimal decision for a welfare maximizing public firm can only be the continuation of its production until price equals its marginal cost. Any deviation between marginal cost and price of the public firm is sub-optimal and the public firm can never make any positive profits.

When the downstream public firm acts as a Stackelberg leader, the relative efficiency and the reactions of the private firm have to be taken into account when it decides its output level. This means $\partial q_2/\partial q_1$ on the right-hand side is no longer zero. For the quantity competition and substitute goods, as it is in our model, $\partial q_2/\partial q_1$ is negative. The sign of the first part must be positive because the private firm is a more efficient producer than the public firm and the increase of a private firm's output with positive profit will increase economic welfare. Therefore the second term as a whole must be negative.

This means that if the downstream public firm follows the *marginal cost pricing* rule, the total derivative becomes negative and the first order condition of economic welfare maximization is violated. Under the assumption of strict concavity in the payoff function of the public firm, the negative sign of the first derivative indicates that the sub-optimal solution is caused by an over-production of the public firm. Thus, the *marginal cost pricing* rule would lead the public firm to produce too much as far as economic welfare maximization is concerned. The reduction of the output of the public firm would lead to an increase in economic welfare.

This result may have important policy implications for the conduct of the public firm. We may argue that in a successive mixed oligopoly with constant returns to scale, the public firm should actively accommodate the private firm by cutting back its output. This is because the private downstream firm turns out to be a more efficient producer at equilibrium under the condition of the asymmetry in the firms' objectives.

4.4. Equilibrium Vertical Structure with Objective Asymmetry

As has been shown in the previous chapters, in a successive oligopoly with symmetric objectives, the individual rationality of Cournot-type behaved firms leads the firms to vertical integration. The question here is whether such conclusion is still valid when the downstream industry becomes a mixed duopoly in which a welfare maximizing public firm and a profit maximizing private firm compete.

For private firms, the only reason to integrate vertically is if the profit of the merged firm is higher than the sum of the profits of the merging firms. This may again depend on the type of games played in the downstream industry. Figure 5.5 is the payoff matrix of the private firms for the vertical integration game with downstream Cournot competition. When the private firms are not integrated, the payoffs are the sum of the profits of the upstream firm and the downstream firm. In this Figure the common factor T is omitted from all expressions and the numbers in brackets are the equation numbers.

Private Firm

Public Firm	Contracts	Integration
Contracts	$\dfrac{(3-\theta^2)(4-2\theta-\theta^2)^2}{(2-\theta^2)^2(8-\theta^2)^2}$ (5.20)+(5.22)	$\dfrac{(4-2\theta-\theta^2)^2}{16(2-\theta^2)^2}$ (5.38)
Integration	$\dfrac{(3-\theta^2)(1-\theta)^2}{4(2-\theta^2)^2}$ (5.29)+(5.30)	$\dfrac{(1-\theta)^2}{(2+\theta^2)^2}$ (5.42)

Figure 5.6. Payoff Matrix of the Private Firm

It can be verified that the profits of the integrated private firm are always higher than the sum of the profits under supply contractual relations and are independent of the strategic choice of the public firm. This means that vertical integration is the dominant strategy for the downstream private firm. A similar pattern of the payoff matrix can be constructed based on the equilibrium results for the Stackelberg game derived in the previous section.

Intuitively speaking, the public firm takes the vertical integration move for several reasons. First of all, it can reduce its marginal costs and improve economic efficiency. Secondly, increased competition in the final goods market strengthens the pressure on the independent upstream firm to lower its profit margin. Both of these factors will have positive impact on social welfare as defined in (5.5). The above discussion, combined with the result in Chapter 1, leads to the following proposition.

Proposition 5.7. *Under a successive duopoly with linear demand and constant returns to scale, vertical integration is Nash equilibrium with both symmetric and asymmetric objectives.*

It should be noted that vertical integration of the public firm may not be easily implemented because of at least two reasons: First of all, there may be some institutional hurdles which prevent the public firm from becoming a vertically integrated firm. Secondly, the private firm in the upstream industry may not be willing to give up without sufficient compensation. If the upstream firm knows the objective of the public firm and knows how much the public firm can gain from vertical integration, the magnitude of the compensation it asks would be substantially higher than its producer surplus. Therefore, it is not known whether vertical integration is feasible in practice, though it is clear that the public firm should integrate with its upstream firm provided that the transaction costs are not too high.

5. CONCLUSIONS

In spite of the prevalence of the mixed oligopoly in some economies, the instances that analyze the competitive public firm competing with the private firm(s) in an oligopolistic setting are rare. Using a simple analytical setting that incorporates the most essential features, new insights are revealed on certain normative as well as positive issues, such as the cost difference between public firms and private firms, the advantage of the first movers in a Stackelberg game and the way of using public firm as an instrument to control a successive oligopoly.

The cost differences between the public firm and the downstream private firm have been endogenized in a mixed successive duopoly when the vertical structure is characterized as a supply contract. The public firm will pay more than the private firm for similar intermediate inputs in equilibrium in all the scenarios that have been looked at. The marginal cost difference is determined endogenously and caused by asymmetric objectives between public and private firms.

An important issue in improving the performance of an imperfectly competitive market is how to use the public firm effectively as an instrument to influence the outcome of an oligopolistic market. The public firm can improve economic welfare by actively participating in the oligopoly industry and acting as a Stackelberg leader. This may increase the profits of the downstream private firm as well since the public firm tends to cut its output to stimulate the more efficient private firm to increase its output.

This will be particularly true when the level of product differentiation is high. Moreover, the private firm may be hurt by the *first-mover disadvantage* if it has to move first by losing this benefit.

It has been shown that there are no universal optimal decision rules for a public firm which can be applied for all types of market structures and for different conducts of oligopolists. A public firm that acts as a Stackelberg leader should set the price above its marginal cost and earn positive profits.

Our analysis also shows that vertical integration is indeed the equilibrium vertical structure. The symmetry or asymmetry in firms' objectives will influence the payoffs of the players, but do not change the equilibrium vertical structure of the industries.

Successive oligopoly with objective asymmetry is complicated and our study is based on a very simple model. Nevertheless, some important insights have been revealed. More importantly, the normative and positive issues in the context of vertical integration with asymmetric objectives have only begun to be explored. Additional effort in this direction is expected to bring fruitful returns.

GENERAL CONCLUSIONS

The topic of vertical integration is at the crossroads of the theory of the firm, the theory of contracts and the theory of markets. To understand the incentives and consequences of vertical integration requires an analytical framework which combines three frequently observed economic institutional arrangements: market transactions, contracts and internal transactions within the confines of a firm. Unlike the existing works on oligopolistic vertical integration, this study explicitly models all three types of alternative vertical relations and investigates their structures in a comprehensive way. By so doing, vertical integration with symmetric and asymmetric objectives in a successive oligopolistic setting can be discussed.

At the outset, by exploring a two-stage game theoretical model with linear demand, fixed coefficients technology and constant returns to scale, we demonstrated that the strategic interactions between firms in the same and adjacent industries determine that vertical integration is the only Nash equilibrium vertical structure for firms competing over quantity. Although vertical integration reduces the total profits of the merging firms as well as the profit of the industry, the competing firms can do nothing but integrate vertically. This is different from the results of Bonanno and Vickers (1988) and Lin (1988) in a price competition scenario. They show that *disintegration* or *separation* is the equilibrium vertical structure in a successive oligopoly. The reason behind our results is that the underlying game has the structure of the *Prisoners' Dilemma* and the competing firms, which integrate first, can gain competitive advantages over their rivals no matter what actions those rival firms take. The rational firms should be able to anticipate that outcome and they will choose the vertical integration strategy as well.

We have also shown that in contrast to horizontal cooperation, merger between vertically related firms increases social welfare by lowering the price of the final products, which increases consumer surplus.

It is then demonstrated that the above conclusion is also true when the market structure is generalized into an n-firm oligopoly. After the horizontal merger effect is excluded from analysis, mixed integration, where some firms are vertically integrated while others are not, is not an equilibrium vertical structure under the assumption of linear demand and constant returns to scale unless there are substantial transaction costs and other types of market imperfections.

We have shown that vertical integration leads to a higher social welfare compared with alternative vertical structures e.g. spot market transactions, exclusive contractual relations and mixed integration. The increases in social welfare are accompanied by the decrease in the profit of the merging firms when the final products are homogeneous, but the reduction in the profits of the firms and the industry may be avoided when the final products are differentiated. The interesting point is that, under full vertical integration, producer surplus may be higher if the final goods are complements or if they are substitutes which are highly differentiated. Vertical integration in these cases satisfies the firm's individual interest and benefits society. The intuition behind this is that if the final goods are highly differentiated, the impact of increasing horizontal competition on the final products market after integration is less important to the competing firms. Instead, the profits may be increased with the gains in economic efficiency by eliminating the double marginalization. The vertically integrated firms benefit from a lower marginal cost and the consumers benefit from a higher level of output of the final products and lower price compared with the case where firms follow other vertical strategies. Therefore, vertical integration leads to a higher profit for the individual firms and a higher magnitude of social welfare.

The merits of vertical integration are not limited only to technology with fixed input proportions. When substitution between the intermediate inputs is possible, vertical integration also results in a larger output than that under the vertical structure of exclusive contracts or spot market transactions. This will naturally lead to a lower price of the final products. It has been shown that the positive impact of vertical integration on social welfare is largely undervalued in the analysis of Abiru (1988), who does not consider the possibility of different pre-integration vertical arrangements between adjacent industries other than vertical integration and spot market transactions.

The total effect of vertical integration from spot market transactions is further separated into the anti-competitive effect of market elimination and pro-competitive effect of pure vertical integration. The former can be represented by an exclusive contract as a type of vertical restraint. When the pre-integration vertical structure in a successive oligopoly is characterized as supply contracts, the market elimination effect of integration is absent and the only impact of vertical integration is the pure integration effect. This pure integration effect increases the level of social welfare. Distinguishing between spot market transactions and exclusive supply contracts as two alternative pre-integration arrangements has important policy implications. When the anti-trust authority reviews a vertical integration case, attention should be paid to the pre-integration vertical arrangement in a specific industry. This point has been largely neglected in the literature of oligopolistic vertical integration.

The significance of the public enterprises in some Western European economies and the trends in the economic reforms in Eastern Europe justify the efforts to analyze the variety of scenarios of a mixed successive oligopoly. Our study shows that when successive oligopoly is characterized by asymmetric objectives, a vertically integrated public firm may improve social welfare substantially. The participation of a public firm with the objective of welfare maximization in an industry otherwise characterized as a successive oligopoly creates a mixed oligopoly. An active participation via the competition among the public firms turns out to be one of the alternative ways to control the profit-maximizing oligopolists. The asymmetry in objectives in the downstream industry not only leads to an increase in the output of the final product, but the (indirect) competition between the intermediate goods suppliers becomes stronger. The upstream firms have to charge both the downstream public and private firms lower prices for similar intermediate goods than the firms with objectives of profit maximization, although the public firm has to pay more than the private firms at equilibrium.

We also showed that the active participation of the public firm, e.g. acting as a Stackelberg leader, proves to be a more effective way to control the successive oligopoly than acting passively as a Cournot player or a Stackelberg follower. More interesting is the finding that the profits of the downstream private firm may be higher when it acts as a Stackelberg follower. The second-mover advantage of the private firm may help to create a *win-win* situation for the downstream firms by limiting the market power of the upstream firms.

In short, this book reveals some fundamental insights concerning the economic impact of vertical integration and the Nash equilibrium vertical structure in a successive oligopoly with symmetric and asymmetric objectives. More importantly, it can be seen as a study which provides the theoretical link between the theory of oligopolistic vertical integration in the spirit of industrial organization and the traditional field of public enterprise economics. This combination is fruitful because, among other things, the imperfect market is one of the basic assumptions and subjects for both branches of economics.

These findings obviously have some important implications for business strategy as well as for public policy. Our results indicate that in an industry with oligopolistic market structure, vertical integration is one way to strengthen the firm's competitive position, provided that it will not cause substantial cost increases. For instance, it has been documented that in the process of rationalization for the VCM-PVC sector in early 1980's, vertical integration is one of the most important factors for the survival of any producers in the European market. All non-integrated producers of PVC went out of business (Paraskevopoulos and Pitelis, 1990). In industries characterized as mixed oligopolies, it may be better for the private firm to take a low profile and act as a follower in the game. Although mergers often arouse the concerns of anti-trust authorities in a number of countries, our study shows that these watch-dogs should take a more relaxed mood towards vertical mergers. The public firm in a mixed oligopoly instead should act as a leader in order to influence effectively the market outcome of a successive oligopoly if the vertical relation is characterized by supply contract relations.

Some of the conclusions developed here are obviously subjects for further empirical investigation. Empirical tests for the propositions related to vertical integration appear to be difficult because of the lack of availability of detailed company data although some advances have been made (Martin, 1986; Lieberman, 1991). Vertical integration in an oligopolistic setting further complicates the issue since the propositions developed are very sensitive towards the assumed conjectural variations. Three possible alternatives may be used to test the validity of the propositions in these circumstances. To overcome data shortage, one can use methods of experiments by collected or generated data. Secondly, detailed case studies on selected industry sectors may provide some empirical evidence. Thirdly, carefully developed questionnaires and detailed interviews with managers in both private and public enterprises can also be used to test some of the propositions developed here.

We are fully aware that in our models there are some restrictive assumptions which can be relaxed. For example, the assumption of constant returns to scale can be generalized to become an increasing marginal cost function. Also, different types of asymmetric objectives can be considered. In addition to these direct extensions, there are a few research directions which should be singled out. First of all, this study can be linked to, and expanded from, the research on the selection of the organizational structures in imperfect competitive environments. The vertical integration decision, in fact, is a decision concerning whether or not to put the successive production processes into the confine of one organization. In this regard, it can only be seen as one of several possible organization forms. Other types of organizational forms, for instance, minority share holdings, equity joint ventures and other types of strategic alliances between horizontally related firms, have emerged as a recent research focal point (Harrigan 1988; Flath, 1991; Veugelers and De Bondt, 1992). Until recently not much work has been done on strategic alliances in vertically related firms. Given that the richness of these organizational forms and the importance of their impacts on competition (cooperation) and welfare implications, the extension along this line should receive priority treatment in the immediate research agenda. Notably, one of the most important purposes of these different types of organizations is to provide a mechanism which could harmonize the asymmetric and (sometimes conflicting) objectives among firms. Our vertical integration model with asymmetric objectives may provide a spring board to generate rich results.

The second possibility for the extension of our research may come with analyzing various forms of vertical restraints, e.g. franchising, resale price maintenance, etc. In this book, exclusive supply contracts are used to explain the impact of the market elimination effect on vertical integration. This can be seen as a simplified presentation of the vertical restraints which are observed very often (Katz, 1989). The mechanisms of vertical restraints are generally believed to be able to provide some benefits of vertical integration without its possible shortcomings. The issue here is the fact that the various forms of vertical restraints are so rich that the competitive (cooperative) and welfare implications of many of these vertical restraints are not yet fully understood and they have not received sufficient theoretical treatment.

The theoretical framework developed here can also be applied to international trade theory and economics of multinational enterprises. Direct investment by one of the vertically integrated multinational enterprises can be seen as an economic activity related to intra-firm trade and the domestic production of non-integrated firms with imported goods and purchased technology can be seen as inter-firm trade. Direct foreign investments by multinational enterprises may lead to a higher economic welfare for the host country than alternative schemes such as technology licensing (Bardhan, 1982; Casson, 1986; Sleuwaegen and Yamawaki, 1990). Although the profits of multinational enterprises may be transferred abroad, the reduction in social welfare, caused by the loss of producer surplus in the domestic firm, may be more than compensated by consumer surplus increases created by stronger competition in the final products market as well as by the decrease in the intermediate goods price for the remaining domestic firms.

As has been pointed out at the very beginning, vertical integration has been a research subject for several strands of economics, including transaction cost economics, information economics, and strategic management. However, their emphases and methodologies differ. We are fully aware of the fact that the assumptions in our model about information structure and transaction costs are largely simplified and stringent. It is true that the issue of vertical integration with asymmetric objectives can also be tackled by somewhat different approaches. In addition to the (noncooperative) game theoretical framework, it can be put into the framework of transaction cost economics (the theory of contracts) (Perry, 1989; Hart and Holmström 1987) and/or information theoretical framework (Shapiro and Willig, 1989). So long as the real world is as complicated as it is and so long as the consumers of the theoretical outputs are versatile, these different approaches seem necessary to grasp certain insights, concealed in appearance, and to satisfy the demand for differentiated explanations in order to improve our understanding of vertical integration.

REFERENCES

Abiru, M., 1988, Vertical Integration, Variable Proportion and Successive Oligopolies, *Journal of Industrial Economics*, 36(3), 315-325.

Allen, R.G.D., 1938, *Mathematical Analysis for Economists*, London: Macmillan.

Arrow, K.J., 1975, Vertical Integration and Communication, *Bell Journal of Economics*, Spring, 173-178.

Bardhan, P., 1982, Imports, Domestic Production, and Transnational Vertical Integration: A Theoretical Note, *Journal of Political Economy*, 90(5), 1020-1034.

Baron, D., 1989, Design of Regulatory Mechanisms and Institutions, in *Handbook of Industrial Organization* vol.1, by R. Schmalensee and R. Willig eds., Amsterdam: North-Holland.

Baumol, W.J. and D. Bradford, 1970, Optimal Departures from Marginal Cost Pricing, *American Economic Review*, 60(1), 265-283.

Beato, P. and A. Mas-Colell, 1984, The Marginal Cost Pricing as A Regulation Mechanism in Mixed Markets, in Marchand, M., Pestieau, P. and Tulkens H. (eds.), *The Performance of Public Enterprises*, Amsterdam: North-Holland.

Bergström, T. and H. Varian, 1985, Two Remarks on Cournot Equilibria, *Economic Letters*, 19, 5-8.

Blair, R. and D. Kaserman, 1983, *Law and Economics of Vertical Integration and Control*, New York: Academic Press.

Blois, K.J., 1972, Vertical Quasi-Integration, *Journal of Industrial Economics*, 20, 253-272.

Boardman, A. and A. Vining, 1989, Ownership and Performance in Competitive Environments: a Comparison of the Performance of Private, Mixed and State-Owned Enterprises, *Journal of Law and Economics*, 32, 1-33.

Bonanno, G. and J. Vickers, 1988, Vertical Separation, *Journal of Industrial Economics*, 36(3), 257-265.

Borcherding, T.E., W.W. Pommerehne and F. Schneider, 1982, Comparing the Efficiency of Private and Public Production: the Evidence from Five Countries, *Journal of Economics/Zeitschrift fur Nationalokonomie*, Supp. 2.

Bös, D., 1989, *Public Enterprise Economics*, 2nd ed. Amsterdam: North-Holland.

Bös, D., 1991, *Privatization*, Oxford: Oxford University Press.

Bulow, J., J. Geanakoplos and P. Klemperer, 1985, Multimarket Oligopoly: Strategic Substitutes and Complements, *Journal of Political Economy*, 93(3), 488-511.

BusinessWeek, The New IBM, December 16, 1991.

Carlton, D.M., 1979, Vertical Integration in Competitive Markets under Uncertainty, *Journal of Industrial Economics*, 27(3), 189-209.

Casson, M., 1986, Vertical Integration and Intra-Firm Trade, in *Multinationals and World Trade*, London: Allen & Unwin.

Caves, R., 1982, *Multinational Enterprise and Economic Analysis*, Cambridge: Cambridge University Press.

Comanor, W., 1967, Vertical Mergers, Market Power and the Antitrust Laws, *American Economic Review*, 57, 259-262.

Cremer, H., M. Marchand and J.-F. Thisse, 1989, The Public Firm as An Instrument for Regulating an Oligopolistic Market, *Oxford Economic Papers*, 41, 283-301.

Cremer, H., M. Marchand and J.-F. Thisse, 1991, Mixed Oligopoly with Differentiated Products, *International Journal of Industrial Organization*, 9(1), 43-53.

Davidson, C. and R. Deneckere, 1986, Long-Run Competition in Capacity, Short-run Competition in Price, and the Cournot Model, *Rand Journal of Economics*, 17(3), p. 404-415.

De Bondt, R. and R. Veugelers, 1991, Strategic Investment with Spillovers, *European Journal of Political Economy*, 7, 345-366.

De Fraja, G. and F. Delbono, 1989, Alternative Strategies of a Public Enterprise in Oligopoly, *Oxford Economic Papers*, 41, 302-311.

Deneckere, R. and D. Kovenock, 1992, Price Leadership, *Review of Economic Studies*, 59, 143-162.

Dixit, A.K. and J.E. Stiglitz, 1977, Monopolistic Competition and Optimum Product Diversity, *American Economic Review*, 67, 297-306.

Dowrick, S., 1986, von Stackelberg and Cournot Duopoly: Choosing Roles, *Rand Journal of Economics*, 17(2), 251-260.

Eaton, C. and R.G. Lipsey, 1989, Product Differentiation, in *Handbook of Industrial Organization* vol.1, by R. Schmalensee and R. Willig ed., Amsterdam: North-Holland.

Farrell, J. and C. Shapiro, 1990, Horizontal Merger: An Equilibrium Analysis, *American Economic Review*, 80(1), 107-126.

Fisher, F., 1990, Games Economists Play: a Noncooperative View, *Rand Journal of Economics*, 20(1), 113-124.

Flath, D., When Is It Rational for Firms to Acquire Silent Interests in Rivals? *International Journal of Industrial Organization*, 9(4), 573-584.

Fortune, Who's Ahead in the Computer Wars, February 12, 1990; The U.S. Chipmakers' Shaky Comeback, June, 20, 1988.

Friedman, J., 1990, *Game Theory with Applications to Economics*, 2nd ed, New York: Oxford University Press.

Greenhut, M. and H. Ohta, 1976, Related Market Conditions and Interindustrial Mergers, *American Economic Review*, 66, 267-277.

Greenhut, M. and H. Ohta, 1979, Vertical Integration of Successive Oligopolists, *American Economic Review*, 69(1), 137-141.

Grossman, S. and O. Hart, 1986, The Cost and Benefits of Ownership: A Theory of Vertical and Lateral Integration, *Journal of Political Economy*, 94(4), 691-719.

Hamilton, J. and S-B. Lee, 1986 a, Vertical Merger, Market Foreclosure and Economic Welfare, *Southern Economic Journal*, 52(4), 948-961.

Hamilton, J. and S-B. Lee, 1986 b, The Paradox of Vertical Integration, *Southern Economic Journal*, 53(1), 110-126.

Harrigan, K., 1988, Strategic Alliances and Partner Asymmetries, *Management International Review*, 28, 53-72.

Harris, R. and E. Wiens, 1980, Government Enterprise: An Instrument for the Internal Regulation of Industry, *Canadian Journal of Economics*, 13(1), 125-132.

Hart, O. and B. Holmström, 1987, The Theory of Contracts, in *Advances in Economic Theory: Fifth World Congress*, by Truman F. Bewley ed., Cambridge, MA: Cambridge University Press.

Hart, O. and J. Tirole, 1990, Vertical Integration and Market Foreclosure, *Brookings Papers on Economic Activity*, 205-286.

Jensen, M. and W. Meckling, 1976, Theory of the Firm: Managerial Behavior, Agency Cost and Ownership Structure, *Journal of Financial Economics*, 3, 305-360.

Johansen, L., 1982, On the Status of the Nash Type of Noncooperative Equilibrium in Economic Theory, *Scandinavian Journal of Economics*, 84(3), 421-441.

Joskow, P. and N. Rose, 1989, The Effects of Economics Regulation, in *Handbook of Industrial Organization* vol.1, by R. Schmalensee and R. Willig ed., Amsterdam: North-Holland.

Kaserman, D., 1978, Theories of Vertical Integration: Implications for Antitrust Policy, *Antitrust Bulletin*, 23, 483-510.

Katz, M., 1989, Vertical Contractual Relations, in *Handbook of Industrial Organization* vol.1, by R. Schmalensee and R. Willig eds., Amsterdam: North-Holland.

Kreps, D. and J. Scheinkman, 1983, Quantity Precommitment and Bertrand Competition Yield Cournot Outcomes, *Bell Journal of Economics*, 14(2), 326-337.

Leibenstein, H., 1966, Allocative Efficiency vs "X-Inefficiency", *American Economic Review*, 56, 392-415.

Lieberman, M., 1991, Determinants of Vertical Integration: An Empirical Test, *Journal of Industrial Economics*, 39(5), 151-466.

Lin, Y., 1988, Oligopoly and Vertical Integration: A Note, *American Economic Review*, 78(1), 251-254.

Lipsey, R.G., and Kelvin Lancaster, The General Theory of Second Best, *Review of Economic studies*, vol. 24, 11-32.

Merril, W. and N. Schneider, 1966, Government Firms in Oligopoly Industry: a Short-Run Analysis, *Quarterly Journal of Economics*, 80, 400-412.

Martin, S., 1986, Causes and Effects of Vertical Integration, *Applied Economics*, 18(7), 737-755.

Martin, S., 1988, *Industrial Economics: Economic Analysis and Public Policy*, New York: Macmillan.

Maskin, E. and Tirole, J. 1982, A Dynamic Theory of Oligopoly: Overview and Quantity Competition with Large Fixed Costs, MIT Working Paper no.320.

McGuire, T. and R, Staelin, 1983, An Industry Equilibrium Analysis of Downstream Vertical Integration, *Marketing Science*, 2(2), 161-191.

Mallela, P. and B. Nahata, 1980, Theory of Vertical Control with Variable Proportions, *Journal of Political Economy*, 88, 1009-1025.

Monteverde, K. and D. Teece, 1982, Appropriate Rents and Quasi-Vertical Integration, *Journal of Law and Economics*, 25, 321-328.

Myerson, R., 1991, *Game Theory: Analysis of Conflict*, Cambridge: Harvard University Press.

Ordover, J., G. Saloner and S. Salop, 1990, Equilibrium Vertical Foreclosure, *American Economic Review*, 80(1), 127-142.

Paraskevopoulos, D. and C. Pitelis, 1990, Capacity rationalisation and Mergers: the Case of the Western European PVC-VCM Industries. Paper presented at the 17th European Association for Research in Industrial Economics Annual Conference, Lisbon.

Parris, H., P. Pestieau, and P. Saynor, 1987, *Public Enterprise in Western Europe*, London: Croom Helm.

Perry, M., 1989, Vertical Integration: Determinants and Effects, in *Handbook of Industrial Organization* vol.1, by R. Schmalensee and R. Willig eds., Amsterdam: North-Holland.

Perry, M. and R. Porter, 1990, Can Resale Price Maintenance and Franchise Fees Correct Sub-optimal Levels of Retail Service? *International Journal of Industrial Organization*, 8(1), 115-141.

Porter, M., 1980, *Competitive Strategy*, New York: Free Press.

Quirmbach, C.H., 1986a, Vertical integration: Scale Distortions, Partial Integration and the Direction of Price Change, *Quarterly Journal of Economics*, 101 (Feb.) 131-147.

Quirmbach, C.H., 1986b, The Path of Price Changes in Vertical Integration, *Journal of Political Economy*, 94(Oct.)1110-1119.

Rees, R., 1984, *Public Enterprises Economics*, 2nd ed., London: Weidenfeld and Nicolson.

Rubinstein, A., 1991, Comments on the Interpretation of Game Theory, *Econometrica*, 59(4), 909-924.

Ruffin, R.J., 1971, Cournot Oligopoly and Competitive Behaviour, *Review of Economic Studies*, 38, 493-502.

Salant, S., S. Switzer and R. Reynolds, 1983, Losses from Horizontal Merger: the Effects of an Exogenous Change in Industry Structure on Cournot-Nash Equilibrium, *Quarterly Journal of Economics*, 98(3), 185-199.

Salinger, M., 1988, Vertical Mergers and Market Foreclosure, *Quarterly Journal of Economics*, 103, 345-356.

Salop, S. and D. Scheffman, 1987, Cost Raising Strategies, *Journal of Industrial Economics*, 36(1), 19-34.

Scherer, F.M. and D. Ross, 1990, *Industrial Market Structure and Economic Performance*, 3rd ed., Boston: Houghton Mifflin Company.

Seade, J., 1980, The Stability of Cournot Revisited, *Journal of Economic Theory*, 23, 15-27.

Shapiro, C. and R. Willig, 1989, Economic Rationales for the Scope of Privatisation, Paper presented at 16th EARIE conference, Budapest.

Shapiro, C., 1989, Theories of Oligopoly Behaviour, in *Handbook of Industrial Organization* vol.1, by R. Schmalensee and R. Willig eds., Amsterdam: North-Holland.

Shapiro, C., 1990, The Theory of Business Strategy, *Rand Journal of Economics*, 20(1), 125-137.

Singh, N. and X. Vives, 1984, Price and Quantity Competition in a Differentiated Duopoly, *Rand Journal of Economics*, 15(4), 546-554.

Sleuwaegen, L. and H. Yamawaki, 1990, Intra-Firm Trade, in A. Keokkoek and L. Mennes eds. *International Trade and Global Development*, Essays in Honor of J. Bhagwati, London: Routledge.

Spence, M., 1976, Product Differentiation and Welfare, *American Economic Review*, 66, 407-414.

Spencer, B.J. and J.A. Brander, 1983, International R&D Rivalry and Industrial Strategy, *Review of Economic Studies*, 50, 707-722.

Stigler, G., 1951, The Division of Labor is Limited by the Extent of the Market, *Journal of Political Economy*, (3), 185-193.

Tirole, J., 1988, *The Theory of Industrial Organization*, Cambridge, Massachusetts: The MIT Press.

United Nations Centre on Transnational Corporations, 1988, *Transnational Corporations in World Development*, New York: United Nations

Van Cayseele, P., 1991, Consumer Rationing and Intertemporal Price Discrimination, *European Economic Review*, 35(7), 1473-1484.

Varian, H. 1984, *Microeconomic Analysis*, 2nd ed., New York: Norton.

Veugelers, R. 1991, International Dynamics in the Belgian Insurance Market, *Management International Review*, forthcoming.

Veugelers, R. and R. De Bondt, 1992, Cooperative Innovative Activities, in C. Antonelli ed., *The Economics of Information Networks*, Amsterdam: Elsevier Science Publishers, 277-299.

Vickers, J. and M. Waterson, 1991, Vertical Relationships: An Introduction, *Journal of Industrial Economics*, 39(5).

Vickers, J. and G. Yarrow, 1991, Economics Perspectives on Privatization, *Journal of Economic Perspectives*, 3(2), 111-132..

Vives, X., 1985, On the Efficiency of Bertrand and Cournot Equilibria with Product Differentiation, *Journal of Economic Theory*, 36, 166-175.

Warren-Boulton, F.R., 1974, Vertical Control with Variable Proportions, *Journal of Political Economy*, 82, 780-802.

Waterson, M., 1982, Vertical Integration, Variable Proportions and Oligopoly, *Economic Journal*, 92, 129-144.

Williamson, O., 1975, *Markets and Hierarchies*, New York: Free Press.

Williamson, O., 1985, *The Economic Institutions of Capitalism*, New York: Free Press.

Williamson, O., 1989, Transaction Cost Economics, in *Handbook of Industrial Organization* vol.1, by R. Schmalensee and R. Willig eds., Amsterdam: North-Holland.

Wolf, C., 1979, A Theory of Non-market Failure: Framework for Implementation Analysis, *Journal of Law and Economics*, 107-140.

Yarrow, G. 1986, Privatization in Theory and Practice, *Economic Policy*, 2, 324-344.

INDEX

PC ABERYSTWYTH
LLYFRGELL